GLOBAL JUSTICE AND DUE PROCESS

The idea of due process of law is recognized as the cornerstone of domestic legal systems, and in this book Larry May makes a powerful case for its extension to international law. Focusing on the procedural rights deriving from Magna Carta, such as the rights of habeas corpus (not to be arbitrarily incarcerated) and non refoulement (not to be sent to a State where harm is likely), he examines the legal rights of detainees, whether at Guantanamo or in refugee camps. He offers a conceptual and normative account of due process within a general system of global justice, and argues that due process should be recognized as *jus cogens*, as universally binding in international law. His vivid and compelling study will be of interest to a wide range of readers in political philosophy, political theory, and the theory and practice of international law.

LARRY MAY is W. Alton Jones Professor of Philosophy, and Professor of Law, at Vanderbilt University, as well as Professorial Fellow at the Centre for Applied Philosophy and Public Ethics at Charles Sturt and Australian National Universities. He is the author of *Crimes Against Humanity: A Normative Account* (Cambridge, 2005), *War Crimes and Just War* (Cambridge, 2007), *Aggression and Crimes against Peace* (Cambridge, 2008), and *Genocide: A Normative Account* (Cambridge, 2010). He is also the editor of *International Criminal Law and Philosophy* (Cambridge, 2009).

D1561426

GLOBAL JUSTICE AND DUE PROCESS

LARRY MAY

Vanderbilt University
Charles Sturt and Australian National Universities

CAMBRIDGE
UNIVERSITY PRESS

CAMBRIDGE UNIVERSITY PRESS
Cambridge, New York, Melbourne, Madrid, Cape Town, Singapore,
São Paulo, Delhi, Dubai, Tokyo, Mexico City

Cambridge University Press
The Edinburgh Building, Cambridge CB2 8RU, UK

Published in the United States of America by Cambridge University Press, New York

www.cambridge.org
Information on this title: www.cambridge.org/9780521762724

First published 2011

Printed in the United Kingdom at the University Press, Cambridge

A catalogue record for this publication is available from the British Library

Library of Congress Cataloguing in Publication data
May, Larry.
Global justice and due process / Larry May.
p. cm.
ISBN 978-0-521-76272-4 (Hardback) – ISBN 978-0-521-15235-8 (Pbk.)
1. Due process of law.   I.   Title.
K3251.M39 2011
347′.05–dc22
2010028667

ISBN 978-0-521-76272-4 Hardback
ISBN 978-0-521-15235-8 Paperback

Contents

Acknowledgements   *page* viii

1 Introduction: understanding global procedural justice   1
   1.1 Magna Carta's procedural rights   4
   1.2 The infirmity of international law   6
   1.3 International outlaws, detainees, and the Stateless   8
   1.4 Procedural justice and the international rule of law   11
   1.5 Summary of the arguments of the chapters in
        this book   14

PART I   PROCEDURAL RIGHTS AND MAGNA CARTA'S LEGACY

2 Magna Carta and the interstices of procedure   21
   2.1 Magna Carta and its twelfth-century background   22
   2.2 Preconditions for the rule of law   26
   2.3 Parallels between Magna Carta and
        international law   30
   2.4 Future directions for the development of
        international law   34
   2.5 Objections   37

3 The nature and value of procedural rights   43
   3.1 Nowheresville and Guantanamo   44
   3.2 Distinguishing procedural and substantive rights   47
   3.3 Instrumental and intrinsic value of procedures   52
   3.4 International procedural rights   57
   3.5 Objections   60

4 International law and the inner morality of law   66
   4.1 Hart on international law   67
   4.2 Fuller on procedural natural law   72

v

4.3 Fundamental procedural rights 75
4.4 Habeas corpus and international law 78
4.5 Objections and replies 80

PART II HABEAS CORPUS AND 'JUS COGENS'

5 Habeas corpus as a minimalist right 87
  5.1 Habeas corpus and the value of procedural rights 88
  5.2 The deterrence argument 90
  5.3 The disappeared argument 93
  5.4 The torture argument 95
  5.5 The Ring of Gyges 98
  5.6 *The principle of visibleness* 100

6 Due process, judicial review, and expanding habeas corpus 104
  6.1 Problems with minimalist habeas corpus 104
  6.2 Due process of law 107
  6.3 Judicial review and habeas corpus 109
  6.4 Assessing the role of judicial review 114
  6.5 Global due process 117

7 Habeas corpus as *jus cogens* in international law 120
  7.1 The idea of *jus cogens* norms 120
  7.2 *Jus cogens* and equity 126
  7.3 Arbitrary incarceration in European
     human rights law 130
  7.4 The Inter-American Commission on Human Rights 133
  7.5 David Hicks and the *MV Tampa* 137
  7.6 An objection 140

PART III DEPORTATION, OUTLAWRY, AND TRIAL BY JURY

8 Collective punishment and mass confinement 145
  8.1 Collective responsibility and punishment 146
  8.2 The Just War tradition and international law 150
  8.3 Collective liability and confinement 154
  8.4 Refugee detention and equity 156
  8.5 Objections 160

9 Non-refoulement and rendition 164
  9.1 The problem of "vicarious dirty hands" 165
  9.2 What is non-refoulement? 168
  9.3 Non-refoulement as a *jus cogens* norm 172

9.4 Expanding the scope of non-refoulement 178
9.5 Objections 180

10 The right to be subject to international law 184
10.1 The concepts of outlawry and Statelessness 185
10.2 Outlawry and Statelessness in international law 189
10.3 Being a subject of international law 191
10.4 Trial by jury 193
10.5 Citizens of what? 197

PART IV SECURITY AND GLOBAL INSTITUTIONS

11 Alternative institutional structures 205
11.1 A world court of equity 206
11.2 Global administrative law 210
11.3 Enhancement of international human rights institutions 213
11.4 A progressive development of alternatives 215
11.5 Due process institutions 217

12 Global procedural rights and security 221
12.1 Human rights, peace, and security 222
12.2 Conflicts between security and rights 225
12.3 Linking the rights of Magna Carta 230

Bibliography 235
Index 244

Acknowledgements

The central guiding idea of this book is that we need to make sense not only of substantive rights to liberty and life at the international level but also of the rights to due process through which appeals of deprivation of substantive rights can be made. I first encountered these issues in both a theoretical and very practical context. In law school, Steve Legomsky first introduced me to many of these issues in a course on human rights law. Later, the courses I co-taught with Jack Knight on the rule of law inspired me to think more carefully about due process than I had before. And then, I had occasion to participate in a few cases of habeas corpus appeal from first degree murder convictions, several involving the death penalty, in the US. This practical experience solidified my belief in the importance of due process matters. In my research about international law I became increasingly convinced that debates about global justice needed more attention to due process as well.

In this book I argue that there is value in due process as constituting a rule of law that exceeds the benefit of protection of substantive rights. And I also argue that international procedural rights can become the corner-stone of an "international" rule of law that will cure many of the infirm-ities of international law today. This book addresses a gap in the political philosophy literature on global justice. Its focus is on procedural issues, whereas most of the literature is on substantive issues. And its focus is on legal rights of detainees, whether at places like Guantanamo or in refugee camps, whereas most of the literature is on economic rights. In inter-national law there is a burgeoning literature on the topics that I will address, but there has also been very little theoretical literature here as well. As in any discussion that fills a gap, it is best seen as a first approach.

Several chapters of this book were published as free-standing essays. Chapter 2, "Magna Carta and the interstices of procedure," was pub-lished by the *Case Western Reserve Journal of International Law* in 2009. Chapter 4, "International law and the inner morality of law," was published in a volume called *The Hart/Fuller Debate in the 21st Century*, edited by Peter Cane (Oxford: Hart Publishing, 2009). This chapter, in a somewhat different form, was also published, under a different title, in the *Leiden Journal of International Law* in 2010. A partial reading and discussion of Chapter 5, "*Habeas corpus* as a minimalist right," was recorded on Public Ethics Radio, in conjunction with the Carnegie Council on Ethics and International Affairs in October of 2008. Chapter 12, "Global procedural rights and security," was published in a volume called *Security: A Multi-Disciplinary Approach*, edited by Cecilia Bailliet (Leiden: Brill Publishers, 2009).

In writing this book I have benefited from the comments of many people who have heard versions of these chapters at conferences and colloquia in 2008–2010 in: Buffalo, Cambridge, Canberra, Carbondale, Chicago, Cleveland, Delft, London, Melbourne, New Orleans, Oslo, Oxford, Philadelphia, St Louis, The Hague, Sydney, and Toronto. I would like to mention the following as having provided especially helpful advice: Susan Appleton, Cecilia Bailliet, Jim Bohman, Tom Campbell, Peter Cane, Hilary Charlesworth, Tony Coady, Adrienne Davis, Toni Erskine, Lenn Goodman, Clarissa Hayworth, Zach Hoskins, Peter Joy, Jack Knight, David Konig, Chris Kutz, Tony Lang, David Luban, Ian MacMullen, Seumas Miller, James Nickel, Philip Petit, Gerald Postema, Andrew Rehfeld, Neil Richards, David Rodin, Kim Rubenstein, Leila Sadat, Nancy Sherman, Ken Shockley, Helen Stacy, Wayne Sumner, and Richard Vernon.

My greatest debt goes to those faithful colleagues and friends who read all or large parts of this manuscript. I am especially grateful to Mark Drumbl, Marilyn Friedman, Bob Goodin, and Kit Wellman, who were often my fiercest critics and also my most supportive interlocutors. I also wish to thank Hilary Gaskin and the staff of Cambridge University Press for encouragement and support of this project. And I am very grateful to Jeffrey Tlumak and Carolyn Dever, from Vanderbilt University, for crucial support during the final stages of this project. I also thank Paul Morrow for supplying an excellent index.

CHAPTER I

Introduction: understanding global procedural justice

No freeman shall be taken or imprisoned or desseised or exiled or outlawed . . .
Magna Carta, 1215, Chapter 29 (39).

No one shall be subject to arbitrary arrest, detention, or exile.
Universal Declaration of Human Rights, 1948, Article 9.

Throughout this book I will discuss issues of global justice from two different perspectives. First, I will address global justice as a matter of morality, especially as a matter of moral fairness. Second, I will also address the issue of global justice from the perspective of international law as an emerging system of norms. This dual perspective calls for an interdisciplinary analysis where philosophical principles and legal practices are brought into conversation with each other as it were. I have employed this approach in my previous books on international criminal law. And I have benefited from employing historical materials from the Just War tradition, which provides a common core for both moral philosophers and international lawyers. In the current work I will also draw much guidance from the historical case of Magna Carta and the debates in many countries about how best to understand and instantiate the rights of Magna Carta's legacy.

The debates about global justice typically concern economic distributive justice or criminal retributive justice. Both of these forms of justice concern substantive justice, namely they concern the substantive rights that people have by virtue of either their economic need or their status as victims. I wish to discuss a third subject matter in the field of global justice, namely the procedural rights that constitute an international rule of law. I will contend that procedural rights provide a moral core to any system of law, and this is even more the case at the international level than at the national level. Such procedural rights provide at least minimalist protection concerning substantive rights as well. In this respect, the moral content of the natural law may very well be best exemplified in the institution of the rule of law.[1] Any substantive rights can be held hostage if the person who would claim these rights can be incarcerated unjustifiably.

My previous work in international law has been about substantive international justice, with volumes on the normative grounding of crimes against humanity, war crimes, the crime of aggression, and genocide.[2] I now turn to procedural issues in international law. In the jurisprudential and political philosophy literature, this is a vastly underdeveloped field, with the global justice literature exploding about substantive rights of victims, as well as economic rights of those who are the worst off, yet with proportionately little attention being given to what I call global procedural justice.

This book will focus on what are sometimes known as "due process" rights. These rights are procedural rights that set a moral minimum on what oversight is necessary for individuals who have been detained or incarcerated by governments. As James Nickel has said:

> Due process rights protect us not only directly when we are accused of a crime, but also indirectly by serving as checks on governmental power. They make less available tempting but tyrannical ways of governing, and thereby promote good government. They do this by requiring that a number of procedural steps be taken before sentencing someone to jail. They also make tyrannical ways of governing less available by making criminal procedure transparent.[3]

In addition, as I will argue, due process considerations prevent abuses in the way that individuals are deported or outlawed within their own countries, in refugee camps or detention centers, for instance. I will focus on due process rights as global rights, not merely rights that exist in particular States. In this sense, I will address due process rights as human rights and as a matter of global justice.

The book is motivated by three concerns. First, in reading the literature on Magna Carta I was struck by the way that the rights secured in the main article of Magna Carta, drafted in the first few years of the

---

[1] See the debate between H. L. A. Hart and Lon Fuller on this point, as discussed later in Chapter 4.

[2] See my previous recent work on these topics: *Crimes Against Humanity: A Normative Account*, NY: Cambridge University Press, 2005; *War Crimes and Just War*, NY: Cambridge University Press, 2007; *Aggression and Crimes Against Peace*, NY: Cambridge University Press, 2008; and *Genocide: A Normative Account*, NY: Cambridge University Press, 2010.

[3] James W. Nickel, *Making Sense of Human Rights*, Oxford: Blackwell Publishing, second edn, 2007, p. 109.

thirteenth century, tracked the same rights that had been denied to those at Guantanamo, Cuba and Bagram, Afghanistan, as well as in many refugee camps, in the first few years of the twenty-first century. In 800 years it looked as if we had made no progress, and indeed had regressed. In part, this is because Magna Carta concerned the rights *inside* England, whereas in Guantanamo and even more in some refugee camps, the rights were said to lie *outside* of a State's jurisdiction. I will argue that since these rights are so important, they should also be enshrined in international law.

Second, I was struck by the fact that the rights of Magna Carta were not substantive, but procedural, although not in the normal sense of that term. The rights were in a sense collateral to the criminal law system, yet provided a foundation, indeed a moral core for that legal system. So, I set out to try to make sense of these rights, especially the right to habeas corpus and the rights against rendition and Statelessness, as rights that are prior to and in some cases more important than even substantive rights. Such procedural rights are most important in times of extreme turmoil, when people's substantive rights are most at risk – largely because of the possibility of indefinite detention in detainee centers and refugee camps.

Third, I was intrigued by possible parallels between the way that the English law had developed since Magna Carta and the way international law has developed since the end of the Cold War. In both cases, law developed in a slow and piecemeal manner where autonomous or semi-autonomous entities struggled in the formation of an overarching legal system: the feudal barons struggling with King John, and the sovereign States struggling with the United Nations (UN). One of my tasks is to try to explain in terms of political philosophy and normative jurisprudence why habeas corpus and other related rights have such a peculiar and significant status, and why they may constitute an international rule of law. These topics are of the utmost importance and yet have received little attention.

In this chapter I will outline in the first section why I find Magna Carta to be a good source for thinking about international law today, especially in its emphasis on procedural rights. In the second section I will explain the ways in which international law is currently infirm and how a Grotian approach to understanding law in general and international law in particular could help cure some of these infirmities. In the third section I discuss the broad category of being an outlaw that informed Magna Carta and can also inform debates in international law today, especially as we seek to find ways to fill in legal black holes that exist in such places as Guantanamo and some refugee camps. I also provide some of the seventeenth-century normative background to my analysis in the rest of the book. In the fourth section I discuss the idea of an international rule of law and the place that procedural rights play in that idea. In the final section I provide a summary of the arguments advanced in the various chapters of the book, as well as a sense of what binds these particular arguments together.

1.1 MAGNA CARTA'S PROCEDURAL RIGHTS

As I said this project is inspired by two events, 788 years apart. The first is the signing of Magna Carta in 1215 and the second is the establishment of US prisons at Guantanamo and Bagram in 2003. It may seem odd to link these two events, but I do not think it is odd at all. Magna Carta established that any person is entitled to due process of law. Guantanamo and Bagram were defended by the idea that certain prisoners can be denied due process if they fall through the cracks in the various extant legal regimes: the criminal justice system of the US and the system of international law. Magna Carta was an agreement extracted from King John of England by feudal barons. Chapter 39 (normally referred to as Chapter 29 in the 1225 revised version of King Henry III) says:

No freeman shall be taken or imprisoned or desseised or exiled or outlawed or in any way destroyed, nor will we go upon him nor send upon him, except by the lawful judgment of his peers or by the law of the land.

There are at least four distinct rights in this document, which came to stand for the core of procedural due process, and all four were violated by the establishment of the prisons at Guantanamo Bay and Bagram Air Base.

The rights enshrined in Magna Carta are: 1) the right not to be arbitrarily imprisoned; 2) the right not to be sent into exile; 3) the right not to be removed from the protection of the law; and 4) the right to trial by jury. At Guantanamo Bay, all four rights were violated. The right of habeas corpus was denied to these prisoners. Several prisoners were sent from Guantanamo to countries that were known routinely to use torture. The prisoners were described by the Bush administration officials as being in a "legal black hole" in that they were neither within the jurisdiction of US courts nor under the jurisdiction of the laws and customs of war, since they were unlawful combatants. And the prisoners at Guantanamo were denied trial by jury.

In many ways, my best case though is not Guantanamo but the refugees and political prisoners of the world who are literally in a legal black hole. Several of the early Articles of the Universal Declaration of Human Rights (UDHR) concern these procedural rights and will help frame my understanding of global procedural justice. In particular, I would mention three articles of the UDHR:

Article 9. No one shall be subject to arbitrary arrest, detention, or exile.

Article 10. Everyone is entitled in full equality to a fair and public hearing by an independent and impartial tribunal, in the determination of his rights and obligations and of any criminal charge against him.

Article 11. 1. Everyone charged with a penal offense has the right to be presumed innocent until proved guilty according to law in a public trial at which he has had all the guarantees necessary for his defense.

2. No one shall be held guilty of any penal offense on account of any act or omission which did not constitute a penal offense, under national or international law, at the time when it was committed. Nor shall a heavier penalty be imposed than the one that was applicable at the time the penal offense was committed.[4]

It seems to me that these rights are basic rights, on all fours with better known economic and retributive concerns. The UDHR is largely hortatory. We will see that these rights have been instantiated in human rights treaties that have wide-ranging scope, but are not afforded the same status commensurate with substantive rights. Indeed, the procedural rights of the UDHR are considered suspendable in times of emergency. I will argue that international law should be changed so as to elevate the status of procedural rights.

I will argue that certain rights, which I contend are best seen as procedural rights, should be the core of global due process. These include:

The right of habeas corpus.
The right of non-refoulement.
The right to be subject to international law.
The right to trial by jury.

One might consider these to be special procedural rights, which can be derived from or gain their normative support from the rights listed in the UDHR. Indeed, some of these rights, such as habeas corpus and trial by jury, are considerably older than the Universal Declaration itself. It is my contention that such rights are the backbone of a minimal respect for

---

[4] Universal Declaration of Human Rights, U.N.G.A. Res. 217A, 3 U.N. GAOR, U.N. Doc. A/810, at 71 (1948).

human rights generally and if recognized globally would significantly fill gaps in an international rule of law.

One of the ideas proposed in this book is that there should be an international legal body that has the authority to hear claims of deprivation of basic procedural rights anywhere in the world that there is a person in detention who claims that the charges against him or her do not support the detention. How this court or other institution would come into being would probably require a multilateral treaty among most of the States in the world. As with other such international courts and institutions, the main reason that States would agree to such a proceeding would be out of concern for the protection of basic human rights across the world. Even the strongest of States, like the US, recognize that they are part of an interdependent world where constraints that protect rights ultimately benefit everyone.

At the moment, the International Criminal Court (ICC) has four substantive crimes as the basis of its jurisdiction: genocide, crimes against humanity, war crimes, and the crime of aggression (the last is currently not operational because of a lack of consensus on what constitutes aggression). These crimes are very specifically defined and are only likely to be prosecuted when there has been a mass atrocity. In addition, the ICC is governed by the important principle of complementarity, which requires that the prosecutor can only take a case if the State that otherwise would have jurisdiction has refused or indicated that it cannot hear the case on its own. I see the global procedural justice rights as corollary to, but also undergirding, the substantive rights already protected at the ICC. And I will argue that there is reason to be cautiously optimistic that sizeable numbers of States would sign on to a multilateral treaty protecting global procedural rights.

1.2 THE INFIRMITY OF INTERNATIONAL LAW

As H. L. A. Hart observed over twenty-five years ago, international law is infirm because it lacks an "international legislature, courts with compulsory jurisdiction, and centrally organized sanctions."[5] The primary rules of the international legal regime, such as against murder, are often virtually the same in content as those of domestic legal systems. But the form of these rules, or at least the form of the underlying secondary rules, especially concerning sanctions, are infirm, calling into question whether

---

[5] H. L. A. Hart, *The Concept of Law*, Oxford University Press, 1984 [1960], p. 214.

international law is indeed a system of law or merely a loose set of laws. In the last decade we have been moving toward an international rule of law, but we are definitely not there yet.

We will not soon have a full-scale solution to the problem of compulsory jurisdiction and centrally organized sanctions. But in the meantime, gap-filling can increase the claim to an international rule of law. Chief among the measures of gap-filling is a system of international procedures including indictments and arrests for violations of international law, especially international criminal law, along with gap-fillers for protecting the rights of those indicted and arrested, such as those found in the call for the institutional protection of the rights of habeas corpus, non-refoulement, and similar measures at the global level. The question posed today about whether the President of the Sudan, Al Bashir, should be indicted and arrested for his role in the Darfur genocide and other atrocities goes directly to the heart of the issue of how best to move toward an international rule of law.

As I said, international law is currently infirm – at best it is a patchwork quilt of norms. The infirmity concerns the lack of coercive sanctions and of centrally recognized authority for resolving disputes. We could add more international substantive norms (e.g., on cluster bombs, anti-personnel bombs, land mines, etc.). Instead, I believe we should work toward an international rule of law by strengthening international procedural norms. These norms are valuable because they add a further layer of protection to substantive norms, but more importantly they fill gaps in the existing system of substantive norms, in that they allow for remedies to rights violations that are not clearly linked to "black letter" substantive norms. Throughout this book, I argue that we can learn quite a lot from historical sources like Magna Carta about how to construct a fully functioning international legal system from the ground up rather than from the top down.

I will begin with a bit of background from the Just War tradition. The most significant figure concerning the ethics and law of war was Hugo Grotius. Writing in 1625, he proposed that there is an "association which binds together the human race, or binds many nations together" and that such an association "has need of law."[6] Grotius then famously defended the idea "that there is a common law among nations, which is valid alike for war and in war."[7] As one commentator has recently noted:

---

[6] Hugo Grotius, *De Jure Belli Ac Pacis* (On the Law of War and Peace) (1625), Francis W. Kelsey (trans.), Oxford: Clarendon Press, 1925, p 17.
[7] Ibid., p. 20.

Grotius, too, is of course fully aware of the importance of independent nations
... However his ultimate frame of reference remains the Ciceronian *humani
generis societas* inherited from Stoicism, a society of mankind rather than States.[8]

Grotius spoke explicitly of such a society bound together "by good faith"
and "tempered with humanity."[9] Grotius recognized that "law fails of its
outward effect unless it has a sanction behind it." Even when there is no
sanction, law "is not entirely void of effect," as long as "justice is approved,
and injustice condemned, by the common agreement of good men."[10] The
conscience of humanity can be affected even without sanctions, but the
international society is even better served if the condemnations of injustice
can be backed by sanctions against those States that act unjustly. Whatever
the sanctions of law, even the sanctions of war, these should be governed by
the singular task of "the enforcement of rights."[11] In this vein, I will argue
for international sanctions for violations of due process rights at the
international level.

The most significant international substantive rights against genocide,
crimes against humanity, war crimes, and aggression are partially protected
by the ICC. I will argue that we also need some other significant addition
to international law that will protect procedural rights like habeas corpus
and non-refoulement. Whether that institution is primarily just an expansion of already existing international human rights committees or councils,
a new administrative regime at the international level, or a full-blown
court, procedural rights need stronger protection than currently exists for
there to be anything that lays claim to an international rule of law.

1.3 INTERNATIONAL OUTLAWS, DETAINEES, AND THE STATELESS

The main focus of this study is the fate of those who in some States have
been deprived of basic rights protection through detention or confinement. The two kinds of case I am most interested in are, first, those
involving individuals in detention centers such as Guantanamo and
Bagram, as well as domestic immigration detention facilities in the US,
Australia, and the UK. Second, I am also interested in those cases where
people are refugees or Stateless, either for political or economic reasons,

---

[8] Peter Haggenmacher, "Grotius and Gentili," in *Hugo Grotius and International Relations*, Hedley
Bull, Benedict Kingsbury, and Adam Roberts (eds.), Oxford University Press, 1990, p. 172.
[9] *De Jure Belli ac Pacis*, pp. 860–861.
[10] Ibid., pp. 16–17.   [11] Ibid., p. 18.

currently occupying camps and who have fled or been exiled from their home countries and yet have not been accepted into the host countries where the camps have been established.

These two groups of cases are similar in that the inhabitants have become " outlaws," people who do not receive the protection of domestic or even international law. They seem to exist in a Hobbesian state of nature or a legal black hole that exists because of the infirmity of international law, which has gaping holes in its system of human rights protection, despite the theoretical guarantee of protection for all. Hobbes famously sets out the infirmities of such a state as follows:

> And because the condition of man … is a condition of Warre of every one against every one; in which case everyone is governed by his own reason; and there is nothing he can make use of, that may not be a help unto him, in preserving his life against enemies; It followeth, that in such a condition, every man has a right to every thing; even to one another's body.[12]

The underlying pessimistic account of human nature need not be accepted in order to see the intuitive idea that without the rule of law people will be strongly tempted to abuse one another and even to take each other's life, despite the theoretical recognition of these rights.

I will say much more about "outlaws" in subsequent chapters. Here let me merely indicate the source of the idea. At about the time of Magna Carta it was apparently a practice in England for those who were disfavored or thought to be dangerous or in some other way suspicious to be exiled either outside or within England itself. For the latter to be accomplished, the person was removed from the normally populous regions of England where the king's law was enforced into a region where no laws were enforced. The term "outlaw" merely refers to those who exist outside the jurisdiction and protection of the law, even though formally they may be rights-bearers. While some outlaws were formally rightless, the cases that interest me are outlaws who remained formally rights-bearers but who were not afforded the effective protection of the law.

The best-known example of an outlaw in England is Robin Hood, who was exiled to Sherwood Forest, an area that was beyond the king's enforcement.[13] There is some question of whether Robin Hood is

---

[12] Thomas Hobbes, *Leviathan* (1651), Richard Tuck (ed.), NY: Cambridge University Press, 1996, Chapter 14.
[13] There is considerable debate about whether the fictional stories about Robin Hood were modeled on a particular actual case.

supposed to have voluntarily exiled himself so as to avoid the king's punishment or whether he was forcibly exiled by the king. But in any event, the effect was the same: Robin Hood was an outlaw in the sense that he was beyond the enforcement of the king's law and this meant, among other things, that anyone in England was free to kill or harm him if they so chose. Robin Hood was in a legal black hole, perhaps somewhat like the situation faced by those detainees at Guantanamo Bay who discovered that they did not have their rights protected by the US, or even by international legal authorities. It is true that Robin Hood was not technically detained, although he was apparently told that if he left Sherwood Forest he would be subject to punishment, perhaps capital punishment, and thereby deterred from leaving and regaining the protection of the laws.

Grotius said: "Violence is characteristic of wild beasts and violence is most manifest in war; wherefore the most diligent effort should be put forth that is tempered with humanity lest by imitating wild beasts too much we forget to be human."[14] There is a sense in which Grotius's remarks direct our attention to the situation that exists when law and its sanctions are not in place, as in some refugee camps. Hobbes stated the point boldly by discussing this as the state of nature as opposed to the state of civil society.[15] There is a wide difference in conceptions of human nature that separates Hobbes's pessimism and Grotius's optimism, yet they both form the same extremely negative assessment of what it is like to be outside of the realm of law.

In detention centers and refugee camps, violence is indeed rampant. Reports regularly circulate about widespread rapes in refugee camps, such as those in Darfur, and of widespread torture in detention centers, such as Abu Ghraib. What is needed is for there to re-emerge the rule of law that among other things seeks to temper the desire to perpetrate violence with a sense of humanity, a civilizing sentiment that is as relevant in domestic as in international matters. Indeed, what the detention centers and refugee camps illustrate is the incredibly depraved way that some people will behave toward those under their care when they are assured that what I will call "visibility" is absent. Visibility encompasses the idea that political practices that affect the rights of people should not be allowed to be conducted in secrecy. When people are assigned to detention

---

[14] Grotius, *De Jure Belli Ac Pacis,* p. 861.
[15] Thomas Hobbes, *Leviathan* (1651), Chapter 13.

facilities or refugee camps where there is no visibility, the effective protection of their rights is potentially undermined.

Being an outlaw was recognized at the time of Magna Carta as something that a person needed specific procedural protections against. Indeed, there is a sense that the entire of Magna Carta's famous Chapter 29 (39) could be understood as an attempt by the barons to extract from the king a set of guarantees that people in England would not be rendered as outlaws, even when they were legitimately confined to prison or sent back to their home countries. I will treat the procedural right not to be rendered an outlaw as similar to the right not to be made Stateless in what follows, and will treat the other rights of Magna Carta separately. But I wish to have my readers remember that all of these other rights are in a sense intimately linked to a wider understanding of the right not to be rendered an outlaw. In international law such a right is the right to be subject to the guarantees of human rights, much like some of the most important rights of the UDHR mentioned earlier, and hence not to be forced outside the effective protection of a legal system.

1.4 PROCEDURAL JUSTICE AND THE INTERNATIONAL RULE OF LAW

The infirmities of international law, especially concerning those who lack rights protection by their home States, can be cured by focusing more on procedural rights than is commonly done in international law. Taking my cue from the development of English law from Magna Carta onward, I will focus on procedural justice as a gap-filling and norm-strengthening basis for the eventual establishment of a robust system of international law. It is very difficult to create a system of law merely by compiling a set of substantive or primary rules, as is seemingly the way international law is proceeding at the moment. Such a set of rules will have gaps both in terms of the reach of its rules and the protection it offers to those who are subject to its rules.

Procedural justice can be understood as Rawls did in terms of fair procedures that all or nearly all would consent to from behind a veil of ignorance.[16] The basic structure of a social order is primarily a matter of understanding what would be acceptable if people did not know their positions in society and yet nonetheless had to design the rules for that society. I find the Rawlsian approach quite helpful on the ideal level, as an

[16] See John Rawls, *A Theory of Justice*, Cambridge, MA: Harvard University Press, 1971.

attempt to make sense of the idea of fairness that any system of law must aspire toward. The Rawlsian ideal is a powerful one, but it is hard to see whether people really would come to a kind of consensus about what the rules should be. Thus, as I will explain, I find the Rawlsian model to be not as useful as some others have in understanding the appeal of procedural justice in non-ideal settings, that is, in the real world, especially at the global level.

In my view, non-ideal procedural justice is better captured by the idea that all are subject to the same rules and that these rules act to provide a minimally fair basis for treating one another with respect in terms of the effective protection of their human rights. Rawls and his followers, or at least some of them, have seen international justice as being a matter of the relations of peoples or of States.[17] Some others, including some who follow Rawls, have seen global justice as a matter of how individuals act toward each other, and so have called themselves cosmopolitans.[18] My own position falls somewhere in between a State-centric and a completely person-centric conception of global justice in general and global procedural justice in particular. We can think of this position as a society of States,[19] much as Grotius did, but one that is aimed at eventually providing a rough equality for all individuals, regardless of which State they reside in. Nonetheless, I do not see the goal of a project of global procedural justice either to be the elimination of States or the continuation of the current strong State-centric approach.

A Grotian society of States approach sees States as instrumentally valuable insofar as they provide protection for the rights of their subjects or citizens and do not jeopardize the rights of non-subjects or non-citizens. The Grotian approach I favor looks to the existing States as often being aids to the development of adequate protection of basic human rights. But at the same time, when a State does not provide such protection or actively undermines such protection, then it loses any claim to receiving the benefit of the doubt. I have made a similar argument concerning a Hobbesian account of international justice.[20] Recently I have come to see my overarching project to be better described in Grotian rather than Hobbesian terms.[21] But on this count there is not a

---

[17] See David Reidy and Rex Martin (eds.), *Rawls's Law of Peoples: A Realistic Utopia?* Malden, MA: Blackwell Publishers, 2006.
[18] See Thomas Pogge, *World Poverty and Human Rights*, Cambridge: Polity Press, 2002.
[19] See Simon Caney, *Justice Beyond Borders*, Oxford University Press, 2005.
[20] See May, *Crimes Against Humanity*, Chapter 1.
[21] See May, *War Crimes and Just War*, especially Chapter 1.

huge difference since on my interpretation both seventeenth-century thinkers arrive at similar conclusions, although from decidedly different premises.

Procedural justice is primarily about equity and equal protection of the law, where this idea has two important components. First and foremost, procedural justice provides people with effective protection of their rights. In the international arena, this means that procedural justice must provide an effective framework for the protection of human rights, especially basic human rights. Second, and nearly as importantly, procedural justice conveys the idea that everyone will be subject to and protected by the same rules. Each person is to be seen as equal before the law. In international law this means that each person must be afforded at least a minimal effective level of protection of his or her basic human rights, regardless of where in the world that person resides. It is this latter condition of procedural justice that makes it constitutive of the international rule of law but also so difficult to instantiate over the objections of strong States that do not want to be subject to anyone else's rule.

There is thus a minimal substantive component to the very idea of global procedural justice, namely that each person will have at least minimal protection of his or her basic human rights. But the substantive part here is quite thin. The emphasis is on the framework for the protection of these rights and especially on the way that dignity is protected through the concept of equality before the law. There must be some rights stating that people have effective universal protection for the idea of equity and equality before the law to make sense at all; the substance of this equality need not be extensive as long as minimal human dignity is maintained.

Here I follow the debates between Hart and Fuller about procedural natural law, as will become clear in later chapters, in thinking that there is "minimal content of the natural law" that any system of law must seek to promote and preserve. While still controversial, this kind of idea can be seen to draw support from very different schools of thought. But, as Hart recognized, there is still room for great iniquity in such a system of law, although perhaps not quite as much as Hart seemed to think was likely to result.[22] In this sense, I follow Fuller more than Hart in thinking that procedural justice will lead to at least minimal respect for people and will rule out some of the worst abuses against individuals.[23] In terms of global

---

[22] Hart, *The Concept of Law.*
[23] Lon Fuller, *The Morality of Law,* New Haven, CT: Yale University Press, 1962.

procedural justice, such a minimum level of respect for persons, especially for their dignity, will lead to a much better world than the one that we currently occupy.

Of the modern equivalents of the four procedural rights of Magna Carta, I will focus primarily on habeas corpus and secondarily on non-refoulement and the right to be subject to international law, with only brief discussion of trial by a jury of one's peers. These rights form the foundation of a system of international law that is primarily a system that strives for the equal minimum protection of the law, making sure that no one is left outside of that protection. As was true at the time of Magna Carta, these international procedural rights could form the basis of a system of due process that aims to guarantee that each person has his or her basic human rights effectively protected as a way of guaranteeing that each person is granted a minimum level of respect for their dignity. I will argue that these rights are key to providing gap-filling so that individuals do not land in places where they have no protection of their basic human rights.

It is in this way that the extraordinary promise of the UN Charter and the UDHR can be achieved, where security and human rights merge together into a system of protections for "human security." Human security is a relatively new term in conceptual debates about global justice, but it is a term that fits well into the context of the themes of this book. Most of the discussion of human security, though, has focused on substantive rights, not on the procedural rights that are the focus of my study. Nonetheless, there is a small but growing literature on conceptual and normative issues concerning the rights that I will address, and I acknowledge my indebtedness to those who have already recognized the importance of procedural matters for the normative development of international law. I will be happy if I can move that debate to a new level.

1.5 SUMMARY OF THE ARGUMENTS OF THE CHAPTERS IN THIS BOOK

In Part I of this book I explore how the model of Magna Carta can help us to develop a robust international legal system, especially concerning the development of such procedural rights as habeas corpus and non-refoulement. In Chapter 2 I engage in some historical reconstruction to tell the story of the reception of Magna Carta from the thirteenth century to the eighteenth century, when Blackstone was able to argue convincingly that habeas corpus was the most important foundational right for the constitution of English law. In Chapter 3 I set out an account of the difference between procedural and substantive rights, articulating the value of each, and arguing that in many situations the two are combined, but that typically one is dominant over the other. In Chapter 4 I discuss the jurisprudential basis of the importance of procedural rights as morally foundational rights by examining and then expanding on the debate between H. L. A. Hart and Lon Fuller over fifty years ago. I stress the way that overcoming secrecy and instilling accountability is indeed the moral core of procedural rights, both domestically and internationally.

In Part II I tackle the issue of how best to conceptualize procedural rights, especially habeas corpus. In Chapter 5 I set out a minimalist understanding of habeas corpus, going back to the earliest formulation of this right by Bracton in the thirteenth century. I explain how even in this very minimalist form, habeas corpus can lay title to be a foundational right. In Chapter 6 I discuss various ways that habeas corpus has been expanded since the time of Bracton, arguing that at least some expansion is highly desirable, but that the current wide meaning of habeas corpus in US jurisdiction is a poor model of how best to conceptualize the international right of habeas corpus. In Chapter 7 I argue in favor of seeing procedural rights like habeas corpus as *jus cogens* norms, the most fundamental norms of international law, and I begin to explore how best to protect such rights internationally as well.

In Part III I explore the other Magna Carta legacy rights, especially non-refoulement. In Chapter 8 I discuss both the Just War tradition and current international law concerning collective detention and punishment. Discussions of war and detention over the centuries have coalesced into a set of common principles of what justice requires. In Chapter 9 I develop a jurisprudential account of non-refoulement, arguing that it too should be seen as a *jus cogens* norm of international law and defending this claim against various objections. In Chapter 10 I return to the idea of international outlaws and show how important it is that the right to be subject to international law be strongly protected.

In Part IV I discuss issues of global security, especially global human security and the institutions that can best protect global human security. In Chapter 11 I explore three different institutional alternatives that could be developed to advance the goal of protecting and promoting international procedural rights. The three alternatives are a global court of equity, an enhanced system of international administrative rules, and an expanded role of the International Rights Committee and Human Rights

Council. I explore the pros and cons of each institutional alternative, ultimately arguing that while a court would be optimal, it is also probably the least likely to happen in the near future. I then suggest that there is nothing wrong with pursuing all three alternatives, allowing for the progressive development of each in a similar manner to the way that English law developed after the time of Magna Carta. In Chapter 12 I describe the elements of security and then explain why habeas corpus and non-refoulement have such an important role to play in advancing the goal of global security. I then pull the disparate threads together into a coherent account of the value of global procedural justice for the development of the international rule of law and the promotion of a system of equality of law and moral fairness or equity in the international domain.

Throughout this book, my aim is to focus attention on a lacuna in the philosophy of international law but also in the practice of international law. My aim is to bridge a gap in the way that global justice is discussed. For just as international criminal law is normally conceived as a matter of the protection of substantive rights, such as the right not to be subject to genocide or crimes against humanity, so global economic disparities are normally conceived as requiring greater protection of substantive rights to food, shelter, and clothing. In both cases it is freedom from harm that is the key, although in one case it is civil or political harm and in the other it is social or economic harm. Procedural justice is able to address both of these forms of harm.

Those who have been deprived of social and economic freedoms, through deprivation of shelter, by being dispossessed, or of basic food, by having their farms burnt to the ground, often find themselves in camps which operate either like detention facilities or like outlaw areas, where raping and pillaging are rampant. Those who have been deprived of civil and political freedoms, through deprivation of speech or association, also often find themselves in detention facilities or as members of the disappeared. In both cases, while much is needed, it is often a good place to start to try to secure certain basic procedural rights of some form of due process where the basis of the deprivation can be challenged. These legal process rights do not necessarily play favorites in the dispute between civil and political rights on the one side and social and economic rights on the other. It has been a mistake in the literature to treat what I will call the Magna Carta legacy rights as primarily civil and political rights. Procedural rights, as we will see, protect many different types of substantive rights. And at least as important is the idea that procedural rights also partially constitute a rule of law that stands against all forms of unfairness and arbitrariness of treatment.

The idea of due process of law is recognized as the cornerstone of domestic legal systems. Various international instruments also recognize due process as a cornerstone of international law. In the chapters that follow I will attempt to provide a conceptual and normative account of due process within a general system of global justice. Due process is also a bridge between moral ideas of fundamental fairness and particular concerns of vulnerable groups whose rights have been trampled by governments. Due process rights thus bring deep-seated considerations against the arbitrary exercise of power into some kind of institutional structure, especially one that connects these moral ideas to legal practicalities. While it may seem that requiring various procedural steps is as mundane and uninteresting a subject as one can think of, it will be shown to be of the highest importance. And as we begin to think about the idea of global justice systematically, discussion of procedures should also come to the fore as at least as important as the heralded substantive rights that have concerned theorists and practitioners in international law.

PART I

Procedural rights and Magna Carta's legacy

CHAPTER 2

Magna Carta and the interstices of procedure

In this chapter I will explain how an understanding of Magna Carta in 1215 might provide an intriguing model for understanding "global procedural justice." I will focus on how extending such rights as habeas corpus to the international community would contribute to the international rule of law as well as help secure other substantive rights. The general idea is that we are currently in a situation where the sovereign States could be seen as similar to the feudal lords at the time in English history when the English State was just beginning to develop. And we might learn from an examination of Magna Carta how a centralized legal system came to emerge from a decentralized set of largely local courts. Most importantly, I hope to show that protection of procedural rights was paramount as a first step toward centralization of a legal system.

The story of how Magna Carta influenced English law gives us a model, but also a cautionary tale, of how international law may develop as well. The process was a very slow and gradual one, and the process largely proceeded through gap-filling, especially in the domain of procedural rights rather than substantive rights. Magna Carta laid the groundwork for the English rule of law by laying out basic procedures that had to be followed, including procedures for challenging arbitrary imprisonment or exile. These procedural rights opened the door for the kind of equitable review of potentially arbitrary use of power by courts and even by the king, so that other more substantive abuses could be exposed and condemned as well. In this way, even as significant substantive rights were lacking in the legal system, procedural rights became gap-fillers. Accountability was the main thing accomplished by Magna Carta and this then led to the possibility of a centralized system of law enforcement across England, just as may be true some day with international law. The process required significant input from Parliament, which extended and solidified Magna Carta's rights. Because there is no international Legislature, other legal institutions will have to play the role of Parliament in extending basic procedural rights globally.[1]

In the first section of this chapter I will provide some historical background on Magna Carta, rehearsing a story that by now has achieved wide consensus among historians. In the second section I will explain why it was that Magna Carta's rights came to be considered fundamental law in England, and why it is especially important that fundamental law be understood in procedural terms for the development of the rule of law. In the third section I draw out some parallels between the development of a legal system in England from the time of Magna Carta and the development of an international legal system today. In the fourth section I explain some of the changes in international law that would be especially important for the eventual creation of a truly international legal system, again drawing on the model of Magna Carta. And in the final section I respond to an especially significant objection, namely that I have displayed unjustified cultural bias in urging that all of international law conform to one particular Western conception of law.

2.1 MAGNA CARTA AND ITS TWELFTH-CENTURY BACKGROUND

In order to set the stage for understanding how Magna Carta might be a model for international law today, we need to understand what gave rise to Magna Carta. The first thing to note is that in twelfth-century England, there was not a strongly centralized State. Indeed, if anything there was strong decentralized power. This decentralization took two significant forms. First, England was a feudal society, which meant that there were often quite strong feudal lords who reigned over large tracts of land in England and many did not feel that they were less powerful or authoritative than the king himself. Second, there were also many courts and systems of courts that had various levels of autonomy and subject-matter jurisdiction.

England had had courts in existence for many years before Magna Carta. One type of older court was called the "Courts of the Hundred." These courts were generally held as open-air meetings in the territorial districts called hundreds, which were larger than villages but not as large as counties or shires. Judges administered the Salic law of the Franks in these courts, and there was a kind of "manual of law and legal procedure for the use or

---

[1] I am grateful for David Konig's help on some of these historical issues.

guidance of free judges" of the hundred court.[2] Here there was a "deliberate attempt to furnish an alternative to violence and bloodshed."[3] These courts were autonomous of the king; the king "is merely represented in it by a class of officers who collect his share of the fines imposed."[4] Only much later does "the popular president of the Hundred Court, the Thingman disappear, and his place is taken by the Graf or Count, the deputy of the King."[5] From the earliest of times, England had autonomous local courts, and this was still true at the time of Magna Carta.

Here is how the distinguished historian Frederick Maitland describes the twelfth-century legal scene:

> At the beginning of the twelfth century, England was covered by an intricate network of local courts. In the first place these were the ancient courts of the shires and the hundreds, courts older than feudalism, some of them older than the English kingdom. Many of the hundred courts had fallen into private hands ... Above all these rose the king's own court. It was destined to increase, while all the other courts were destined to decrease; but we must not think of it as a court of first instance for all litigants; rather it, like every other court, had its limited sphere of jurisdiction.[6]

And at the beginning of the thirteenth century, the great jurist Bracton "is forced to make something like an apology for the activity of the king's court."[7]

In the twelfth and thirteenth centuries there was great distrust for the king's court, as well as for the king's growing political and military power. Here is just one example of the difficulty faced by the growing strength of the crown:

> The problem of local government, then, was fast taking a new form, namely, how best to protect the weak from unjust fines and oppressions inflicted on them by local magistrates. The sheriff's local power was no longer a source of danger to the monarch, but had become an effective part of the machinery which enabled the Crown to levy with impunity its always increasing taxation.[8]

King John and the feudal barons had been warring about such matters for several years when things came to a crisis point. The barons refused to pay

---

[2] Sir Henry Maine, *Dissertations on Early Law and Custom*, NY: Henry Holt and Company, 1886, p. 168.

[3] Ibid., p. 169.   [4] Ibid., p. 171.   [5] Ibid., p. 172.

[6] Frederick W. Maitland, *The Forms of Action at Common Law*, Cambridge University Press, 1971 [1909], p. 10.   [7] Ibid., p. 12.

[8] William Sharp McKechnie, *Magna Carta: A Commentary on the Great Charter of King John*, Glasgow: John Maclehose and Sons, 1914, p. 16.

the king's taxes or to provide him with soldiers to fight for lands in Normandy that the king claimed as his by right. By the time of Magna Carta, the barons were in open rebellion and "John found himself, for the moment, without power of effective resistance."[9] The barons "asked a plain acceptance of their plainly expressed demands" and John was "constrained to surrender."[10]

Magna Carta was a charter, a kind of compact, drafted on June 15, 1215 and agreed to by the feudal lords on one side and King John on the other. The compact came to take on mythical proportions by the seventeenth century, especially due to the writings of Edward Coke. But it is not terribly controversial to say that Magna Carta was originally thought of as an agreement between parties that were roughly de facto equal in order to help dispel distrust and provide for harmonious relations within England. As one historian put it: "The barons on that day renewed their oaths of fealty and homage: this was the stipulated price of 'the liberties.'"[11] Magna Carta, the Great Charter between King John and the feudal barons, was primarily a bargain struck so that the king could retain his crown and the barons could get assurances that the king would stop abusing his power. Both parties paid a high price to get what they desired from the compact. Initially, Magna Carta did not appear to be anything other than an agreement struck between the leaders of England in the very early years of the thirteenth century.

King John bristled under the terms of the Charter and tried to extricate himself from its terms by enlisting the aid of the Vatican, which attempted to annul Magna Carta. But events intervened, making quite a difference. Here is William McKechnie's analysis:

At a critical juncture, when fortune still trembled in the balance, John's death at Newark Castle, on the morning of 19th October 1216, altered the situation rendering possible, and indeed inevitable, a new arrangement of parties and forces in England. The heir to the throne was an infant, whose advisers found it prudent to reissue voluntarily, and to accept as their rule of government, the essential principles of the Charter that had been extorted from the unwilling John.[12]

So, in the very early years after its adoption, the character of the charter changed.

Magna Carta was an agreement between semi-autonomous feudal lords and the king, and was in some respects like a multilateral treaty among sovereign States. Indeed, I will later look at the way that Magna Carta

---

[9] Ibid., p. 35.   [10] Ibid., p. 38.   [11] Ibid., p. 40.   [12] Ibid., p. 47.

may help us in understanding such treaties. But Magna Carta as a historical document probably would not have had such an enormous impact if not for the fact that successive kings and parliaments continued to reaffirm it, each time allowing the Great Charter to live up to its name by both expanding its reach and confirming its permanency. The seventeenth-century jurist Edward Coke claims that there were twenty-nine reaffirmations of Magna Carta between 1215 and the early seventeenth century.[13] By the early seventeenth century the Charter was said to have established fundamental or constitutional law in England, despite its humble original meaning. Over time, the Charter or "treaty" was expanded in scope and jurisdiction, and given a life of its own that would be one of the bases of many other founding documents such as the American Bill of Rights.

What is often cited as the most important provision of Magna Carta, and that which is closest to a provision of the American Constitution, is that of Chapter 39 (normally referred to as Chapter 29, from the 1225 revised version of King Henry III):

No freeman shall be taken or imprisoned or desseised or exiled or outlawed or in any way destroyed, nor will we go upon him nor send upon him, except by the lawful judgment of his peers or by the law of the land.

These liberties are described at the beginning of Magna Carta, in Chapter 1, "to be had and held by them and their heirs, of us and our heirs forever."[14] This supposedly fundamental character of being final and immemorial probably did much to cement the importance of Magna Carta when the document was referred to over the centuries.

As I said in Chapter 1, there are at least four distinct rights in Chapter 29 (39) of Magna Carta. First is the right to trial by jury, which is so important that the other rights cannot be abridged unless a jury determines that such abridgement is justified. Second is what came to be called the right of habeas corpus – the right not to be arbitrarily imprisoned. Third is the right not to be desseised, which meant the right not to be arbitrarily dispossessed or deprived of citizenship rights, including the rights to certain "of any free tenements or of his liberties or free

---

[13] Faith Thompson, a contemporary historian, corrects this figure upward to a total of forty-four including both parliamentary and royal decrees of affirmation of Magna Carta. See Faith Thompson, *Magna Carta – Its Role in the Making of the English Constitution 1300–1629*, Minneapolis, MN: University of Minnesota Press, 1948, p. 10.

[14] Note that this wording also conveys the idea that the Charter initially only applied to those who signed and their heirs, not to all those living in England.

customs."[15] And fourth is the right not to be outlawed or exiled arbitrarily, at least in part what is today called the right of non-refoulement, namely the right not to be arbitrarily sent out of a country where one resided to another country where one was likely to be harmed. These rights, including the vaguer right not to be destroyed in any other way, are the core rights that were thought to be necessary to protect any substantive freedoms. For if one could be arbitrarily sent to prison, outlawed, or exiled, what good would substantive rights to property or the receipt of compensation for military service do?

The phrase "by the law of the land" came to be understood as "due process of law" by the fourteenth century. Indeed, Magna Carta is now so closely associated with due process rights that it is surprising that the term "due process" does not appear in it, except in this wide interpretation of the phrase "by the law of the land." The first explicit mention of due process of law as an interpretation of Chapter 29 (39) seems to be in 1352 with the second of the six statutes during Edward III's rule:

Whereas it is contained in the Great Charter of the Liberties of England, that none shall be imprisoned ... unless it be by indictment of good and lawful people of the same neighborhood where such deeds be done, *in due* manner, or by *process* made by writ original at the common law.[16]

Thus, in just a few years, Magna Carta is cited to stand for the right of due process in a number of English statutes and cases, even though the phrase itself does not appear in it.[17] It is not at all clear that this is what was foremost on the minds of the barons who sued to get the king to agree to this compact. Yet, although the phrase 'habeas corpus' does not appear in Magna Carta either, surely the root idea, barring arbitrary imprisonment, is there in Chapter 29 (39).

2.2 PRECONDITIONS FOR THE RULE OF LAW

The rights contained in Chapter 29 (39) of Magna Carta are what are sometimes referred to as fundamental law. It is interesting to speculate, as I will do in subsequent sections, how such fundamental law could serve as a model for international law today. A number of historians, including Holdsworth, date the idea of habeas corpus to an earlier time than Magna

---

[15] This wording was added in the 1225 version of Magna Carta. See Thompson, *Magna Carta*, p. 68.

[16] Faith Thompson, in her book, *Magna Carta*, p. 91, claims that this is the first mention of due process in the context of Magna Carta. My italics.

[17] Ibid., p. 92.

Carta. And interestingly, the earliest uses of habeas corpus also do not stand for such a broad right as due process, but only for the right to challenge one's imprisonment, a purely procedural right. Such rights do not specify any right to a particular form of treatment or liberty that the State must protect. Rather, these rights are simply what minimally must be done so that arbitrariness does not creep into the way that people are deprived of their liberty by being incarcerated, outlawed, or exiled. What is not initially clear, but what I will explore in the following sections, is how pure procedural rights could come to be thought of as fundamental or constitutional law.

By the time of the seventeenth century, those who defended limitations on sovereignty found in Magna Carta a symbolic way to make their case that customary rights formed an immemorial law that restricted the prerogative of kings. As Pocock said:

In this way there grew up – or rather, there was intensified and renewed – a habit in many counties of appealing to "the ancient constitution," of seeking to prove that the rights it was desired to defend were immemorial and therefore beyond the king's power to alter or annul.[18]

These rights were imbued with a power stronger than reason, namely immemorial custom that no one could deny. Nonetheless, Coke chose to add to the legitimacy of Magna Carta's rights the fact that many times Parliament had affirmed them as checks against sovereign prerogative, and he also appealed to the fact that an early English king had voluntarily restrained himself in conformity with these ancient rights.[19] Thus, the great rights of Magna Carta were not merely legitimated by the Charter but more importantly by immemorial custom, a moral constitution, which in effect is merely expressed in the Charter rather than founded by it.

The great rights in Chapter 29 (39) of Magna Carta are best seen as procedural rights. They are not themselves what people sometimes mean by "due process rights" and they are not those listed in the canonical treatment of the rule of law by Lon Fuller.[20] Fuller does mention habeas corpus in passing, as part of the congruence between official action and declared rule. He lists this right along with the right to appeal, not as part of "procedural due process," but as rights "in part directed toward the same objective" as due process, in that a lack of such rights can contribute

---

[18] J. G. A. Pocock, *The Ancient Constitution and the Feudal Law*, Cambridge University Press, 1957, p. 16.
[19] Ibid., pp. 44–45.
[20] See Lon Fuller, *The Morality of Law*, New Haven, CT: Yale University Press, 1969 [1964], Chapter 2.

to a broken or arbitrary system.[21] This seems right, if a bit more under-stated than I will put it later in the chapter.

Perhaps the provisions of Magna Carta's Chapter 29 (39) should be seen as "purely procedural," but in any event, they are not substantive in the normal sense of the term, since they do not secure any particular liberty. Purely procedural rights would be those that are necessary for the efficacy of procedural rights, but do not have the normal features of being procedural themselves. Habeas corpus says only that there must be some ability of a prisoner to be made visible, to get his case reviewed, and this right can act in a way that deters the most egregious forms of arbitrariness. But it does not specify what that procedure should be. Nonetheless, I will generally continue to talk about these rights as procedural, but it should be noted that I do recognize the distinction between procedural rights that are a precondition even for other procedural rights and procedural rights that are not a precondition for other rights, as I discuss in Chapter 3.

When the great struggles over English sovereignty took place in the seventeenth century, the part of Magna Carta that people focused on were these rights in Chapter 29 (39). Here is how one legal scholar characterizes this later development:

Thus the Habeas Corpus Act [1679] provides heavy penalties against all who offend against its provisions: judges who refuse to issue the writ, officers who send a prisoner out of England. The right of the penalty is a private right, enforceable like any debt; and the King has no power to pardon, at any rate after the proceedings have been commenced. In other cases the right of action is given to the "common informer," that is, any member of the public who chooses to take proceedings; in others, again, to some corporation which represents profes-sional interests, such as the Law Society or Goldsmiths' Company.[22]

The provisions of Chapter 29 (39) were seen as crucial for "enforcing the law," especially for making sure that the legal rights were not denied by spiriting a potentially complaining party away, either into jail or out of the country altogether. No rights would be secured without these rights of habeas corpus and other similar rights being enforced.

Consider for instance the practice of basing conviction merely on the king's claim of "notoriety" of the deeds of the accused. Magna Carta was cited to show that there must be some kind of judicial proceedings, with the accused present, for conviction and execution to be lawful.[23] What

---

[21] Ibid., p. 81.
[22] W. M. Geldart, *Elements of English Law*, London: Thornton Butterworth, 1933 [1911], p. 233.
[23] See Faith Thompson, *Magna Carta*, p. 73.

transpired over the centuries after Magna Carta was "the long slow progression toward the 'rule of law.'" Even kings such as Edward II would declare that they could not act "contrary to Magna Carta and the common law of the realm,"[24] although initially kings used the cover of Magna Carta to rule in ways they wanted to on other grounds. Procedure was incredibly important in giving legitimacy to what would otherwise seem to be controversial, even for those who were kings.

Henry Maine well stated the most important point I am trying to establish in this section:

So great is the ascendancy of the Law of Actions in the infancy of Courts of Justice, that substantive law has at first the look of being gradually secreted in the interstices of procedure; and the early lawyer can only see the law through the envelope of its technical forms.[25]

The substantive rights of liberty, especially the right to be free in one's bodily movements, are indeed first approached in a system of law that moved beyond the purely local, in this somewhat surprising way. Perhaps a similar kind of move can be made in international law today. Rather than focusing directly on substantive rights, perhaps it is procedural rights, such as habeas corpus to which we should turn, since the substantive rights developed much more slowly in medieval English legal debates.

It is also true that many other types of early law, including Irish and Indian legal systems, give "an extraordinary prominence" to procedure.[26] When early legal systems focus on procedure, they display an awareness that what is most important is that "service to mankind was to furnish an alternative to savagery, not to suppress it wholly" by limiting but still partially allowing private remedies. As long as the appropriate procedures are followed, these private remedies were important, since early tribunals often lacked the "power of directly enforcing their own decrees."[27] Procedures, like those that set limits on the arbitrary use of power, nonetheless allow a wide variety of enforcement mechanisms, something that is especially important when there is no centralized sovereign power, as of course is true of international law today.

Maitland tells us how the forms of action were absolutely crucial in determining whether there even was a wrong that had been committed. As Maitland put it, one did not see a wrong and then look for a form of

---

[24] Ibid., p. 84.
[25] Sir Henry Maine, *Dissertations on Early Law and Custom*, NY: Henry Holt and Company, 1886, p. 389.
[26] See, ibid., pp. 374 and 386.   [27] Ibid., p. 387.

action, but one first had to find a form of action before there was any wrong that was legally actionable. Maitland also explains how the growing importance and consolidation of forms of action contributed to the gradual increase in sovereign power within England. Here is how he characterized the incremental move toward centralized sovereignty:

Had the worse come to the worst, the king might have claimed these things: jurisdiction over his own immediate tenants, jurisdiction when all lords have made default, a few specialty royal pleas known as pleas of the crown. To this he might have been reduced by feudalism ... That his court should throw open its doors to all litigants ... is a principle that only slowly gains ground.[28]

Magna Carta did not instantly transform English legal culture into a centralized system. Instead, procedural consolidation merely set the stage by restricting the form of law so that later a consolidation of substance could proceed. Indeed, the whole process took at least four centuries and to a certain extent has not ended yet.

There is no doubt, though, that Magna Carta came to be seen as hugely important. A. E. Dick Howard makes the point quite succinctly, if quite controversially:

Magna Carta had established itself as more than simply a venerable statute; by then it was fundamental law. In 1368, for example, a statute of Edward III commanded that the "Great Charter and the Charter of the Forest be beholden and kept in all Points; and if there be any Statute made to the contrary, it shall be beholden for none." Here we see Magna Carta treated as a superstatute, in other words as a constitution ... an obvious similarity ... to the language of the American Constitution ... and to the doctrine of judicial review."[29]

Parallels to the Rome Statute are also apt.

2.3 PARALLELS BETWEEN MAGNA CARTA AND INTERNATIONAL LAW

In this section I will discuss some of the parallels between the development of English law after Magna Carta and the development of international law after the end of the Cold War. I am interested in the parallels between the way in which the semi-autonomous feudal barons and their courts were eventually brought together under a single umbrella of

---

[28] Maitland, *Forms of Action at Common Law*, p. 11.
[29] A. E. Dick Howard, *Magna Carta: Text and Commentary*, Charlottesville: University of Virginia Press, 1998 [1964], pp. 24–25.

English sovereign law and the way in which the sovereign States and their legal systems seem to be very slowly being brought under the umbrella of a system of international law in the twenty-first century. In both cases, what was sought was a way to make it less likely that individuals could fall through the cracks and have no forum where abuse of their rights can be redressed.

First, there is an interesting parallel in the way that provisions of Magna Carta were enforced and the way that enforcement works in international law. Recall that initially there were both public enforcement mechanisms and also several types of private enforcement. Universal jurisdiction in international criminal law has also meant various forms of universal prosecution and punishment, that is, where any State that has the where-withal can prosecute and attempt to punish flagrant human rights violations such as those that occur in genocide or crimes against humanity, or in grave breaches of the rules of war. It is interesting to contemplate what it would mean to have truly private outsourcing of enforcement of international criminal law. Perhaps think of private bounty hunters who would attempt to find and bring indicted political leaders to The Hague. But at the moment, things are less radical, in that the ICC's principle of complementarity allows for multiple trial forums and also for multiple enforcement mechanisms, while still providing the beginnings of a uniformity to such trials.

Second, there is a parallel concerning the development of jurisdiction. Perhaps it was inevitable that when the ICC opened its doors seemingly to all litigants, it would be seen as moving too quickly, at least by the US and other major powers like China. If the progress of international criminal law takes four centuries or even eight centuries, I would not be surprised. In the meantime, as also in the case of Magna Carta, changes are occurring nonetheless, even though they do not constitute a complete break with the past. And as time passes slowly in this progress, it is the procedural provisions that may do the most work, by filling gaps in the substantive system of rules. So there are two issues: who is to be addressed by a system of law and what are the types of norm that the law seeks to enforce. In both cases, we are at the very beginning of a recognition that international law might some day address all people concerning a variety of causes of action, just as was claimed to be true at the time of Magna Carta, but where the realization of this goal took a very long time.

Third, what is "secreted in the interstices of procedure" may indeed fill the gaps left because of an incomplete system of substantive rights in international law, just as Sir Henry Maine said was true of the time of

Magna Carta. I have in mind that the recognition of such things as an international right to habeas corpus could stand in for due process considerations that may come to include even substantive due process. Indeed, the line between procedural due process and substantive due process is often hard to draw. Substantive norms are concerned with the proper aims or ends to be sought by legal rules. Procedural norms relate to what makes something a rule, or a system of rules, in the first place. "Purely procedural" norms may be different again, having to do with enforcement of the norms of both sorts set out above.

Fourth, Chapter 29 (39) of Magna Carta and other early forerunners of due process did at least two significant things: the elimination of the most egregious forms of arbitrary power over individuals and the harnessing of various forms of private enforcement mechanisms in the service of a single conception of justice. It is easy to see how international criminal procedures today have been accomplishing these goals as well, even if still only in a preliminary way. The diminishing of arbitrariness has mainly come in the form of prosecutions of those who would otherwise achieve impunity. But surely another way would be for international criminal tribunals to hold out the prospect of intervention to deal with arbitrary incarceration and deportation, as was one of the chief goals of the famous Chapter 29 (39) of Magna Carta. Another way that international criminal tribunals are having an effect is in the harnessing of "private" enforcement mechanisms so that international tribunals do not have to provide such enforcement themselves, which would be well beyond their means, as was also true of the beginning of the king's courts in England just after Magna Carta.

I must enter a cautionary caveat about the use of "private" enforcement mechanisms. There was a worry that the private enforcement mechanisms at the time of Magna Carta (and this included the way in which even criminal trials proceeded) could abuse the system for personal revenge or gain, especially concerning the use of "common informers." Similarly, today we should worry about prosecutors in Spain and Belgium who take upon themselves the task of enforcing international criminal law, with a similar possibility of abuse. Vigilante justice is the term most often used for the abuse of these types of "private" enforcement of the norms of international criminal law.

But there is a sense of "private" enforcement that was less controversial at the time of Magna Carta and the first centuries after its adoption, even as it was still a source of some abuse. The Law Society monitored and enforced standards of professional conduct of lawyers, and the Goldsmiths' Company performed a similar task concerning the enforcement of statutes regulating the weighing and selling of gold and silver, as well as the general professional standards of goldsmiths in England. In both cases, these private groups were given the right to enforce the statutory standards against their members, with attendant due penalties. Such systems of private enforcement have their parallels in the systems of private arbitration and dispute resolution in international law that have the blessing of the various international tribunals and political bodies. I will say more about this general point when addressing the international administrative law movement in Chapter 11.

Despite some reservations, I would also endorse the more robust way that international law has incorporated the municipal courts of States into the system of enforcement of international law. The English political leaders at the time of Magna Carta realized that it would be a huge mistake to try to dismantle the local courts in favor of national courts. Instead, as I have indicated, the king gradually inserted himself into these local courts, eventually replacing the Thingmen and other local magistrates with those who were employees of the crown. But this process took a very long time, and in the period of transition the king simply exercised a little oversight and collected fees from these courts, rather than disbanding them or taking them over completely. The transition was a gradual and largely uncontroversial one, at least after the death of King John and the subsequent reaffirmations of Magna Carta discussed earlier. It has been important that international tribunals have been composed of judges from around the world as a way to indicate that the tribunals are not merely Western attempts at hegemony.

In addition, the ICC, for instance, has not sought to abrogate the right of State courts to prosecute individuals for international crimes such as genocide and crimes against humanity. Indeed, the Court's principle of complementarity specifically allows for States to prosecute and only asserts the Court's jurisdiction when a State is unable or unwilling to prosecute international crimes through its own courts. So far, such a system has made the ICC not nearly as controversial as one might otherwise have predicted. The experience of Magna Carta is that a gradual process is needed in such a transformation. The king's sheriff intrudes gradually into a local process that is otherwise left pretty much unchanged. This experience helps explain why a similar process in international law is much less controversial than might have been anticipated.

The experience of the reception of Magna Carta in England can help us understand the recent reception of the internationalization of criminal courts. One cannot stress enough though how historical events can make such a difference in an otherwise seemingly impossible situation. If King John had not died a year after Magna Carta, he would have continued to resist the reforms of the barons, and if the Cold War had not come to an end, the Security Council would have remained stalemated in its attempt to form international tribunals. Of course, gradualism is one of the key lessons. But one can be a good deal more specific by looking at parallels between aspects of the reception of Magna Carta and the reception of international multilateral treaties like the ICC's Rome Statute. In the next sections I will also offer some thoughts about what needs to happen next in international law for the idea of procedural protections to go forward and for new international institutions to develop, in spite of the lack of international governance structures.

2.4 FUTURE DIRECTIONS FOR THE DEVELOPMENT OF INTERNATIONAL LAW

Magna Carta was a compact in 1215 that was somewhat similar to the ICC's Rome Statute, which was a multilateral treaty in 1998. Seven hundred and eighty-three years separate these two treaties, yet the former can still give guidance for the development of the latter. I have been focusing on the importance of procedural matters in the reception and development of Magna Carta and will here offer some suggestions about procedural matters at the ICC as well as other international institutions. There has been quite a lot of focus on procedural matters at the ICC itself, that is, concerning how prosecutions are to be run once a case arrives at The Hague. I want to focus on a somewhat different matter, namely how to deal with cases that are unlikely to make it to The Hague on substantive grounds, but which are nonetheless matters concerning which the ICC or some other international institution could begin to exercise some over-sight over basic procedural rights protection, so that "visibility" results for abusive State practices.

The first matter to discuss is what might be called international habeas corpus rights. The leading American law hornbook on habeas corpus describes the unusual status of habeas in the US as "a civil, appellate, equitable, common law, and statutory procedure."[30] Hertz and Liebman go on to explain that habeas corpus has become a broad "surrogate for

---

[30] Randy Hertz and James S. Liebman, *Federal Habeas Corpus Practice and Procedure*, Charlottesville: Lexis Law Publishing, 1998, fourth edn 2001.

Supreme Court review"[31] of whether the petitioners' "constitutional rights have been preserved."[32] Indeed, some courts and individuals have said that the right of habeas corpus is simply the right to due process of law.[33]

The International Criminal Tribunal for Rwanda (ICTR), in its appellate decision in the *Barayagwiza* case, declared that the right of habeas corpus "is a fundamental right and is enshrined in international human rights norms, including Articles of the Universal Declaration of Human Rights."[34] Yet, currently, the right of habeas corpus is only recognized by international tribunals and courts in a limited way. On May 23, 2000 the ICTR held that "the notion of habeas corpus at the international level is limited to a review of the legality of the detention" of those held by the ICTR, seemingly not for those held in custody in other settings such as Guantanamo or Bagram.[35]

A second, and related, idea is to set up international institutions so that they act as much on considerations of equity as on statute. The Chancery Courts in England developed into courts of equity, which sat alongside courts of common law. The Chancellor was considered the conscience of England. In a similar vein, one writer has proposed that we need an international habeas corpus court that would be "the keeper of the world's conscience."[36] International criminal tribunals have seen themselves on this model, but have mainly restricted their role to prosecuting substantive mass crimes. I envision expanding this domain so that a range of serious violations of due process would also fall under the domain of these courts. Equity considerations would involve, among other things, egregiously unfair rulings by national tribunals and courts, along with the denial of basic human rights.

And in this respect, again returning to the Guantanamo case, it should not be permissible for an individual to fall between the cracks of legal jurisdictions. The Bush administration declared that it need not provide procedural rights protection at Guantanamo since it was a black hole – where neither US criminal law nor the Geneva Convention and other

---

[31] Ibid., p. 23.

[32] Ibid., p. 86, quoting Justice Oliver Wendell Holmes in *Moore v. Dempsey*, 261 U.S. 86, 87–88 (1923).

[33] *In re McDonald*, 16 F. Cas. 17, 21 (E.D. Mo. 1861) (No. 8, 751): habeas corpus is designed to ensure that "no arbitrary authority might act without warrant, or 'due process of law.'" Quoted in Hertz and Liebman, *Federal Habeas Corpus*, p. 20.

[34] *Jean-Bosco Barayagwiza v. Prosecutor*, ICTR Appeals Chamber, November 3, 1999, para. 88.

[35] *Prosecutor v. Joseph Kanyabishi*, ICTR Trial Chamber, Case No. ICTR-96-15-1, May 23, 2000, para. 28.

[36] Luis Kutner, *World Habeas Corpus*, Dobbs Ferry, NY: Oceana Publications, 1962, p. 14.

aspects of international law applied. In my view, this is the kind of unfairness that an international court of equity or similar international institution should take up, and where the purpose of such proceedings is to fill the gaps that occur as we move very slowly away from a system of law completely dependent on States toward one that will some day, perhaps, be independent of States.

A third new direction is for there to be international oversight and possibly prosecution of State leaders who violate non-refoulement by engaging in deportation of individuals to countries where they will be tortured or otherwise harmed, or who engage in extraordinary rendition of prisoners of war or others captured on the battlefield. There are international instruments that recognize the right of non-refoulement, but they have not often been enforced, as was true at Guantanamo. In my view, what is needed is for an international court like the ICC, or some other international institution, to have this as part of its subject-matter jurisdiction as a way to protect some of the most vulnerable of people, those who are currently Stateless. I would extend non-refoulement further than it is recognized now, so that all refugees are under its purview.

A fourth new, highly controversial direction is for international institutions to promote trial by jury. In many Western countries, trial by jury in criminal matters is an acknowledged right. And this is probably the most controversial of the four proposals I have put on the table. For there have not yet been major international instruments that have recognized trial by jury as a requirement of criminal proceedings. This was one of the lynchpins of the evolving Magna Carta doctrine. It is my view that the right to trial by jury of one's peers is crucial for justice. Yet today there are no international jury trials, so this right is a long way from being recognized and enforced, although the recent US Supreme Court opinion in *Boumediene* seems to be on the road to recognizing this as a universal right.[37]

As the development of the rights recognized in Magna Carta took a long time to be enforced in English courts, so I would envision a slow process of recognition and enforcement of these rights as properly enforced through international courts and other international institutions. Like the development of Magna Carta, this process will probably involve

---

[37] *Boumediene v. Bush*, 128 S. Ct. 2229, 2256 (2008). Kennedy cites Harlan's concurring opinion in *Reid v. Covert* as criticizing *In re Ross*, 149 U.S. 453 (1891), in wondering "whether jury trial *should* be deemed a necessary condition of the exercise of Congress' power to provide for the trial of Americans overseas." *Reid v. Covert*, 353 U.S. 1, 75 (1955).

the extension of the reach of rights protections to an increasing circle of individuals. That the process will be slow, perhaps very slow, is no reason not to start working toward this eventual goal now.

I would think that the order of these rights is that habeas corpus and non-refoulement are the ones that should be put first on the agenda today, with the others taken up in turn only as an international climate for such considerations changes over time. The first of these rights, habeas corpus (at least as a right to be brought out of secrecy and into visibleness), is already given some recognition by both the UDHR and the International Covenant on Civil and Political Rights, whereas the fourth is not recognized by these instruments. Non-refoulement and certain other equity considerations are recognized, but are not currently enforced in an effective way. As international institutions move from the first to the fourth of the Magna Carta legacy rights, we will move increasingly toward an international rule of law and at least piecemeal cosmopolitanism.

2.5 OBJECTIONS

Critics of my view have voiced the objection that I am engaging in a kind of cultural imperialism in assuming that what is good for certain Western countries should be simply applied wholesale to the rest of the world as well.[38] This criticism is especially strongly put in the case of trial by jury, which is not recognized as an important right in most of the world at the moment. But this criticism has also been voiced about habeas corpus, which in its Western form at least is not recognized as an international right. The idea here is that various societies have gotten along quite well over the centuries, if not the millennia, with customary forms of procedure that are especially well suited to the cultural traditions of those societies.[39] Indeed, there is a sense that the Magna Carta rights I have trumpeted grew out of a set of customs that were suited for situations in England. Why should we assume that this set of English practices should be applied to the rest of the world?

---

[38] Leila Sadat has been an especially sharp critic of my view in this respect. Mark Drumbl and Helen Stacy have also voiced this criticism. I am grateful to them all for forcing me to see the importance of this point.

[39] See Laura Grenfel, "Legal Pluralism and the Challenge of Building the Rule of Law in Post-Conflict States: A Case Study of Timor Leste," in *The Role of International Societies After Conflict*, Brett Bowden, Hilary Charlesworth, and Jeremy Farrall (eds.), Cambridge University Press, 2009, pp. 157–176.

I agree that Magna Carta grew out of a particular set of cultural and social conditions in England in the Middle Ages. But over time Magna Carta gave rise to a set of procedural norms that were adopted in diverse societies and that came to be the model for various international instruments that have been found acceptable by a significant proportion of States across the world. Of course, this still could be said to place priority on what States as opposed to communities have found acceptable. But at least this is a start at trying to show that the Magna Carta legacy rights I have been discussing are not merely acceptable to those in England who had already adopted many of these rights in their customs. In the end, the proof of the value of the Magna Carta legacy rights is in their usefulness as protectors of substantive rights and as constituents in a reasonable conception of a minimalist rule of law.

The critique of cultural imperialism has also been raised against the human rights movement generally, not merely against those of us who are pushing for global procedural rights. In its most famous form, scholars from African and Islamic societies criticized human rights, especially social and cultural rights, as also imposing Western values on the rest of the world in a "one size fits all" manner. The criticism of cultural imperialism is especially apt, say my critics, since I rely on a specific historical document from so long ago to stand as a model for all of contemporary international law. Indeed, one scholar has said that all of international law is merely an attempt to "civilize" non-Western States in an especially harmful form of colonialism.[40] I will attempt to respond to this important line of criticism in the remainder of this chapter.

The larger criticism of the human rights movement is an interesting place to start in dealing with the more specific objection to my defense of Magna Carta legacy rights as international procedural rights. In an earlier work I tried to respond to this line of criticism at the beginning of my textbook on applied ethics seen from a multicultural perspective.[41] The first point to note is that a cultural diversity approach has the disadvantage that it has trouble strongly condemning practices such as female genital mutilation that have been supported by certain cultures. The point is that it is strongly counter-intuitive to allow cultural pluralism to dominate

---

[40] See Martti Koskenniemi, *The Gentle Civilizer of Nations: The Rise and Fall of International Law 1870–1960*, Cambridge University Press, 2001.
[41] Larry May, Kai Wong, and Jill Delston (eds.), *Applied Ethics: A Multicultural Approach*, fifth edn, Upper Saddle River, NJ: Pearson/Prentice Hall, 2010.

these debates about human rights so that no criticism is possible of a wrongful practice if it has support in a given society.[42]

In the context of the Magna Carta legacy rights, habeas corpus and non-refoulement are especially prone to be denied in certain societies, and yet their deprivation constitutes, as I will show in later chapters, quite a serious wrong, perhaps a wrong of the same order as substantive wrongs such as genocide and crimes against humanity. And the tendency to deny these rights is as true of Western as of non-Western States. It may well be true, as multicultural proponents such as John Mohawk have said, "that we are going to have to make peace with those who are different from us."[43] But it would completely upset the very idea of human rights as universally applicable if respecting difference means that serious wrongs cannot be criticized or proscribed when a society disregards those rights for whatever reason, especially if the reason is not a good one.

Concerning habeas corpus in particular, I think that the cultural imperialism objection somewhat misses the mark. I am not necessarily advocating that all of the world should conform to the specific wording of this right that comes down to us from 800 years ago in a very particular historical context. As I will argue in later chapters, the various components of a habeas corpus right are recognized by an assortment of international documents and customs. And there is a core minimalist right that is very hard to argue against, in that it is so strongly associated with giving minimal protection to a host of substantive rights that have garnered universal acceptability, such as rights against genocide, torture, and crimes against humanity.

There is another component of my response that is equally important, namely it is much harder to make cultural arguments against procedural rights than against substantive rights. Substantive considerations, such as that some individuals can be legitimately harmed for religious rituals, are one thing, but it is hard to see what cultural traditions would be seriously offended if habeas corpus or non-refoulement rights were to be protected globally. Rather than offending deep-seated cultural norms, it is far more likely that the objections will come from government leaders who find the increased transparency or "visibility" in their societies that comes from respecting procedural rights to be inconvenient or downright

---

[42] See Martha Nussbaum, "Judging Other Cultures: The Case of Genital Mutilation," in *Sex and Social Justice*, Oxford University Press, 1999, reprinted in *Applied Ethics: A Multicultural Approach*, Larry May, Shari Collins-Chobanian, and Kai Wong (ed.), Englewood Cliffs, NJ: Prentice Hall, fourth edn, 2006, pp. 15–26.

[43] John Mohawk, "Epilogue: Looking for Columbus," in *The State of Native America*, M. Annette Jaimes (ed.), Boston, MA: South End Press, 1992, p. 443.

obstreperous in their attempts to suppress their populations. It is not my intention to argue against the need to consider contextual differences in the way that procedural rights are protected. But that certain procedural rights should achieve universal protection is not obviously opposed to cultural practices in the way that the similar protection of substantive rights has been opposed on cultural imperialism grounds.

A more practical variation of the cultural imperialism objection is that there may be other and even better ways to protect individuals than to insist that Magna Carta legacy rights are protected everywhere. I am not in principle opposed to the thrust of this variation of the cultural imperialism objection. I would, though, say two things. First, it is unclear to me what would be the specific cultural pluralism objection to habeas corpus that should cause one to back off from a full-throated defense of such rights at the global level. Second, I am certainly willing to accept cultural variations of the rights I will be addressing in great detail in subsequent chapters. I will defend what I will call "a minimalist" approach to these procedural rights that leaves room for significant cultural variation. Indeed, my model is the complementarity principle in international criminal law, where international institutions only get involved at all if it is clear that States are unwilling or unable to provide their own protection for the core of these rights.

One last variation of the objection under consideration is that I have too closely allied myself with a "liberal" orientation to rights and am thereby showing a theoretical bias that is open to cultural imperialism charges. My response here is simply to admit that my approach is quite broadly liberal in the sense that I am working within a context of rights of individuals that is largely Western. But I would also point out, as others have as well, that most if not all major non-Western theoretical perspectives are also supportive in principle of the kind of rights that form the background of my thinking about procedural issues.[44] So, I am willing to

---

[44] See Abdullahi Ahmed An-Na'im, "Islam, Islamic Law, and the Dilemma of Cultural Legitimacy for Universal Human Rights," in *Asian Perspectives on Human Rights*, Claude E. Welch and Virginia Leary (eds.), Boulder, CO: Westview Press, 1990, reprinted in *Applied Ethics: A Multicultural Approach*, pp. 101–110. See also Claude Ake, "The African Context of Human Rights," *Africa Today*, vol. 34, no. 142, 1987, 5–13, reprinted in *Applied Ethics: A Multicultural Approach*, pp. 111–116; Joseph Chan, "A Confucian Perspective on Human Rights for Contemporary China," in *The East Asian Challenge for Human Rights*, Joanne R. Bauer and Daniel A. Bell (eds.), Cambridge University Press, 1999, reprinted in *Applied Ethics: A Multicultural Approach*, pp. 117–132; and Kenneth K. Inada, "A Buddhist Response to the Nature of Human Rights," in *Asian Perspectives on Human Rights*, 1990, reprinted in *Applied Ethics: A Multicultural Approach*, pp. 133–142.

take the cultural imperialism objection quite seriously, but fail to see it undermining the approach I adopt in this book.

There is also a methodological variation of the above objection, namely that my approach is liberal and Western in that it is rationalistic rather than impressionistic, or some such. Again, it is unclear to me how my project can go forward in providing a philosophical analysis of procedural rights in international law if it were only impressionistic rather than analytic. Nonetheless, I suppose I will simply have to accept this criticism – if anyone makes it – and acknowledge the limitations of my study as well as my own limitations as a thinker and writer. Nonetheless, I continue to think that my approach can have merit even if it displays some of the biases that I have attempted to address in this section.

Ian Langford has challenged the idea that there is anything universal about the idea of the right to a fair trial or the use of the idea of fairness as involving specific procedures that must be followed.[45] He argues that it is not even true that the idea of a fair trial is unique to all Western legal systems. Rather, he contends that this idea is only of very recent vintage even in Western societies. It is primarily a twentieth-century concept and one that is confined to certain Western societies even today. On the basis of his empirical work on the usages of the idea of a fair trial, Langford concludes that "fair trial is like rugby, the boy scouts, and television, simply a diffused cultural trait." The idea that there is an "inherent nature of human rights in all people is a kind of secular utopianism, an attempt to foist a single ideology on the world."[46]

Like many of the critics of the universality of human rights, Langford seems to confuse normative claims with empirical claims. Even if it were *empirically* true that specific human rights, such as the right to a fair trial, were only discussed in the West in the twentieth century, it does not follow that *normatively* the idea of a right to a fair trial is merely supported by a particular ideology. One could similarly show empirically that it was not until the late nineteenth century, and primarily in Western countries, that slavery was condemned as violating the rights of slaves. But this does nothing to blunt the normative claim that slavery violates the rights of slaves. Universal normative truths are not dependent on their being recognized at all, although one hopes that once the case is made for particular rights, they will be seen as largely compelling. If there is

---

[45] Ian Langford, "*Fair Trial*: The History of an Idea," *Journal of Human Rights*, vol. 8, no. 1, January–March 2009, 37–52.
[46] Ibid., p. 51.

anything utopian about claims concerning universal rights, it is mainly that they will indeed one day be recognized as such by all people. But the normative status of such claims does not turn on empirical facts about the diversity of practices across cultures and times.

In this chapter I have been inspired by events nearly 800 years apart – the signing of Magna Carta on the one hand and the creation of the prison in Guantanamo Bay as well as refugee camps on the other hand – to consider what might be significant in the piecemeal movement toward an international rule of law. Eight hundred years is not much time in evolutionary terms, and in many ways it is not much time in terms of legal progress. But perhaps the lessons learned from these events can propel us forward, incrementally, toward global procedural justice. And the place to start is in the interstices of procedure. In the next chapter I will tackle abstract issues rather than the highly practical issues of the current chapter. In this respect the most significant issue is to delineate the difference between substantive and procedural rights and to clearly articulate the value of procedural rights.

CHAPTER 3

The nature and value of procedural rights

In the debates about Guantanamo, one of the central questions is whether or not the denial of habeas corpus to the detainees is a serious violation of their human rights. The denial of habeas corpus is the abridgement of a procedural right, at its most minimal the right to be brought out of prison and to have the charges against one publicly proclaimed. And while it may be that the abridgement of such a right also violates substantive rights to liberty of the detainees, it may not if, as the Bush administration claimed, the detainees were guilty and highly dangerous, and hence deserving of being detained. But what are we to make of the denial of a procedural right, like habeas corpus, when no substantive right is also denied? To begin to answer this question, I take a step back and ask what is the nature and value of procedural rights, as distinguished from substantive rights?

I will begin this chapter by discussing Joel Feinberg's thought-experiment about Nowheresville. Feinberg said it was characteristic of a place where there are no rights that people do not make claims since they "do not have a notion of what is their due."[1] In recent cases at Guantanamo and Bagram, the lack of procedural rights is not a matter of failing to see what is one's due, but rather of having officials recognize what are their duties in light of claiming by inmates and detainees under their care. Being able to claim is only part of what rights involve. And if there are places where only claiming goes on, without corresponding recognition of the claiming person's status, that is another instance of Nowheresville. Guantanamo and Bagram are unfortunately like Nowheresville in this latter sense, as is also true of some refugee camps and of those who are held as political prisoners.

The dividing line between substantive and procedural rights is not always easy to see. One reason for this is that it is often the case that a given right has both a substantive and a procedural component. And there

[1] Joel Feinberg, "The Nature and Value of Rights," *The Journal of Value Inquiry*, 1970, 249.

43

is often considerable disagreement about whether a given right should be seen as substantive or procedural, even as primarily so. The main example that I will examine in this chapter is the right of habeas corpus. Most minimally, habeas corpus involves the right of a prisoner to be brought out of prison and to have the charges against him or her publicly proclaimed. This right is sometimes seen as a substantive right insofar as it protects the liberty of those who have been detained. But others, myself included, see habeas corpus and other Magna Carta legacy rights as procedural rights insofar as they establish a requirement that a particular set of rules must be followed if one has been detained, but having followed these rules does not necessarily mean that the person incarcerated will indeed regain liberty. Yet there is nonetheless enormous value here.

At the beginning of this chapter I re-examine an influential essay by Joel Feinberg on the nature and value of rights. I then attempt to explain some of the special puzzles that arise when we consider procedural rights as opposed to rights in general. I here draw on the example of the incarcerations at Guantanamo Bay just after the 2001 bombings of the US World Trade Center towers. In the second section of this chapter I will set out various attempts to draw the line between procedural and substantive rights, ultimately defending one of these approaches. In the third section I examine the value of procedural rights, spending time considering various objections to seeing procedural rights as having value independent of the value of promoting a corresponding substantive right. In the fourth section I examine the role that procedural rights play in the rule of law, ending this section by discussing the international rule of law. In the final section I discuss some objections from the perspective of Robert Nozick, Lawrence Solum, and David Estlund to some of what I have argued and also apply some of these criticisms to international procedural rights.

3.1 NOWHERESVILLE AND GUANTANAMO

In his celebrated essay "The Nature and Value of Rights," Joel Feinberg began with a thought experiment, asking his readers to imagine "a world very much like our own except that no one, or hardly any one (the qualification is not important), has *rights*."[2] Feinberg describes the state of Nowheresville as follows:

---

[2] Feinberg, 243.

Nowherevillians, even when they are discriminated against invidiously, or left without the things they need, or otherwise badly treated, do not think to leap to their feet and make righteous demands against one another, though they may not hesitate to resort to force and trickery to get what they want. They have no notion of rights, so they do not have a notion of what is their due; hence they do not claim before they take.[3]

Feinberg gives us an account of rights as a form of claiming, where claiming is an "elaborate sort of rule-governed activity . . . which is public, familiar, and open to our observation."[4] Feinberg then gives us his analysis of having a right: "To have a right is to have a claim against someone whose recognition as valid is called for by some set of governing rules or moral principles."[5] One can have a claim even if one does not make a claim. The important point is that if one has a claim, then others have a duty to respond appropriately when the claim is indeed made or voiced.

I wish to use this account of rights and the description of Nowheresville as a springboard for my analysis of procedural rights. To imagine what the world would be like if there were substantive rights but not procedural rights is seemingly a very difficult thing given the way that Feinberg has set up the issue. But in other respects it is not as hard as it might seem, since on my view people could make claims but no one would be specifically required to recognize them. Indeed, there was a real-life example of Nowheresville for procedural rights, and that was the situation at Guantanamo Bay, Cuba from 2002 until 2009.

In Guantanamo the detainees made claims in protest of their denial of liberty and the abusive conditions of their detention, but the Bush administration said they were in the "legal equivalent of outer space." This meant that there was no one who recognized a duty to respond to the putatively valid claims of the detainees. Most importantly, there was no one who regarded himself or herself as required to determine if the claims of the detainees were valid, and not even anyone who was required to determine if a detainee was indeed still in detention and why his or her substantive claims were being ignored. At Guantanamo, by design, no one recognized certain governing rules or moral principles that clearly applied, at least not ones that would require that valid claims were recognized. And with the lack of recognition, it was *as if* the detainees at Guantanamo were in Nowheresville. But this is not because they did not think they were entitled to make claims, but because no one

---

[3] Ibid., 249.   [4] Ibid., 250.   [5] Ibid., 257.

believed he or she had the rule-based duty to respond appropriately to these claims.

That there may be people making claims but no one is thought to be required to listen is to highlight one way of thinking about the distinction between substantive rights and procedural rights. In a sense, one does not have rights at all, at least not in Feinberg's sense, unless one is entitled to make substantive claims *and* also there are rules and principles that assign duties to other people to recognize or at least to determine if recognition is called for, and hence whether the claims themselves have validity. There may be hortatory ways in which one has rights or one may wish to say that one does have rights that are in need of recognition, but in Feinberg's perceptive treatment of the subject, one does not really have rights unless one can make substantive claims and procedurally there are people who are duty-bound to respond. Guantanamo seems to epitomize what it is like to lack the procedural dimension of rights or, in other words, to lack procedural rights.

But does it make sense, in Feinbergian terms, to speak of procedural rights at all? Is there both an "entitlement to claim" and a "duty to recognize" component of a procedural right? In one sense this question can be clearly answered in the affirmative. A person can claim to have procedures recognized and followed. This is like claiming to have one's substantive claims recognized. While this is a kind of meta-claiming, it still certainly involves a form of claiming. Procedural rights involve a claim to have the proper procedures followed, where the procedures themselves are also a kind of claim of recognition. Yet, since this claim is really a kind of meta-claim, there is also a sense that procedural rights are not claims proper, that is, that they do not fully stand on their own without there being some substantive rights at issue. Of course, in Feinberg's analysis, substantive rights do not stand on their own without procedural rights either.

Returning to Guantanamo, and especially to the issue of the procedural right of habeas corpus, may help us better understand how to conceptualize procedural rights. In Guantanamo the detainees were said to fall through the cracks of extant legal systems. When these detainees claimed that a habeas corpus review of their situations should take place, they certainly were looking for recognition of substantive claims to liberty and against abusive treatment. But they were also claiming a certain kind of status – as someone who is subject to a legal system where members are entitled to make claims that have to be recognized, something which was being denied them. The nature of procedural rights is primarily that a certain kind of status or standing is afforded to those who have these rights. The status is one of being recognized to make claims to have certain rules followed, independent of the outcome of those rules being followed. We will explore precisely what that status is in subsequent sections, but mainly at the very end of this chapter.

Having a certain status can have value instrumentally, as we will see later, in terms of the protection of the substantive rights of one who has this status. Yet it is also true that the claiming to have status or standing is itself a value, and its value is independent of the value of those substantive concerns, as we will also see in subsequent sections of this chapter. By making habeas corpus claims, the Guantanamo detainees were in a sense asserting procedural rights independent of their substantive rights. They were saying that they should be afforded equal treatment in terms of being subject to rules that others who were similarly placed were afforded. It is certainly also true that they were hoping to get their liberty back, which they believed had been arbitrarily taken from them, and in this sense they were also pressing procedural rights as a means to promote their substantive rights to liberty.

3.2 DISTINGUISHING PROCEDURAL AND SUBSTANTIVE RIGHTS

Michael Bayles provides us with a very good place to start in distinguishing between procedure and substance. He says:

Most people have a common-sense grasp of the difference. Procedure concerns the process or steps taken in arriving at a decision; substance concerns the content of the decision. The two are conceptually distinct, for one can use different procedures for the same substantive issue and the same procedure for different substantive issues. Hence, a substantive topic cannot imply a procedure, nor a given procedure imply a particular substantive topic.[6]

Processes, or steps, to a given result are here distinguished from the result itself. Even if the result may be that it occurred through a certain means, we can still distinguish the means from that result, even if the entirety of the means is part of the result. However, things get increasingly complicated when results are largely about means, e.g., that things be decided justly.

Another strategy is to distinguish between form and content as a way to help draw a distinction between procedure and substance. Here it is useful to think of the role of the copyeditor. Copyeditors are trained to make

---

[6] Michael D. Bayles, *Procedural Justice*, Dordrecht: Kluwer Academic Publishers, 1990, p. 3.

changes to the form or style of writing so as to make it clearer, but without much changing the content, or the ideas expressed, in the written material. Here we can seemingly distinguish form from content. Yet the form of the writing, especially in content-lite fields like logic and critical reasoning, is nonetheless often very hard to distinguish in practice from the content. The form and content distinction suggests that practically we might not be able to separate substance and procedure as easily as the quote from Michael Bayles (at the beginning of this section) suggests.

We could also try to draw a distinction between procedure and substance in terms of primary and secondary rules, which is the way that H. L. A. Hart drew that distinction.[7] According to Hart, primary rules tell ordinary people what they have an obligation to do, whereas secondary rules tell officials how to go about interpreting, enforcing, or changing the primary rules. Hart insists that primary rules set out what people are obligated to do, whereas secondary rules, even as addressed to officials, are not best thought of as obligations. If, as Hart suggests, there is no clear sanction in the case of secondary rules addressed to officials, then there is a good question about how procedures function. In the next chapter I explore Hart's idea that secondary rules derive their bindingness by consensus among the officials.[8] It seems to me that similar kinds of things can be said of procedural rules and rights. Indeed, we can go quite a way in distinguishing between substantive and procedural rights by considering who the addressee is of each type of right, although not quite as far as some might hope.

My view is that a somewhat better strategy is to distinguish procedural from substantive rights in terms of weighty rules. If there is to be a bright line between procedural and substantive rights, the most plausible view is that procedural rights differ from substantive rights in that substantive rights are especially weighty rules that aim to promote a particular human good or end, whereas procedural rights are especially weighty rules that aim only at a certain kind of formal fairness. Formal fairness is best understood in terms of equal treatment of like cases and of a minimal consideration of equity, in that one gets quite minimally what one deserves within a context of rules that apply to all. One question to ask is as follows: why not think of fairness, even formal fairness, as a human good? In the remainder of this section I will explore this issue. I do not

---

[7] H. L. A. Hart, *The Concept of Law*, Oxford: Clarendon Press, 1961.

[8] Also see Larry May, "International Law and the Inner Morality of Law," in *The Hart/Fuller Debate in the 21st Century*, Peter Cane (ed.), Oxford: Hart Publishing, 2009, pp. 79–96.

think that ultimately I can give an account of even formal fairness that does not make reference to aiming at a human good. Hence, my strategy will not provide a bright line between all cases of substantive and procedural rights. What we will have is only a way of saying whether a given right is more or less procedural than substantive.

It does not seem that fairness is best thought of as primarily a substantive right; therefore, if it is a human good, it is a distinctly different one from such goods as health or well-being. Fairness is not a state or outcome, but a way or method to reach states or outcomes – and here is where status enters in. Fairness concerns equity and equality in the way that decisions are reached: equity in terms of being treated as someone deserving of even-handedness; equality in terms of being treated the same as all others similarly situated, and not subject to disparate consideration unless on the basis of relevant criteria. Fairness in this sense is not primarily about outcomes but about status.

There is value in having certain ways of achieving ends rather than other ways. Some ways are fairer than others, despite the fact that both ways could lead to exactly the same human good. Since different ways can lead to the same human good, the difference among these ways or methods is not just in what human good they promote. Indeed, fair procedures can lead to seemingly unjust results insofar as substantive goods are denied or diminished rather than advanced. Here it is useful to think of dividing a pie fairly by dividing it into equal slices. It may be that all are thereby satisfied, yet it may also be that some of the recipients of pieces are not hungry and hence do not want or need a slice. And it may be that other recipients are so famished that their portions will not help them sufficiently to stave off starvation.

I here employ the idea of formal fairness as distinguished from contentful fairness that aims at a certain end or content. As I suggested above, the form/content distinction overlaps the procedure/substance distinction at least in this one respect. Procedures in and of themselves aim at something that is independent of content. There is indeed a good that procedures aim at, but it is formal fairness. And since the good is a formal good – a status – it is not part of what is normally thought to constitute human well-being. There is, as we will see, a kind of fairness that is part of normal human well-being, but it is not because of the ends of formal fairness that it plays a role in human well-being, but because of its means. Means are seemingly independent of ends, but not completely so, since there is an end of procedural rights that involves equity and equality. And yet equality and equity are ends of a formal sort but ends nonetheless.

Let me quote from one of the early twentieth-century attempts to understand the distinction between procedure and substance. Walter Wheeler Cook argued that most authors had misidentified the problem of distinguishing procedure from substance:

> Nearly every discussion seems to proceed on the tacit assumption that ... the object is to find out, as one writer puts it, "on which side of the line a set of facts falls." This way of stating the problem, if taken literally, seems to the present writer to start us off on the wrong scent, and so to divert our attention from the fact that we are thinking about the case precisely because there is no "line" already in "existence" which can be "discovered" by analysis alone ... our problem turns out not to discover the location of a pre-existing "line" but to decide where to draw a line.[9]

I do not here wish to dispute Cook's claim that in many cases the hunt to distinguish between procedure and substance is a line-drawing rather than a line-discovering exercise. But of course this does not take anything away from the problem, at least on the assumption that where there are lines, drawn or discovered, there is conceptual difference that may indeed make a practical difference. In many cases the reality of the situation is that procedure is only a subset of substance, where both aim at the protection of certain liberties, procedures doing so indirectly.[10] Yet in other cases a line can be drawn nonetheless, especially if status rather than a result is the aim.

I am not committed to seeing a bright line, whether discovered or constructed, between procedure and substance. Indeed, there is not such a bright line in most cases. Various rights can be conceived as more procedural or more substantive, and yet such a designation is an important one in how we eventually come to regard the rights associated with them, especially in debates in international law. I am most especially interested in the way that gaps can be filled so that a seamless rule of law results. And in this respect, rules and rights that are mainly procedural can play an important, although not well-recognized, role. That role is to put a stop to arbitrariness of the actions of rulers and their agents, and the case of habeas corpus illustrates this well.

I wish to offer just a few remarks on whether to think of habeas corpus in particular as a procedural or substantive right and what is at stake in this debate at the global level. In the context of detention of persons by a

---

[9] Walter Wheeler Cook, "'Substance' and 'Procedure' in the Conflict of Laws," *Yale Law Journal*, vol. 42, 1933, 333–357, especially 335–336.
[10] I am grateful to Kit Wellman for pressing me on this point.

State, the substantive question is whether the State has justifiably restricted the liberty of the person detained. The procedural issue is whether the State has followed reasonable rules in affording the detained person the ability to challenge the basis of his or her detention. In this sense, the procedural issue is second-order since it does not concern whether the person has indeed been justifiably detained. The procedural issue, and the corresponding procedural right, becomes more than second-order when it is realized that certain procedures are at least partially constitutive of a rule of law. And when reasonable procedures of this sort are not in place, then the rule of law may itself be jeopardized.

Insofar as habeas corpus is primarily conceived as a right protecting people from arbitrary deprivation of liberty, and insofar as liberty is a basic human good, then habeas corpus resembles a substantive right in that it aims at the promotion of a significant human good. But insofar as habeas corpus merely calls for a certain rule to be adhered to, where a person must be brought out of the detention and have the charges against him or her recited publicly, habeas corpus more closely resembles a procedural right. Habeas corpus is in this latter sense primarily a procedural right – a right that can remain fixed even as the particular substantive crimes that could lead to arrest and incarceration might vary quite significantly over time. Indeed, habeas corpus does not stipulate any particular conditions that must be included as part of the procedure although, as I will argue, whatever the conditions are, they must satisfy minimal principles of equity and equality. Habeas corpus can be both a procedural and a substantive right, but I will focus on it as a procedural right.

In the debates about global justice, for some theorists it will matter whether habeas corpus is merely procedural or also substantive. If habeas corpus is a right to certain forms of liberty, then habeas corpus can be defended in the same way as other substantive rights. But if habeas corpus is primarily a procedural right, then different forms of protection may be needed for it than for substantive rights to liberty. In addition, we may need to change how we regard human rights protection in general. This is because substantive rights are considered to be the core of human rights and where most international attention should be focused. It is my contention, though, that some procedural rights are also extremely important human rights that the international community should protect as vigilantly as certain better known substantive rights. But to understand why this issue is an important one, there must be some way to distinguish procedural from substantive rights and to explain the value of each.

For some theorists like Thomas Franck, procedural fairness need not be moral at all and in any event can certainly differ, with moral distributive justice seen as a substantive matter.[11] We shall next see that there is considerable disagreement about what precisely is the normative value of procedural rights, as well as whether the value of procedural rights can be understood as independent of the value of substantive rights. Conforming to procedural rights can still leave room for great iniquity. Yet, as we will see, there is still considerable value in having a regime where procedural rights are strongly protected.

3.3 INSTRUMENTAL AND INTRINSIC VALUE OF PROCEDURES

At this stage in a fairly abstract chapter, let me summarize where we are. Procedural rights are of value because of the two primary goals that they serve: protecting substantive rights, especially the right to liberty, and partially constituting the rule of law. First, procedural rights have instrumental value as complements to substantive rights. Procedural rights offer protection for substantive rights and are often "stops" against certain forms of wrongdoing. Procedural rights protect the means by which substantive rights violations can be brought to public light and redressed. Thus, procedural rights have instrumental or derivative value in that they promote and support substantive rights. Nearly everyone agrees that procedural rights have instrumental value, although there is quite a bit of disagreement about how significant this value is.

Second, procedural rights have intrinsic value as partially constituting the rule of law. Procedural rights allow for a system of law to emerge out of a set of substantive rules and to minimize arbitrariness. A *system* of law is different from a *set* of laws in that there are means to decide conflicts among substantive rights and also to provide a coherent order to the rules and rights that are elements of the law. In this way, procedural rights have *intrinsic* value in that they are partially constitutive of a rule of law. In this latter sense, procedural rights may not have content and while they aim at a certain good, that good, fairness and nonarbitrariness, may also have no content, unlike the goods that substantive rights aim at, such as property rights or free speech rights which have content and aim at the human good of liberty. Fairness may have no content when it is strictly a formal

---

[11] Thomas M. Franck, *Fairness in International Law and Institutions*, NY: Oxford University Press, 1995, p. 22.

matter, that is, where the relevant critical question is whether a particular set of rules is reasonable and has been reasonably followed.

The best way to characterize the intrinsic value of procedural rights is as a stop to arbitrariness. Non-arbitrariness is related to a type of fairness that involves complying with a rule conjoined with a system of overseeing that the rule is complied with. This topic is generally discussed under the heading of the rule of law. Lawrence Solum has persuasively argued that procedures are able to promote such fairness to the extent that they allow individuals to participate in decisions about their welfare, and hence to monitor those decisions to make sure that they are fair. Solum calls this the Participation Principle which, he says, "stipulates a minimum (and minimal) right of participation, in the form of notice and an opportunity to be heard, that must be satisfied (if feasible) in order for a procedure to be considered fair."[12]

Joseph Raz has argued that not all forms of arbitrariness are inconsistent with the rule of law and the kind of procedural rights I have been discussing. For Raz, arbitrariness is a subjective notion, either having to do with intending to act contrary to the purposes which would justify the use of power or with indifference to those purposes. Because Raz thinks that arbitrariness is subjective, he is able to say that "It all depends on the state of mind of the men in power. As such the rule of law does not bear directly on the extent of arbitrary power."[13] But Raz thinks that there is a "hard objective edge" to "the subjective core" of the concept of arbitrariness:

Since it is universally believed that it is wrong to use public powers for private ends any such use is in itself an instance of arbitrary use of power ... the rule of law does help to curb such forms of arbitrary power.[14]

When we are addressing political authority, a legal rule must conform to the rule of law if it is to respect human dignity, even though other valuable considerations can be inconsistent with the rule of law.

Political orders are arbitrary when they involve rule by the whim of a person or persons, instead of by a rule, or when they involve no oversight. Yet the independent value of non-arbitrariness is hard to characterize. There is a kind of formal protection that is achieved when procedural

---

[12] Lawrence B. Solum, "Procedural Justice," Public Law and Legal Theory Research Paper No. 04–02, in possession of author, 1–126, at p. 9.
[13] Joseph Raz, *The Authority of Law*, Oxford University Press, 1979, p. 219.
[14] Ibid., p. 220.

rights are respected. In particular, there is a predictability that allows individuals to plan with an eye toward their own agency when they are assured that various means of appealing mistreatment can be called upon. Predictability is crucial for exercising agency and, when it is denied, a person's normal human capabilities are disrupted.[15] When people cannot exercise their agency, they are not afforded proper respect as persons. Arbitrariness is a disvalue in the sense that it disrupts such predictability and ultimately disrupts the proper and respectful functioning of human agency.

To illustrate this point, let us return to the example of habeas corpus. Habeas corpus provides a minimal rule that calls for the detainee to be brought out of the detention and given the opportunity to hear the charges against him or her as well as to respond to those charges. Habeas corpus thus provides a way, through a minimal hearing, for deciding whether one's incarceration is proper, and also a rudimentary system for oversight, through the public hearing, of the process leading up to the incarceration and of the conditions of the incarceration itself. In this sense, habeas corpus epitomizes procedural fairness, even as the kind of arbitrariness that it rules out is not the worst form of abuse that rulers can perpetrate on their subjects. I will now say more about why arbitrariness is a disvalue as I take up three challenges to my view.

First, let us consider an argument that David Estlund has made in the context of debates about whether democratic procedures have intrinsic value independent of their outcomes. In arguing against the intrinsic value of procedures, Estlund discusses coin tosses. There is a sense that coin tosses are the purest form of procedural fairness – everyone is treated exactly the same and no one is treated according to a standard that is biased. Estlund makes such an argument in order to show that procedural fairness is not itself intrinsically valuable, since coin tosses, the purest example of procedural fairness, are not always valuable.[16] He makes this argument to show that democratic processes do not have intrinsic value. But this is just the point – some procedures have value in one context even though they lack value in another context. In some contexts procedures can have intrinsic value, even though these procedures would lack such value in different contexts. Intrinsic value can be linked to context without this value becoming merely instrumental.

---

[15] On this point see Colleen Murphy, "Lon Fuller and the Moral Value of the Rule of Law," *Law and Philosophy*, vol. 24, no. 3, 2005, 239–262.
[16] David Estlund, *Democratic Authority: A Philosophical Framework*, Princeton University Press, 2007.

Coin tosses have value in terms of how they are used, that is, in terms of their context. There can be value, especially intrinsic value, due to that context. If there is nothing else that could be a relevant basis of decision making, then coin tosses have value in that they provide a fair way to reach decisions, and that value is independent of the outcome of the process. But if there is some other method that could relevantly be used to make a fair decision, then coin tosses simply look arbitrary, as Estlund implies. In democratic decision making, expertise could be relevant, except that it turns out to be very hard to see how to figure out who has expertise. Preferences are arguably relevant to democratic decision making and, if they are relevant, then it makes no sense to use coin tosses rather than voting. Both are procedures and both have value in certain contexts, not because of consequences but because of what is a relevant basis for decisions about disparate treatment.

Second, one could argue that procedures like habeas corpus directly promote a substantive human good, namely that we should not be forced to assume certain risks. Larry Alexander has denied that procedural rights have value, or even status, independent of substantive rights. His position is that "procedural rights just are substantive rights, albeit substantive rights of a special (but quite numerous) kind: rights against risks."[17] He argues that "procedural rights are in some sense secondary to substantive rights because they are rights about official determinations of the facts governing the application of substantive rights."[18]

The examples Alexander gives are of the same sort: "the right to a court appointed attorney," "the right to compel witnesses to testify," and "the right to a jury trial." And he argues that the goal of such procedural rights is "Minimizing the risk of mistaken conviction" which then "increases the risks associated with crime."[19] The kind of fairness that Alexander concerns himself with is thus a kind of substantive fairness – minimizing the risk of mistaken conviction. This kind of fairness has largely derivative status, as he argues. Concerning rights like habeas corpus, Alexander contends that these procedural rights have value only as that value derives from the substantive right "to liberty from confinement."[20]

I do not deny that sometimes procedural rights like habeas corpus have value insofar as they promote the liberty of the detainee. But I think that the more important and more interesting value of habeas corpus has to do

---

[17] Larry Alexander, "Are Procedural Rights Derivative Substantive Rights?" *Law and Philosophy*, vol 17, no. 1, January 1998, 19.
[18] Ibid., 23.   [19] Ibid., 24.   [20] Ibid., 31.

with its intrinsic value as part of the rule of law by protecting people against arbitrariness. It may be that the liberty from confinement is unaffected by habeas corpus rights, since the prisoner may have only very temporary removal from confinement associated with this right. Alexander may be right that there is a worry about certain risks, but specifying what the risk is in the case of a denial of habeas corpus rights is not always easy to do. And it is sometimes unclear what substantive right is risked when the rule of law is denied. Think of Jacobo Timmerman and assume that he is never tortured or otherwise harmed. There is a loss of status in his occupying a cell without a number and being a prisoner without a name. The loss is one of status not necessarily one of liberty – indeed, as I will later argue, it is best understood as a loss concerning one's status as a human, as a bearer of human rights.[21]

Third, one could argue that the human good of fairness is what procedural rights promote and what is at jeopardy when rights like habeas corpus rights are denied. If a human good is achieved by a fair method and the same human good is produced by an unfair method, there is a normative superiority of the fairly achieved human good, but not merely because that good is indeed achieved, since that good can also be achieved by an unfair method. A fair method is often one that is open to all parties and that proceeds in a publicly open manner. Formal fairness, as I have said, epitomizes equality and minimal equity in just this way.

Consider the way that treats can be awarded to one's children. I can award children treats based on a private calculation of who I like best, or based on an open competition for the treats, the terms of which the children are aware. It may turn out that by both methods the treats are awarded to the same children. Therefore, the fair method is not better because of what it achieves. There is something about the allocation process, or the process to decide how to engage in allocation, that itself has value in such cases. I have tried to put the best case forward for the independent value of procedural rights. But like the analysis of the difference between substantive and procedural rights in the previous section I have not fully succeeded. We can draw a conceptual distinction between the value of procedural and substantive rights, but practically there may not be a bright line.

Fair methods are generally ones that are open to public scrutiny – they conform to what I have called "the principle of visibleness." This principle

[21] Jacobo Timmerman, *Prisoner Without a Name, Cell Without a Number*, Toby Talbot (trans.), Madison, WI: University of Wisconsin Press, 2002.

does not have overriding weight, but it is a significant consideration. And the value is that when visibleness is part of a continuing process, where people can expect that their actions will be open to public scrutiny, arbitrariness is diminished. Arbitrariness is a disvalue that again is not fully understood in terms of outcomes or goods. For the same result could be achieved arbitrarily or non-arbitrarily. Procedural rights create a bulwark against arbitrariness and for this reason they have value, and that value is independent of what human goods are promoted. The rule of law is merely what is constituted by a reasonable, coherent, and efficacious set of practices involving procedural rights. There is a close link between the rule of law and procedural fairness, and on my account the Magna Carta legacy rights, such as habeas corpus, play a significant role in the rule of law; indeed, they are partially constitutive of the rule of law in certain situations.

3.4 INTERNATIONAL PROCEDURAL RIGHTS

If there is to be an international rule of law, certain core procedural rights will have to be protected against abuse wherever that abuse occurs. A good example is the failure to provide core procedural rights at the prisons in Guantanamo Bay, Cuba, and Bagram Air Base, Afghanistan, as well as at refugee camps. It seemed as if there was a legal black hole, and indeed that was just what certain members of George Bush's administration actually advocated. If human rights are to be protected globally, protecting Magna Carta legacy procedural rights across the world is utterly crucial.

For a variety of reasons, international law has focused mainly on substantive rather than procedural rights. Perhaps the most obvious reason is that the popular imagination is easily inspired by substantive rights violations such as those that occur in genocide or crimes against humanity cases. The popular imagination is not easily aroused by violations of procedural rights at the international level, such as those that occurred at Guantanamo or Bagram. Yet this is itself a very good reason to think that international procedural rights are especially in need of protection, even more than is true of international substantive rights. Without the popular concern about procedural rights, even more attention needs to be given to protecting these rights through international courts and tribunals. Indeed, this also seems to have been William Blackstone's view in 1765 when he said this about habeas corpus: "Confinement of the person, by secretly hurrying him to gaol, where his sufferings are unknown and forgotten; is a less public, a less striking, and therefore a more dangerous engine of arbitrary government."[22]

Procedural rights, such as those denied at Guantanamo, should be protected internationally in such a way that no one slips into the legal black hole where procedural rights claims are not recognized. When procedural rights claims are not recognized, then two things happen. First, it is much harder for substantive rights claims to be recognized, or even for anyone to tell if such claims are being made. And, second, there is a serious impediment to the establishment of the rule of law. There are many dark corners of the world where vulnerable individuals can be spirited away, like Guantanamo and Bagram, as well as some refugee camps, and where these individuals may easily fall into becoming as if they are rightless, at least in the sense of not having their status recognized. Feinberg and others who have followed his lead have seen recognition as a necessary condition of having rights. Especially if we are interested in human rights, namely the rights a person has by virtue of their status as being a member of humanity or the human community, people's rights will not be effectively protected unless there is a gapless system of enforcement that extends across the globe.

In the protection of human rights, one of the most significant considerations is that there is protection of the minimal procedural right that a person's claims are heard. And, on an even more basic level, there must be protection that an individual is not taken from public view and incarcerated as a prisoner without a name and in a cell without a number, again to use the powerful image from Jacobo Timmerman.[23] International procedural rights protect the status of persons as deserving of respect and recognition as rights-bearers. In this sense, international procedural rights have value, as they provide obvious protection for substantive rights like the right against indefinite incarceration or the right against torture while in confinement. And there is also intrinsic value in international procedural rights insofar as they are part of what constitutes an international rule of law.

Let me just say a bit about the very idea of global justice in terms of procedural rights. In his important book on fairness in international law, Thomas Franck distinguishes between process fairness and moral fairness, arguing that moral fairness is largely a matter of distributive justice

---

[22] William Blackstone, *Commentaries on the Laws of England* (1765), University of Chicago Press, 1979, vol. I, p. 132.
[23] Timmerman, *Prisoner Without a Name*.

and is not necessarily satisfied (and may be in conflict with) having fair procedures.[24] Especially at the international level, procedural rights provide the kind of stability that the rule of law generally supports. But, according to Franck, there is a sense that in some cases the rule of law may impede the advancement of justice, understood as a matter of moral distributive allotments or as rectification for wrongs of the past. In this way, protecting procedural rights may promote a very thin morality but leave untouched, and perhaps work against, a thicker conception of moral justice.

I do not dispute this possibility. Indeed, on a very minimalist construal of habeas corpus, the prisoner may be brought out of detention where the jailer publicly proclaims the charges against the prisoner, but the prisoner can then legitimately be returned to detention without anything further having happened. It may even be that having followed these procedures to the letter makes it much harder to raise substantive justice questions about the rightness of having incarcerated the prisoner in the first place. More likely is the possibility that the focus on procedures will make it very hard to see systemic problems in a society that might have led to the incarceration of this prisoner and his or her cohorts rather than another group from a different stratum of that society.

However, I disagree with Franck's view that procedural fairness is not a form of moral fairness. Procedural fairness can be at least minimally moral in that even moral fairness has both its substantive and procedural aspects. Not all of morality is a matter of distributive justice, as even John Rawls admitted at the beginning of his book *A Theory of Justice*.[25] And if we are considering the morality of institutions and practices, distributive justice is not all there is to morality either. There is a moral minimum where we expect to treat people in a consistent manner and also not to ignore their claims. Here there is something like a substantive component to even a rudimentary procedural right. There is both a sense that the person should be treated according to the same rules as everyone else, and also the idea that those rules must meet some kind of minimal threshold, in terms of minimal equity or even-handedness.[26]

Thus, for procedural rights to be respected, individual humans must be afforded the status of rights-bearers: they cannot be consigned to

[24] Franck, *Fairness in International Law and Institutions*, p. 22.
[25] John Rawls, *A Theory of Justice*, Cambridge, MA: Harvard University Press, 1971.
[26] I thank Tom Campbell for discussion of this point. See also Lon Fuller, *The Morality of Law*, New Haven, CT: Yale University Press, 1963.

Nowheresville or to Guantanamo Bay and Bagram Air Base, where their claims will be unrecognized. Just as no one should be consigned to the status of being Stateless, as Hannah Arendt so strongly argued,[27] it can also be said that no one should be denied other basic procedural rights either, especially since Statelessness itself is largely a function of being deprived of certain procedural rights. For, when basic procedural rights, like habeas corpus, are denied to a person, it is as if that individual ceases to be a rights-bearing member of humanity. It should not be allowed that we can be forced to occupy legal black holes even as other morally problematic things may occur in our dangerous and diverse world.

3.5 OBJECTIONS

In this section I will respond to criticisms that have arisen over the sort of positions I have taken in this chapter. First, let me consider some of Robert Nozick's writings. Nozick's account of procedural rights raises an important objection to the view I hold, even as Nozick also supports other aspects of my view.[28] Nozick considers whether we have a moral right that others first use reliable procedures to determine our guilt before these others are justified in punishing us. Nozick argues that there is a moral right not to be punished unless the punishment is based on a reliable procedure. In this respect, Nozick's view and my own are similar. But Nozick then explains that reliable procedures are important because they limit exposing people to unacceptably high levels of risk, such as being forced to play Russian roulette.[29] In what follows I will explain why I think Nozick has not adequately captured what is wrong with unreliable procedures, and why the Russian roulette example actually supports my own account of what is wrong with them.

I agree with Nozick that it is unacceptable to punish on the basis of unreliable procedures and that this is true even if one is actually guilty. I also agree that part of the explanation is that one's substantive liberties are unjustifiably put at risk by such procedures and that such riskiness is problematic regardless of whether one deserves to be punished. I might even agree with Nozick that he has captured the most important element of what makes such procedures problematic, and yet still think his analysis to be seriously flawed because of what it leaves out. What Nozick has not

---

[27] Hannah Arendt, *The Human Condition*, University of Chicago Press.
[28] I am grateful to Kit Wellman for calling this objection to my attention.
[29] Robert Nozick, *Anarchy, State, and Utopia*, NY: Basic Books, 1974, pp. 96–108, especially p. 105.

fully captured is the systemic reason for why such procedures are problematic. Indeed, if risk is solely the problem, then it would be hard to see why in the case where it is known that the punished person is guilty, an objection to this practice should still be that there is an unjustified risk of punishing the innocent. Risk of being unjustifiably punished would not actually matter in this case, since the person in question was actually guilty.

Let us consider the Russian roulette case in this context. Assume that we know somehow that the person will not hurt himself or herself because the bullet to be fired is simply not in the cylinder. What is problematic is that in other cases of Russian roulette some people may be harmed by such situations and that in general people should not have to face such situations. To be sure, this rationale is connected to the general riskiness of Russian roulette. But the generalized riskiness is of a different sort than the specific risk the person faces (or does not face) in the actual case. And the issue is not merely one of whether or not we can know that the person is indeed guilty. Procedures can have value independent of the particular case they are being applied to, even as that value connects to the minimization of particular risks.

Russian roulette is generally problematic because of the utterly misplaced incentives where life is forced to be risked for things far less valuable. Even when we know that the particular person's life is not so risked, because there is no bullet in the chamber about to be fired, the incentive structure of Russian roulette is still problematic. The world is a better place where Russian roulette is not played, regardless of whether anyone is actually ever killed. The "institution" of Russian roulette belittles the value of life and liberty. Even though the belittling of life and liberty is due to the inappropriate risking of life and liberty on the part of those who play Russian roulette, the belittling is ultimately independent of whether anyone's life is truly risked or not.

This is related to whether a person can be harmed by being forced to consider a beneficial offer. Clearly accepting or rejecting the offer does not in itself run the risk of harming the person, since either the person is no worse off than before by rejecting the offer or the person is better off than before by accepting the offer. But there are systemic reasons why we might think nonetheless that there is harm when it is procedurally allowed that certain kinds of offers can be made, especially in cases where the offer is in some sense inappropriate. Consider a situation where a professor can offer a better grade in exchange for the student washing his car. If the offer is rejected it looks like no one has been harmed, since in terms of pre-offer situations everyone is seemingly in the same position. Nonetheless, there is now a problem with the system of how grades are distributed that did not exist in the pre-offer situation.

In a sense, the inappropriate offer has poisoned the well and rendered the whole grading system problematic. I here make use of an idea I have developed elsewhere concerning structures of incentives that can be assessed somewhat independently of the risk at the moment of harm.[30] In international law, what happens at the systemic level is often as important as what happens at the level of individual cases. What is at stake is whether or not a rule of law is encouraged or discouraged from being developed.

Second, consider some of the writings of Lawrence Solum. Solum suggests that there is a fuzzy line between procedural and substantive rights, although one function is "dominant or characteristic." To figure out which is dominant, he proposes a thought experiment where there is a "possible world in which citizens know only the content of the substantive law, and only legal officials know the content" of the procedures. This is similar to Hart's way of distinguishing primary from secondary rules that was examined earlier in this chapter. In this way, legal institutions and their procedures can be "acoustically separated from ordinary citizens."[31] Acoustical separation means that neither officials nor ordinary people can hear what the other is saying in terms of a given practice.

Solum then proposes separating functions and rights based on whether they are recognizable by those outside the system. If they are not recognized outside the system, then they are primarily procedural. By using this method, it appears that habeas corpus would straddle the divide between substance and procedure, not be primarily procedural as I have suggested, since the functioning of habeas corpus has to do with rules of conduct of officials that are also recognizable to non-officials.[32]

I have suggested that I do not see habeas corpus as a pure procedural right. So, the worry is only that I have mischaracterized whether habeas corpus is primarily procedural or substantive. If we could acoustically separate the prisoner and the warden, it is unclear to me that the prisoner

---

[30] See Larry May and John C. Hughes, "Is Sexual Harassment Coercive?" in *Moral Rights in the Workplace*, Gertrude Ezorsky and James Nickel (eds.), Albany, NY: State University of New York Press, 1987, pp. 115–122.

[31] Lawrence Solum, "Procedural Justice," Public Law and Legal Theory Research Paper Series, Research Paper No. 04–02, Spring 2004, pp. 22–23 (paper in possession of author).

[32] See also Meier Dan-Cohen, "Decision Rules and Conduct Rules: On Acoustic Separation in Criminal Law," *Harvard Law Review*, vol. 97, 1984, 625.

would not recognize how habeas corpus functions. For at least minimal habeas corpus is a very simple procedure, calling only for the prisoner to be brought out of detention into the light of day in order to have the charges against him or her publicly declared. Given how simple habeas corpus is, and that it mainly calls for a kind of visibility of the prisoner, the way in which this right is procedural is not best captured by thinking about whether one or the other party involved in this right can be acoustically separated from the other.

I will show in Chapters 5 and 9 that the focus of the Magna Carta legacy rights is not just about whether the officials made good decisions about the incarceration or rendition of the detainee. Rather, the additional conduct of these officials, in terms of how the detainee is treated, especially in terms of torture, is also the focus. But since the focus is on the officials, not the non-officials, it makes sense to talk of habeas corpus as primarily a matter of procedural rather than substantive rights. And this is true even though the rights in question aim at such liberties as the right not to be tortured, and also that the detainee can surely get a sense of what is at stake in these procedures.

Third, consider one last objection, namely that I still have not managed to explain the reason why a lack of procedures like habeas corpus increases the likelihood of arbitrariness. Indeed, there remains a question about what specialized use I am making of the idea of arbitrariness. To make this objection more specific, we can turn to recent debates on democratic legitimacy. It is sometimes said that only democratic decision making is non-arbitrary politically. This is because democratic decision-making procedures best exemplify the politically legitimate use of authority. In the words of David Estlund, "No one has authority or legitimate coercive power over another without a justification that could be accepted by all qualified points of view."[33] Non-arbitrariness results from democratic or quasi-democratic procedures, not the sort I have been describing as epitomized in the Magna Carta legacy rules and rights.

Estlund and others such as Thomas Christiano agree about the "thin and only occasional value" of procedural fairness.[34] Christiano says that the fairness of a procedure "varies in part depending on the nature of the enterprise."[35] Christiano looks to the outcome of the procedure; Estlund

---

[33] David Estlund, *Democratic Authority: A Philosophical Framework*, Princeton University Press, 2007, p. 33.
[34] David Estlund, "Debate: On Christiano's *The Constitution of Equality*," *The Journal of Political Philosophy*, vol. 17, no. 2, 2009, 241–252, especially 249.
[35] Thomas Christiano, "Debate: Estlund on Democratic Authority," in ibid., 228–240, especially 231.

looks to "epistemic" considerations that include outcomes. But they also seemingly recognize that there is more to it than this. As Christiano says, "we put some weight on the procedure itself, inasmuch as each is thought to be entitled to a fair go," and he admits that fairness involves a certain kind of constraint that is "grounded in some fundamental moral principles regarding the relations of persons to one another."[36]

I have contended that one of the non-instrumental values of procedural fairness is that possible arbitrariness of Executive rule is disrupted, which includes rule by officials of various sorts who do the bidding of the "sovereign" power. I should add that this non-instrumental value of procedures is only true in certain fairly limited contexts, especially where individuals are most vulnerable to the whim of persons in the Executive branch of government, and most especially when a person is incapacitated and subject to the complete control of such officials.

Arbitrariness has to do with treating people in a way that denies them a "fair go" in that the unpredictability and lack of openness deprives them of their agency as well as diminishing their status in terms of equity and equality. And procedural or formal fairness can be an effective restraint in those situations where visibleness is likely to help the person overcome irrelevant or improper treatment. As we have seen in this chapter, procedural rights have significant value, even if they cannot be completely separated from substantive rights. And in the international domain, the lack of protection of procedural rights is especially problematic.

I began this chapter by discussing Joel Feinberg's thought-experiment about Nowheresville. Feinberg said it was characteristic of a place where there are no rights that people do not make claims since they "do not have a notion of what is their due."[37] In discussing Guantanamo and Bagram, we have seen that the lack of procedural rights protection is not just a matter of failing to see what is one's due, but rather of having officials recognize what are their duties in light of claiming by inmates and detainees under their care. Being able to claim is only part of what rights involve. And if there are places where only claiming goes on, without corresponding recognition of the claiming person's status, that is another instance of Nowheresville. International law is unfortunately like Nowheresville in this latter sense. In the remainder of the book, I will try to indicate what can be done to correct this problem.

---

[36] Ibid., 232.
[37] Feinberg, "The Nature and Value of Rights," 249.

As we have seen in this chapter, procedural rights have significant value, even if they cannot be completely separated from substantive rights. In the next chapter I will discuss in more detail the morality of a system of procedural rights. And in the international domain the lack of protection of procedural rights is especially problematic. The full discussion of the international right of habeas corpus, along with other Magna Carta legacy rights, will take up the sections of the book that follow the next chapter. In the meantime we will delve more deeply into the philosophical concerns that have caused some theorists to postulate that a system of law must have a moral minimum of fairness. This will set the stage for a full defense of such procedural rights in international law. But it will not be until the final part of the book that comparative institutional remedies will be discussed fully.

CHAPTER 4

International law and the inner
morality of law

In this chapter I will connect the previous discussion of procedural rights with the debates about the rule of law. In Book V of the *Nicomachean Ethics*, Aristotle gives one of the first accounts of the rule of law when he says: "we allow only reason, not a human being, to be ruler."[1] Aristotle then divides political justice into two parts. "One part of the politically just is natural, and the other part legal. The natural has the same validity everywhere alike, independent of its seeming so or not."[2] This characterization of the natural part of justice is sometimes associated with the so-called natural duties of justice, specifically with the substantive duties to promote just institutions. But, it seems that Aristotle, at least at that point in his *Ethics*, is referring to something procedural, what might be called "natural fairness."

I am interested in seeing what the normative jurisprudential support is for a minimalist version of habeas corpus in international law. In my view, the writings of H. L. A. Hart and Lon L. Fuller about the internal aspect of rules or the inner morality of law concern an issue that is similar to what Aristotle meant by the natural part of justice, namely that part of natural fairness that stays the same from society to society, and perhaps even outside of particular societies – for instance, in the international arena. Indeed, Hart spoke of "natural procedural justice"[3] and Fuller spoke of a "procedural version of natural law."[4] In this respect one could ask whether there is something like a natural duty to support procedures, such as habeas corpus, that provide minimal fairness for those who have been incarcerated or detained. And if there is such a duty, is it part of the inner morality of law? In his eighth desiderata of the rule of law, Fuller

---

[1] Aristotle, *Nicomachean Ethics*, 1134a35.   [2] Ibid., 1134b20.
[3] H. L. A. Hart, "Positivism and the Separation of Law and Morals, *Harvard Law Review*, vol. 71, 1958, 623.
[4] Lon Fuller, *The Morality of Law*, New Haven, CT: Yale University Press, 1969 [1964], pp. 96–97.

mentions such things as habeas corpus as an aspect of procedural due process,[5] but he does little more than mention it; Hart does not mention it at all. But in my view both legal theorists focus as much on procedural as substantive justice.

In what follows I will investigate what Fuller called "procedural natural law" in contemporary international criminal law. I will argue that procedural rights are part of what constitutes the rule of law and are especially important as gap-fillers in creating an international rule of law that respects fundamental fairness. International criminal law will not come to maturity as a system of law unless protections of fundamental fairness, such as a global right of habeas corpus, are put in place. I will use some of Hart's and Fuller's writings as a springboard for assessing procedural rights within the context of the international rule of law. In the first two sections I will rehearse some of Hart's and Fuller's views as they pertain to the subject of international law and also to the inner morality of law. In the third section I will set out some of my views on these matters, drawing on both Hart and Fuller, concerning the value of fundamental procedural rights. In the fourth section I will discuss the right of habeas corpus as a good test case of how to think about these issues. In the final section I will expand on these remarks by considering various criticisms of my view.

4.1 HART ON INTERNATIONAL LAW

H. L. A. Hart draws a distinction between primary rules, in which "human beings are required to do or abstain from certain actions," and secondary rules, which may introduce, extinguish, or modify primary rules.[6] Hart is often interpreted as requiring a rule of recognition, which involves secondary rules that establish how primary rules are to be recognized as valid law; indeed, Ronald Dworkin talks about the rule of recognition as a "master rule" for Hart.[7] Yet, in Hart's treatment of international law in the final chapter of his book *The Concept of Law*, he does not deny that international law is law, even though international law, at least in the early 1960s, seemed to Hart to lack a rule of recognition. In this respect, consider the final sentence of his book:

Bentham, the inventor of the expression "international law," defended it simply by saying that it was "sufficiently analogous" to municipal law. To this two

---

[5] Ibid., p. 81.
[6] H. L. A. Hart, *The Concept of Law*, Oxford: Oxford University Press, 1994 [1961], p. 81.
[7] For example, see Ronald Dworkin, "The Model of Rules I," in *Taking Rights Seriously*, London: Duckworth, 1977, p. 41.

comments are perhaps worth adding. First, that the analogy is one of content not of form; secondly, that in the analogy of content, no other social rules are so close to municipal law as those of international law.[8]

This is not to say that formal features of a system of rules were unimportant to Hart. However, on the penultimate page of his book, Hart spoke of emancipating "ourselves from the assumption that international law *must* contain a basic rule."[9]

Hart himself often says that law is best understood as the "union of primary and secondary rules." But by the last chapter of his book, the chapter on international law, Hart is at pains to point out that while this union provides a "sufficient condition for the application of the expression 'legal system'" he has not claimed "that the word 'law' must be defined in its terms." Instead, he says that the "idea of a union of primary and secondary rules … may be regarded as a mean between juristic extremes."[10] Arguably, what is even more important to Hart for establishing that a set of rules is a legal system is whether the people who live under the set of rules have an internal perspective or point of view toward these rules, where one is concerned with rules "as a member of a group which accepts and uses them as guides to conduct."[11]

For Hart, the internal perspective is crucial for legal systems, but there are arguably two candidates for this perspective, only one of which is truly so. What is crucial for distinguishing "social rules from mere group habits" "is that there should be a critical reflective attitude to certain patterns of behavior as a common standard, and that this should display itself in criticism (including self-criticism), demands for conformity, and in acknowledgement that such criticism and demands are justified."[12] Taking this internal perspective is crucial for the proper functioning of a system of rules that is considered authoritative and deserving of obedience.

In Hart's view, international law can be law properly so called. In the early 1960s Hart already recognized that international law very closely resembled domestic municipal law in its content, although not in its form, since international law lacked a rule of recognition. Indeed, Hart probably would say something different today, especially with the institution of the ICC and its complex statute, as well as with the growing recognition and acceptance of the legitimacy of international law in nearly all quarters. But there is another way to

---

[8] Hart, *The Concept of Law*, p. 237.   [9] Ibid., p. 236.   [10] Ibid., p. 212.
[11] Ibid., p. 89. I am grateful to Jack Knight for discussion of this point.   [12] Ibid., p. 57.

understand the legitimacy of the claim that international law is law properly so called.

International law is easier to understand if one focuses on such things as "the internal aspect of rules" rather than sovereignty which creates or enforces a master rule. As Hart recognized, there is an "absence of an international Legislature, courts with compulsory jurisdiction, and centrally organized sanctions." These absences have inspired "misgivings" about whether international law is properly called law, especially since the absence of such things seems to indicate a lack of a rule of recognition.[13] Hart was seemingly not one of the people who had these misgivings, at least not in a way that made him doubt that international law could be law properly so called. The fact that Hart recognized that many saw international law as a "doubtful case"[14] and that he placed international law in his last chapter indicates that he also saw it as a hard case. But, as I have been arguing, he probably also saw international law as a good example for discussing the relative importance of the internal point of view as opposed to the union of primary and secondary rules in identifying when there is a system of law.

In eventually taking up the case of procedural rights like habeas corpus it will be important to remember that Hart stressed the importance of "demands for conformity" with primary rules, as well as a "centrally organized system of sanctions." In international law, especially international criminal law, both of these factors are currently hard to satisfy in a rigorous way since there is no sovereign international State that can accomplish or facilitate these things. But gaps in sanctions can be filled without a fully centralized system in place, especially if the relevant officials take an internal perspective toward the law. Especially in high profile cases, indictment and arrest procedures that are piecemeal can go a long way, as can other piecemeal ways, to protecting substantive rights internationally.

At the end of the chapter I will take up the case of the Guantanamo detainees who tried to get their substantive rights protected even though there was no centrally organized international sanctioning power. The Guantanamo detainees filed habeas corpus petitions in order to put public pressure on the US government to protect their substantive rights. In addition, habeas corpus appeals sought to prevent the "legal black holes" that had seemingly opened because of a lack of a gapless international legal system. In this sense, habeas corpus was a gap-filler that helped

---

[13] Ibid., p. 214.   [14] Ibid., p. 3.

establish an international rule of law even though there are still no Executive and Legislative branches of an international government.

As international law comes to have more institutional arrangements that are like municipal law, Hart was right to think that it will resemble municipal law in form as well as in content. And we are certainly moving in this direction with the creation of the ICC with some compulsory jurisdiction and centrally organized sanctions, at least for those States that have ratified the Rome Treaty. And as the Security Council acts more and more like a world Legislature, similarly international law moves closer to municipal law. There is still a lack of fully centralized sanctions in international law, although the various appellate courts at the International Criminal Court for the Former Yugoslavia (ICTY), the International Criminal Tribunal for Rwanda (ICTR) and the ICC have been striving valiantly to create a piecemeal uniformity of sanctions, despite lacking a fully centralized mechanism of enforcement of their indictments and judgments. But in the meantime, what has been most striking since the early 1960s, when Hart wrote his book, is how far the world community has moved in developing an internal perspective on international law, especially international criminal law. And with the development of this perspective, some of Hart's worries about international law have been addressed.

In Chapter 9 of *The Concept of Law*, Hart launches his own positive discussion of natural law by explaining that there is a "rational connection between natural facts and the content of legal and moral rules." Without a minimal natural content to the law, "men, as they are, would have no reason for obeying voluntarily any rules."[15] At least some members of the society must voluntarily accept the rules. "Without their voluntary cooperation, thus creating *authority*, the coercive power of law and government cannot be established."[16] And for the system to be most stable, these people "must conceive of themselves as morally bound to do so."[17] The natural facts must be satisfied for such an acceptance, and their acceptance is then expressed in "internal statements," but this does not mean that they "are thereby committed to a moral judgment."[18]

In another of his writings, Hart discusses "procedural requirements" that include what he calls "rules of natural justice." These rules specify what law "except in special circumstances" is required to be. There are two perspectives from which one can see the value of procedural requirements

---

[15] Ibid., p. 93.   [16] Ibid., p. 201.   [17] Ibid., p. 203   [18] Ibid.

of natural justice: the perspective of the officials who run the legal system and the perspective of the individual citizen. Concerning the latter he says:

Thus, general rules clearly formulated and publicly promulgated are the most efficient form of social control. But from the point of view of the individual citizen, they are more than that: they are required if he is to have the advantage of knowing in advance the ways in which his liberty will be restricted in the various situations in which he may find himself, and he needs this knowledge if he is to plan his life.[19]

Jeremy Waldron has helpfully commented on these passages that it is at least plausible that Hart here allows that some aspects of the rule of law have moral value which is severable from their legal value.[20] This may only be true of the requirement that law be general in form. But it seems to me that it may also be true of procedural requirements that concern natural justice. Alternatively, it may be that Hart's comments in this relatively obscure encyclopedia entry are not definitive of how far his soft positivism took him. As we will see, Lon Fuller's position is less equivocal and provides a better springboard for my later discussion of the importance of respecting habeas corpus for there to be a system of law.

So, for Hart, there is a relationship between the minimal content of natural law and the internal perspective, but what is unclear is exactly what the relationship is. More importantly for my project, why restrict the relevant natural facts to the *content* of rules instead of also to the minimal *form* of these rules? Would Hart recognize the kind of procedural natural law that Fuller discussed and that Aristotle also seemed to embrace? Hart seems to suggest that the form also matters when he addresses Fuller directly by claiming that "in general [rules] must not be retrospective, though exceptionally they may be."[21] Hart even allows that such considerations may properly be called "the inner morality of law," yet he couches this acceptance of Fuller's terminology by then stipulating "It is unfortunately compatible with very great iniquity."[22]

Some content and also some form, in terms of formal properties as well as procedural requirements, seem to be required for law to attain the

[19] H. L. A. Hart, "Problems of the Philosophy of Law," *The Encyclopedia of Philosophy*, Paul Edwards (ed.), NY: Macmillan Publishing, 1967, vol. 6, pp. 273–274.
[20] See Jeremy Waldron, "Positivism and Legality: Hart's Equivocal Response to Fuller," *New York University Law Review*, vol. 83, no. 4, 2008, 1135–1169, especially 1153–1154.
[21] Hart, *The Concept of Law*, p. 203.   [22] Ibid., p. 207.

voluntary acceptance of some of the population. Hart has put his finger on a crucial point – certain things are required for any system of rules to attain sufficient voluntary acceptance in a population to be called a system of law. And Hart's own emphasis on secondary rules as involving largely procedural matters points us toward what must be better secured in international law if there is to be a system of law in the international domain that achieves acceptance as well. Or at least this is one, perhaps controversial, way to interpret Hart's claim that international law resembles municipal law in content but not yet in form. When international law acquires municipal law's form, it will then have a claim to be a mature system of law. In my view, as I will indicate in the ensuing discussion of Fuller, the form that is most important is that there is a guarantee of formal fairness that largely comes from the protection of procedural rights.

4.2 FULLER ON PROCEDURAL NATURAL LAW

Lon Fuller was critical of many of the theses and arguments advanced by Hart, but there is nonetheless a striking similarity in how they regarded the internal perspective of a system of law. Hart does recognize the connection between the internal perspective and what he called the minimal content of the natural law, and Fuller makes this connection more explicit and in that sense moves us forward in understanding what needs to happen for international law to become a mature system of law. Whether or not Fuller really does fit into the natural law tradition, he does link something like Hart's internal perspective to certain minimal natural law – and what he also calls moral – considerations that have historically been identified with the rule of law.

For Fuller, there are eight desiderata that when not satisfied lead to disaster for the rule of law. Here are the ways failure can occur:

(1) a failure to have rules at all;
(2) a failure to publicize ... the rules;
(3) the abuse of retroactive legislation;
(4) a failure to make rules understandable;
(5) the enactment of contradictory rules;
(6) rules that require conduct beyond the powers of the affected party;
(7) introducing such frequent changes in the rules that the subject cannot orient his action by them;

(8) a failure of congruence between the rules as announced and their actual administration.[23]

Moreover, Fuller helps us understand what is necessary for a set of rules to be a legal system when he says that his eight desiderata concern:

> a procedural, as distinguished from a substantive, natural law. What I have called the internal morality of law is in this sense a procedural version of natural law, though to avoid misunderstanding the word "procedural" should be assigned a special and expanded sense so that it would include, for example, a substantive accord between official action and enacted law.[24]

For Fuller, "substantive natural law" concerns "the proper ends to be sought through legal rules."[25] Procedural natural law is necessary for rules to be rules at all and for them to form a system. In this respect, there appears to be a connection between the internal perspective on rules that Hart identified and Fuller's inner morality of law.

The inner morality of law is a set of procedures, such as non-retroactivity, that rules must conform to in order for there to be a system of rules at all. As Hart pointed out, to call this an inner "morality" is questionable, especially since it is compatible with great iniquity. Fuller contends that a system of rules that satisfied his eight desiderata would not be a system that could be gravely iniquitous. Whether properly moral or not, there is no doubt that these desiderata are procedural constraints on rules that when adhered to make these rules into a system of rules that is deserving of respect. One way to begin to understand the possibility of common ground between Hart and Fuller is to see that the inner morality of law must be satisfied in order for people within the system of rules to take an internal perspective toward these rules.

In my view, Hart and Fuller did not really disagree much about what constitutes the inner morality of law. Rather, they disagreed about whether and to what extent it really was a "morality" that connected to ideas such as justice and fairness in a way that blocks iniquity within a system of law. In another place I have suggested that this was at best a minimal moral notion, but that is not to disparage its moral character.[26] Perhaps this is merely to say that these requirements must be satisfied for a system of law to deserve our fidelity to it, where this might capture what

---

[23] Fuller, *The Morality of Law*, pp. 39 and 96.   [24] Ibid., pp. 96–97.   [25] Ibid., p. 98.
[26] See my treatment of this topic in the first few chapters of my book *Crimes Against Humanity: A Normative Account*, Cambridge University Press, 2005.

both Hart and Fuller wanted, although they both failed to recognize an important aspect of these procedures.

In his exchange with Hart in the *Harvard Law Review*, Fuller at one point illustrates what he sees to be Hart's failure to deal with the issue of fidelity to law by reference to what makes constitutions deserving of respect. He says that "we should keep in mind that the efficacy of our work will depend upon general acceptance and to make this acceptance secure there must be general belief that the constitution itself is necessary, right, and good." Fuller then goes on to make this important observation:

We should think of our constitution as establishing a basic procedural framework for future governmental action in the enactment and administration of laws. Substantive limitations on the power of government should be kept to a minimum and should generally be confined to those for which a need can be generally appreciated. In so far as possible, substantive aims should be achieved procedurally, on the principle that if men are compelled to act in the right way, they will generally do the right thing.[27]

Here Fuller indicates why he thinks that following procedures can lead to substantive moral aims that would elicit fidelity to law. Following right procedures leads people to do the right thing. And if right procedures are not followed there is a sense that people will be more likely to do wrong to one another. As we will see later, the failure to grant habeas corpus rights to the detainees at Guantanamo made it more likely that the substantive rights of these detainees would be abused.

For Fuller, "If one wished to summarize all this [about the inner morality of law] in one phrase, it would be hard to find a better expression than 'due process of law.'"[28] Fuller gives as an example "judicial review."[29] And he says "What law must foreseeably do to achieve its aims, is something quite different from law itself."[30] But why does Fuller think that certain procedural matters are not properly part of the legal system, rather than merely being different types of procedure within a system of law? Perhaps some procedures directly protect substantive rights and others do so in a less direct, although no less important way. Indeed, that is what he says of the eighth desiderata. There may be due process rights that guarantee that legal systems have a substantive fairness. But there may also be

[27] Lon L. Fuller, "Positivism and Fidelity to Law: A Reply to Professor Hart," *Harvard Law Review*, vol. 71, 1958, 643.
[28] Fuller, *The Morality of Law*, New Haven, CT: Yale University Press, 1964, 1969, p. 103.
[29] Ibid., p. 104.   [30] Ibid., p. 108.

other procedural matters that protect the formal fairness of a system of law without having much to do with any particular substantive right. And yet the formal fairness of a system of law is itself highly valuable and in a sense undergirds the other values of specific procedures within a system of law.

Fuller says that "It is precisely when the legal system takes up weapons of violence that we impose on it the most stringent requirements of due process." Fuller then says that whenever people embark on "subjecting certain kinds of human conduct to the explicit control of rules" "they come to see that this enterprise contains a certain inner logic of its own, that it imposes demands that must be met (sometimes with considerable inconvenience) if its objectives are to be attained."[31] But Fuller did not seem to see that some rules, like those of habeas corpus, could be very important and yet not necessarily protect any substantive rights. Indeed, habeas corpus is just the kind of procedural right that would protect formal as opposed to substantive fairness of a system of law, since what habeas corpus primarily protects against is arbitrariness of decisions.

For Fuller, following his eight desiderata would require that there be stringent rules of due process for there to be international criminal law. And this includes judicial review, something currently lacking. As I will argue later, I believe that one of the best things to do to begin to bridge this gap is for there to be an institutionalized international version of procedural natural law including a right of habeas corpus. In criminal matters, habeas corpus functions as a rudimentary basis of something like judicial review. Interestingly, Fuller does mention habeas corpus once in *The Morality of Law* and links it to "procedural due process" under his eighth desiderata, the "Congruence Between Official Action and Declared Rule."[32] And he did recognize that it is in this eighth desideratum that there would be rules that were not necessarily themselves part of the legal system. But he did not put these pieces together and hence missed an important point for law in general and international law in particular.

4.3 FUNDAMENTAL PROCEDURAL RIGHTS

In considering the idea of formal or procedural natural law, one wonders whether Hart would recognize a "minimal *form* of the natural law" similar to the "minimal *content* of the natural law." Would Hart regard certain procedural matters, such as the right to habeas corpus, as similar to the substantive prohibitions on murder or theft, as key components for any

[31] Ibid., pp. 150–151. [32] Ibid., p. 81.

legal system, given what we know of humans? While neither Hart nor Fuller addressed this issue directly, I believe that key components of the rule of law would indeed be seen by both theorists as important for the natural justice of a legal system. In what follows, I am sympathetic to Fuller's brief suggestion that a version of procedural natural law involves a right of habeas corpus, among other basic due process rights. In criminal matters, habeas corpus functions as a rudimentary basis of something like judicial review.

I will argue that a version of procedural natural law involves a rudimentary right of habeas corpus, among other basic procedural rights, and that such rights form the basis for at least a minimal moral fairness in a system of law. Some procedural rights, such as habeas corpus, have been considered part of fundamental law as a way to indicate how important they are for the fundamental fairness of a system of law and also that their value is not merely derivative from protecting substantive rights. Fundamental law today most frequently refers to the formal constitution of a given legal system. But this is misleading for several reasons. First, it implies that systems of law that lack a formal constitution lack fundamental law. And, second, it makes it seem as if the written document itself is fundamental law rather than the principles which are contained therein or even merely assumed in the written document. Instead, fundamental law concerns first principles for a given legal order.

When there is no constitution, fundamental law typically refers to certain long-standing customs, perhaps even being "fixed and unalterable."[33] The customs themselves may articulate principles, but they are not the same as the principles and certainly do not gain their authoritativeness merely from being long standing.[34] The principles are moral principles that derive their authority in the way all moral principles do – because of their claim to legitimacy. Typically, there is a small set of substantive principles that are thought to be definitive of a particular political society, such as freedom of speech, press, and association, or nondiscrimination on the basis of race or gender. Like the principles that undergird a constitution, in a society without a constitution there are principles that also provide a foundation for the political and legal system.

"Fundamental law" is a phrase that came to have its most important meaning in seventeenth-century England. Habeas corpus and similar procedural rights are not themselves fundamental law in the sense of

[33] J. W. Gough., *Fundamental Law in English History*, Oxford University Press, 1955, p. 15.
[34] See my discussion of the problems with custom in my book *Crimes Against Humanity*, Chapter 3.

being a body of substantive principles undergirding a legal system, but they can be significantly intertwined with fundamental law. Procedural, not merely substantive, rights are significant in fundamental law because of the two important roles procedural rights play. As we saw in the previous chapter, some procedural rights are instrumentally valuable as they complement substantive rights. One way that they can do this is by gap-filling. Again following Aristotle, equity relies on such gap-filling insofar as the substantive rules of any system of rules will not always fit the specific case in the way that the drafters of the rules envisioned. In particular, procedural rights can be a gap-filler in that they may inhibit kings and presidents from finding loopholes by which prisoners can be abused, or where other forms of unfairness can creep into the system of law.

While it may be that substantive rights undergo change over time, having procedural rights remain constant is crucial, especially since there is much less need for procedural rights to change over time. Habeas corpus is a right of this sort – a procedural right that can remain fixed even as the particular substantive crimes that could lead to arrest and incarceration might vary over time. Basic moral fairness is achieved in the system of law when there is such a fixed set of procedural guarantees as that provided by habeas corpus. Here habeas corpus, which guarantees that no prisoner is locked away for arbitrary reasons or as a way to deny other important moral rights of the prisoner, helps secure a foundational moral minimum.

The idea of fundamental law has been somewhat controversial over the last few centuries, since some have seen reference to fundamental law as an attempt to limit what duly elected Legislatures can do. The worries about fundamental law have mainly been voiced concerning substantive principles, such as the right to privacy supposedly discovered as a substantive right undergirding the American system of law. But such a criticism is harder to mount if we are discussing fundamental procedural rather than substantive rights. Procedural rights typically do act as a restraint, but most frequently, at least in the US, on the Executive rather than the Legislative branch of government. Even when they restrict democratically elected Legislatures, these rights are less controversial than substantive rights because they do not clearly overrule the will of the people.

The will of the people is normally expressed substantively and procedural rights can accommodate changes in what the people think are the fundamental substantive norms of the society. If there is a popular vote to overturn the right of habeas corpus, and a court overturns this popular decision, the will of the people may be thwarted, but this is much less antidemocratic than overruling the populace on substantive grounds. Procedural rights, unlike substantive rights, are much less likely to be abused in an antidemocratic way. Indeed, since most procedural rights are minimal protections of fairness, it is hard to see why a populace would object to them.

Both Hart and Fuller recognized the importance of procedural considerations to the rule of law. Hart saw these procedures as secondary rules and Fuller saw them as desiderata for the rule of law. Arguably, both theorists saw these procedures as a minimal moral core, although Hart continued to downplay the sense of morality here. In taking as my point of departure this part of the work of Hart and Fuller, however, what I have stressed is the point of seeming agreement between them that if there is to be a *system* of criminal law (whether domestic or international), not merely a *set* of laws, then attention needs to be placed on procedural not merely substantive rights.

The works of Fuller highlight the importance of procedural rights and also raise the question of whether there is a sense that fundamental fairness requires certain procedures, placing limits on constructivist approaches to procedural justice. Whether we call the fundamental rights properly moral or not, certain procedural rights must be contained as secondary rules if there is to be a fair system of law. As I will next claim, in international law in general, and international criminal law in particular, attention needs to be placed as much on procedural or secondary rules and rights as on primary or substantive rules and rights. And there is a very practical benefit to this attention. Looking to the global right of habeas corpus provides a way to fill gaps and prevent legal black holes such as existed at Guantanamo Bay and Bagram Air Base.

4.4 HABEAS CORPUS AND INTERNATIONAL LAW

Several recent international criminal decisions have addressed habeas corpus rights, but only in the context of specific proceedings already begun at The Hague or Arusha, not in a broader context that would apply habeas to cases like that at Guantanamo Bay, where a gap existed in the system of international law. In the *Kanyabashi* case, the ICTR recognized the international right of habeas corpus, but confined it to "a review of the legality of detention" of those accused who are currently held by the

ICTR.[35] In this way, habeas corpus is restricted in two significant respects. First, there is an attempt to restrict the scope of habeas corpus proceedings so that it only concerns the prima facie legality of the arrest and incarceration, preventing habeas corpus petitions from being granted where there is a prima facie case for the conviction of the person who is incarcerated. Secondly, habeas corpus is restricted only to arrest and detention of those who are currently held by international tribunals and courts. I take up the first issue in the current section and the second issue in the next section.

Two very important things come out of the ICTR decisions in the early part of the first decade in the twenty-first century. First, the right of habeas corpus was there recognized as a fundamental, or *jus cogens*, right. This in effect gives habeas corpus the status of fundamental international law. In Chapter 7 I will provide a more developed account of what it means for habeas corpus to be *jus cogens*. But, second, this right was greatly limited, making it a much more restricted procedural right than is true in Anglo-American common law. Indeed, in the *Barayagwiza* case, the ICTR Appeals Chamber ultimately reversed the dismissal of the charges against Barayagwiza with prejudice, reinstating the case, despite the seemingly egregious violations of habeas corpus.[36]

For my purposes, one of the most important findings of the string of cases at the ICTR is that habeas corpus is a fundamental right of international humanitarian law. It is not surprising that there was such a ruling, given that the International Covenant of Civil and Political Rights had listed the right against arbitrary arrest. But it is one thing to have the substantive right against arbitrary arrest recognized and quite another matter to have a specific procedure, like habeas corpus, protected as a fundamental right as well. There is in my view a significant difference between the recognition that people have a substantive right not to be arbitrarily incarcerated and the procedural right to what is necessary to enforce the substantive right through a review to determine if one has been arbitrarily incarcerated. In the case of habeas corpus there is also a noninstrumental reason to elevate it to *jus cogens* status, as we will see in subsequent chapters.

---

[35] *Prosecutor v. Kanyabashi*, International Criminal Tribunal for Rwanda, Trial Chamber II, Case No. ICTR-96-15-I, May 23, 2000, Decision of the Defence Extremely Urgent Motion on Habeas Corpus and for Stoppage of the Proceedings, para. 28.

[36] See *Prosecutor v. Fernando Nahimana, Jean-Bosco Barayagwiza, and Hassan Ngeze*, International Criminal Tribunal for Rwanda, Case no. ICTR-99-52-A, Appeals Chamber Judgment, November 28, 2007.

As will become clear in the next part of the book, my view is that more is needed to enforce such procedural rights than is currently on offer. Part of the difficulty is that violations of procedural rights simply do not capture people's imagination in the way that violations of substantive rights do. When the substantive crimes of genocide or ethnic cleansing occur, the "conscience" of the world's community is easily aroused. And so it matters less whether the protections offered are regional or global, although with the institution of the ICC, there is what promises to be an effective global enforcement mechanism for these substantive rights violations to go along with the regional bases of protection. Procedural rights need a similarly global protection institution.

4.5 OBJECTIONS AND REPLIES

It could be objected that I have not shown that habeas corpus in particular needs to be protected for there to be an international rule of law. I will attempt to make such an argument in the next part of the book. But let me say now that I do not regard habeas corpus in particular as necessary for a rule of law. It is possible that other procedural rights could play many of the roles that habeas corpus has played in the Anglo-American legal system over the years since Magna Carta. I am not quite sure what those other procedures would be, but I certainly cannot rule out the possibility that there are other, perhaps even better, ways to protect fairness and nonarbitrariness in the way that people are detained and incarcerated. What I will claim is that when habeas corpus is included along with other Magna Carta legacy rights, there is at least a partial constitution of a rule of law that will support the goals of moral fairness and nonarbitrariness.

As we will see, what habeas corpus does, and what perhaps some other procedural rights could do as well, is to render transparent the reasons for incarceration as well as the conditions of incarceration of some of the most vulnerable members of society. In Chapter 12 and elsewhere I will explore whether there can be emergency exceptions to such rule of law constraints on sovereign power. But that there might be emergency exceptions does not undermine the need for procedural constraints that are held in very high esteem. Procedural rights that increase transparency, or visibleness, make systems morally fair in ways that it is very hard to create in other ways. What the long history of the development of Magna Carta legacy rights like habeas corpus shows is only that one particular set of rights has stood the test of time, but not that it is the only or even the best set of rights. Nonetheless, for a critic the burden has shifted to describe a better system for protecting moral fairness in a system of law.

Another criticism to consider is that I have not been fair in interpreting Hart and Fuller who, after all, did not really address the issues in this chapter. Chris Kutz has argued that Hart is in the end not interested in moral norms but only social norms, namely the recognized social practices that the officials in any putative legal system acknowledge. The norms "remain thoroughly positivistic" and hence will not support the kind of normative foundations that I have in mind. This is especially true, Kutz argues, when we realize that States now routinely engage in the suspension of the very rights that I am concerned with. While Hart recognizes the importance of procedural fairness, in the end it is far too narrow a notion to support the more robust conclusions about fundamental procedural norms that I am arguing for. As for Fuller, Kutz argues that very specific rights like habeas corpus or non-refoulement are not necessary for Fuller's minimal idea of a rule of law even with a bit of judicial review. Fuller cannot in the end provide a reason for thinking that just the procedural rights I have identified are necessary for a system that lives up to being a rule of law.[37]

I am not in strong disagreement with Kutz about Hart. Indeed, it is part of my critique of Hart that he did not recognize the importance of specific procedural rights for the establishment of the rule of law. However, I do disagree with Kutz more strongly about the centrality of fairness and of specific fair procedures for Fuller's understanding of the rule of law. Fuller spends quite a lot of time talking about highly specific procedures and even mentions habeas corpus as an example of a procedure that would be crucial, if not also necessary, for satisfying his eighth desideratum. But here I also agree with Kutz that Fuller would need more argumentation to show the necessity or at least very strong need for something like habeas corpus in satisfying the rule of law.

A third objection could reasonably be made to my characterization of Hart's view in the early sections of the chapter. Hart places quite a lot of emphasis on whether or not there are secondary rules, that is, rules of adjudication, change, and interpretation. And while it may be true that Dworkin has overemphasized the role of these secondary rules as forming

---

[37] See the commentary on my paper that was the ancestor to this chapter in Christopher Kutz, "On Visibility in International Criminal Law," in *The Hart-Fuller Debate in the Twenty-First Century*, Peter Cane (ed.), Oxford: Hart Publishing, 2010, pp. 97–105.

a "master rule," my account of Hart's view underemphasizes this aspect of his theory. More attention needs to be given to the interplay of secondary rules and the internal aspect of a system of law. And when such a nuanced reading of Hart is constructed, international law is not as clearly supported as I have indicated.[38]

I admit that my reading of Hart is idiosyncratic and has been so since I focused on Hart in the final chapter of my doctoral dissertation in the late 1970s. It certainly is true that Hart sees himself as engaged in a project that is "both descriptive and general."[39] Moreover, as pursuing a descriptive project, Hart does not see himself as involved in a normative or interpretive project. But none of this tells against seeing a minimal set of procedural rules as necessary for any system of law to be properly so called. For as Hart himself is so clear about, he is also interested in the general question of what makes for a system of law wherever we can properly talk of such a system.

I would be the first to admit that I follow Dworkin and Fuller more closely than I follow Hart, especially concerning the importance of evaluative matters in the overarching project of jurisprudence and philosophy of law. But what I am trying to do in referring to Hart is to explain that even for someone who eschews the evaluative enterprise, there is room for discussing international law as law, and for wondering whether there is a minimal form of the natural law that corresponds to the minimal content of the natural law that Hart famously discussed. Indeed, it can be part of a descriptive jurisprudence to ask such a question.

This brings us to a fourth, related objection, namely that I have overstated Hart's support for seeing international law as being properly law. Hart says that the lack of a rule of recognition in international law means that the rules of international law at his time constituted a set of laws, not a system of law. And I have failed to realize that this is an important difference between international and municipal law, making international law considerably more infirm than I recognize and calling into question whether international law is indeed law properly so called for Hart.

My sense is that Hart's text in Chapter 10 of *The Concept of Law* admits of several interpretations and I do not want to prejudge the case one way or the other. In fact, it is not so important to me that Hart sees international law as very or only somewhat infirm as it is why he thinks that international law is infirm and what it would take to make it less so. Hart clearly

---

[38] I am grateful to Thomas Mertens for this objection and the next.
[39] See H. L. A. Hart's Postscript to *The Concept of Law*, pp. 240 ff.

recognized that international law and municipal law were very close in certain regards, as he also recognized that the form of international law was what stood in the way of it being a less infirm legal system. This is all I need to get out of Hart for getting us started in thinking about how to reform international law in terms of its formal and procedural dimensions.

A fifth objection is that I have misunderstood the value of habeas corpus. Habeas corpus is so clearly valuable as a bulwark against assaults on individual liberty that it is a mistake to muddy the waters by discussing the way that habeas corpus is also a bulwark against arbitrary and unfair treatment. In emphasizing the procedural value of habeas corpus I have seriously undervalued its essential function of guaranteeing that people are not arbitrarily deprived of liberty when they are incarcerated.[40]

This objection is right, at least partially. Habeas corpus is indeed of great value as a bulwark against arbitrary deprivation of liberty. Nothing I have said in the chapter is meant to deny this fact. Indeed, in the next few chapters I will explore the value of a minimalist version of habeas corpus and how that minimalist construal does not provide the kind of protection that has historically been that which habeas corpus has become famous for providing.[41] But in the current chapter I have only sought normative jurisprudential support for the idea of habeas corpus as a minimalist right in international law on the way toward a more robust international right of habeas corpus some day.

A sixth objection is that my plan to change the way that international law deals with habeas corpus complaints is either utterly unrealistic or underdeveloped. I seem to call for something that would virtually require a world State in order to police the actual States of the world that deny habeas corpus to their citizens or residents. Alternatively, if my proposal does not call for something so unrealistic, it is not clear what precisely I do think would be a realistic way to solve the problem of the lack of habeas corpus protection and other procedural problems in international law.

I readily admit that I do not have a good sense of what would work at the moment that would solve the international problems I have identified. In Chapter 11 I will suggest that the solution may not even be a court but rather some kind of international administrative review, or some kind of expanded domain of the international human rights council.[42] But I have my doubts that any of these alternatives will fully respond to the glaring problem of the procedural gaps that exist today

---

[40] I am grateful to Harmen van der Wilt for this objection and the next.
[41] See Chapters 5 and 6.   [42] See Chapter 11.

in international law, especially international criminal law. Only some kind of world court is likely to meet the incredible needs that currently exist. Yet it is true that a world court of equity, as I have sketched it, is indeed not something that is likely to be developed in the near future.

In these first few chapters, we have begun to see how the seemingly innocuous right that a prisoner be brought out of detention and have the charges against him or her publicly proclaimed is indeed crucial for the protection of many other substantive rights, but it is also a value in itself insofar as it is a crucial component of the rule of law. As we will see, the slightly more robust habeas corpus right to have minimal judicial review and due process adds to this a process that has as its primary aim the protection of those, like those in Guantanamo and Bagram, whose rights are not being respected by any State. And when thinking about the international rule of law, habeas corpus should be one of the first rights protected. Natural justice, as understood from Aristotle's time to the present, demands as much. I strongly support the idea that procedural natural law needs to have the full attention of international legal scholars. I next turn to a detailed discussion of habeas corpus and other procedural rights that should be protected internationally.

PART II

Habeas corpus and jus cogens

CHAPTER 5

Habeas corpus as a minimalist right

In the first part of this book I explored the value of procedural rights in the debates about global justice. In this and subsequent parts of the book, I will discuss a handful of specific procedural rights. I will begin with a discussion of the right of habeas corpus as it was understood just prior to Magna Carta. Habeas corpus was at first merely the right to be brought out of detention and to have the charges against one publicly read. One could be immediately returned to detention after the reading and no other rights were involved. Yet Bracton and Blackstone, the great legal theorists of the thirteenth and eighteenth centuries, say that habeas corpus was fundamentally important, as have many legal theorists since.

Habeas corpus, at least in this first and most minimal version, is oddly procedural since there is no clear set of rules that need to be conformed to, except the one rule that a detainee can petition to be brought out of detention and have the charges against him or her read. But it is definitely not substantive in that there is no clear human good that is directly aimed at, or even one that is risked. Indeed, minimalist habeas corpus rights seem to be consistent with fairly great iniquity. Nonetheless, there is something very valuable indeed to this right. One only needs to think about Guantanamo in order to see what can happen when this right is systematically abridged – the challenges against detention at Guantanamo were all drawn in habeas corpus terms. Habeas corpus sets out a simple rule to be followed, and a rule that is so innocuous that it is hard to see why it would be of such importance for domestic or global justice. In this chapter I try to explain why this procedural right may be of the first importance for global justice.

In an earlier part of the book I explained how procedural rights came to be gap-fillers in the emerging system of law in post-Magna Carta England. At present, I wish to get us thinking conceptually about the value of very rudimentary procedural rights. The ensuing exercise is meant to be merely an introduction to the subject about which I will have quite a lot more to say in a developed manner. But I begin with a fairly simple puzzle, namely how the innocuous right that an individual is to be brought out of detention and read the charges against him or her has come to assume such near-mythical characteristics in legal theory.

In the first section I attempt to explain why it is so problematic to understand the value of a minimalist habeas corpus right. In the second section I rehearse one of the main arguments used to explain the value of habeas corpus, namely that it deters arbitrary acts by rulers, but I also explain why this is itself problematic. In the third and fourth sections I discuss other reasons to think that habeas corpus has value by examining its role in preventing the disappearance or torture of detainees. In the fifth section I discuss Plato's famous "Ring of Gyges" example as a model for understanding the value of minimalist habeas corpus. In the final section I discuss the important concept of visibleness in grounding procedural rights like habeas corpus. Throughout this section I restrict the scope of habeas corpus to see its pure value; in the next chapter I discuss a broader right of habeas corpus.

5.1 HABEAS CORPUS AND THE VALUE OF PROCEDURAL RIGHTS

In certain countries, those who are in prison may get out of prison and have the charges against them made public by filing a habeas corpus petition. For over 800 years in the English-speaking world, the right to file such a petition has been sacrosanct. Important legal theorists such as William Blackstone have said that this procedural right is the cornerstone in the "preservation" of personal liberties, since without protection of habeas corpus a prisoner can be incarcerated in such a way that his or her "sufferings are unknown or forgotten."[1] But why is this so important? If one is guilty and properly sent to prison, where most people would suffer, why is it that if one cannot make such a petition, then all of that person's liberties, indeed, all of everyone's liberties, are adversely affected?

In thinking about this puzzle, one place to start is simply to substitute the word "dungeon" for "prison" in the above account. Webster's unabridged dictionary defines dungeon as "a place of confinement, especially a subterranean chamber or other dark and gloomy cell." It is perhaps not so odd to think that everyone has a strong interest in getting

---

[1] William Blackstone, *Commentaries on the Laws of England* (1765), University of Chicago Press, 1979, vol. I, p. 132.

out of a dark and gloomy underground cell. But again, if one deserves to be in such confinement, why is it of paramount significance that one must be once brought out? Why think that all of one's other rights depend on the right to petition to be brought out of the dungeon and have a reading of the charges against one? Yet, at least since just before the time of Magna Carta, habeas corpus has been given such a position of pre-eminence.

Compounding the puzzle is the fact that the rudimentary idea of habeas corpus is not that an individual has a right to get out of jail or prison altogether, but only that the prisoner's jailer must "produce the body" of the prisoner, bring him or her out of the dungeon temporarily, merely so that the prisoner can be seen, and have the charges against him or her publicly declared. In its most rudimentary form, the form that was given just prior to Magna Carta, it may be acceptable to take the prisoner back to the dungeon immediately afterwards. The right to be only temporarily removed from jail is such an innocuous right that it is difficult to figure out why habeas corpus has been thought to have such importance.

Bracton clearly lists the writ in his *De Legibus et Consuetudinibus Angliae* (c. 1230) and specifies its form as follows:

that he produce his body ["et nunc praecipietur vicecomiti quod habeat corpus"] on another day by a writ of this kind: The king to the viscount greeting. We enjoin you before our justiciaries &c. on such a day the body of A., to answer to B. concerning such a plea.[2]

Here we see the writ described as addressing the official who is detaining or jailing a person, requiring him or her merely to produce the body of the prisoner and provide an answer concerning why the prisoner should continue to be deprived of his or her freedom. So, the right of habeas corpus is not a "get out of jail free" card, but only a right to be brought out of the dungeon quite temporarily, where it may be that the prisoner is then subjected again to incarceration and suffering soon thereafter.

The folk history of habeas corpus has it that there are three things that are important about this right. First, the body must be produced to demonstrate that the person has not merely been killed. Second, bringing the body into the light of day allows one to see if there are marks on the body indicating torture or other forms of physical abuse. Third, the

---

[2] 6 Bracton 474–477, Sir Travis Twiss (ed.), Bracton, *De Legibus et Consuetudinibus Angliae* (London: Longmans, 1883), quoted in William F. Duker, *A Constitutional History of Habeas Corpus*, Westport, CT: Greenwood Press, 1980, pp. 16–17.

public reading of the charges against the prisoner is meant to act as a deterrent against arbitrary or unlawful incarceration. It is the third factor that is often said to be the most important as a cornerstone of all other rights. But it seems to me that the full value of a minimalist habeas corpus right cannot be seen unless one takes into account all three of these considerations.

Today, habeas corpus in the US means much more than the rudimentary concerns I have been discussing, and includes an examination of any violations of a person's constitutional rights. Initially, and most fundamentally, habeas corpus is not such a broad right. It is indeed very simple, almost simplistic, and highly innocuous. Yet why should the mere display of the prisoner and the public reading of the charges against him or her, with no other procedural considerations required, deter arbitrary or unlawful incarceration and be necessary for the efficacy of all other rights? Was Blackstone right to think that habeas corpus would deter tyranny? And, short of deterring tyranny, how exactly will habeas corpus deter wrongful acts at all since it is such an innocuous right? These are the questions I shall be pursuing in this chapter.

Let us consider three possibilities. First, habeas corpus might literally be necessary for deterring all other rights abuses since if one could lock someone away for no good reason, it could be done whenever one might complain about other rights violations. Second, it may be that being made to disappear is so feared that one would be willing to trade away nearly anything to prevent it, including one's most valuable freedoms. Third, habeas corpus might be important for deterring something else, such as torture, which must be deterred in order to secure all other rights. In what follows I will take up each of these possibilities, ultimately arguing that they fail to explain the inordinately widespread acceptance of the high value of a minimalist or stripped down habeas corpus right, and then supply my own explanation, which is indebted to Plato's tale of the Ring of Gyges. Ultimately, I defend the view that the key normative principle is that of visibleness, the very thing that is lost if prisoners can be secretly incarcerated. And I will also begin the argument that such a right must be protected globally.

5.2 THE DETERRENCE ARGUMENT

In my view, each of the three above arguments has some plausibility, and I will build on each of these in this chapter in support of my own account of the value of habeas corpus. To begin, there is an obvious deterrence argument that I will present here that has quite a few problems and that adversely affects its plausibility as an explanation of the high value placed on the right of habeas corpus. The idea seems to be that even tyrants will be dissuaded from violating the rights of their subjects if the subjects have the right to bring those deeds to public attention. As we will see, even with its problems, this deterrence argument contains quite a bit of truth.

There are two initial problems with the deterrence argument. First, bare bones habeas corpus rights do not include the right to trial or even the right to respond to the charges brought against one in some other forum than a trial. Rather, the right is merely to have the jailer publicly set out the charges in the presence of the prisoner. There is nothing explicit here that requires that the rights violations against the prisoner should be disclosed, except perhaps that there were trumped-up charges that landed the prisoner in jail. And because of this fact, there is seemingly little that a leader would fear, and which would hence be the basis of deterrence, due to having a habeas corpus petition recognized.

Second, it is not clear why tyrants would care if those who they abused had to be produced occasionally and the charges against them read in public, even if the charges are thereby shown to be trumped up. This issue is the heart of the matter. For if the minimalist or stripped-down habeas corpus right merely means that a bit of publicity is given to the misdeeds of a tyrant or other political leader, the question is why this would matter so much that the tyrant would calculate that it is not worth the risk of such a public disclosure by having violated the rights of the prisoner in the first place. At its core, this rationale for the high value of habeas corpus turns on a psychological claim about how humans respond to publicity, especially publicity about their putative misdeeds. And for the argument to work, the claims about publicity would have to be true of all rulers – not just benevolent and sensitive leaders, but also the tyrants of the world who are those most likely to abuse the rights of subjects.

Deterrence is here linked to the fear of being publicly shamed or embarrassed. And the issue I am raising is whether some political leaders might not be beyond shame or embarrassment. Feeling shame is different from feeling guilt, in that it is related to how an audience responds or how an anticipated audience would respond. Think of the Greek chorus in the plays of Sophocles, always watching the action and passing judgment on the deeds of the actors. Oedipus is so concerned about the reactions of others to his misdeeds of sleeping with his mother and killing his father that he pokes out his eyes so that he can not be shamed by fellow Greeks.[3]

For such shaming to act as a deterrent, the person to be shamed must have eyes to see the reaction. In the case of anticipated reactions, the agent must at least have the kind of normal sympathies that would make him or her responsive to the reactions of others, to care about how others might react. But not all political leaders are like Oedipus in this respect, and none that I know of has gone to such extreme lengths to avoid being shamed. Degrees of susceptibility to shame or embarrassment seem to me to run across a fairly wide spectrum, especially in the class of those who are political leaders. And while it may be that no one is completely shameless, it certainly seems that some political leaders have come pretty close and would not care very much if their misdeeds were made public.

I suppose the other possibility is that political leaders will fear being turned out of office if their misdeeds are publicized. This would be most relevant to those political leaders who must stand for election, but every political leader is subject to recall or at least to civil rebellion, and must care what the populace, or at least part of the populace, thinks of him or her. Deterrence could indeed work through such fears more straightforwardly than through shame or embarrassment. Here the idea would be that public disclosure of one's misdeeds will weaken a leader's hold on the reins of power by sowing seeds of discontent among the populace. To make sure that this does not happen, political leaders, even tyrants, may be willing to restrict rights abuses out of fear that they will be disclosed when those whose rights have been abused are brought into the light of public scrutiny. So there is some truth to the deterrence argument, but it is not as strong as some have assumed.

The problem again is why we would think that merely having the charges read publicly, without more of an exposure of the circumstances leading up to the filing of those charges, would be likely to weaken the hold on the reins of power that political leaders desperately want to retain. Why would the lack of habeas corpus rights make for a greater likelihood that subjects/citizens would rebel against their political leaders? To answer this question, more is needed than the slender argument based on the questionable moral psychology of political leaders. It needs to be shown that something highly valuable is lost when arbitrary incarceration is never made public, which would motivate such possible rebellions or serious

---

[3] See my discussion of shame and moral taint in my book *Sharing Responsibility*, University of Chicago Press, 1992.

criticism of rulers. In the next two sections I will sketch several possible ways to understand that value, a value which may be so important that people would be willing to risk their lives in rebellion against political leaders who denied their subjects such a right.

5.3 THE DISAPPEARED ARGUMENT

In his book *Prisoner Without a Name, Cell Without a Number*, Jacobo Timmerman evokes the situation feared by so many in Latin America and elsewhere: that one will become a member of the disappeared.[4] In a sense, if one is made to disappear so that one's identity is unknown to anyone, one has no real rights.[5] This is because rights need some kind of enforcement mechanism to be real. If you are held secretly in prison, where no one knows whether you are alive or dead, or if you are alive who you are, and where no one knows that you have rights in need of protection, the protection of your rights is so at the whim of another that it is as if you had no rights. This is one possible way to understand Blackstone's famous defense of habeas corpus:

To bereave a man of life, or by violence to confiscate his estate, without accusation or trial, would be so gross and notorious an act of despotism, as must at once convey the alarm of tyranny throughout the whole kingdom. But confinement of the person, by secretly hurrying him to jail, where his sufferings are unknown or forgotten, is a less public, a less striking, and therefore a more dangerous engine of arbitrary government.[6]

Blackstone does not explain precisely why it is more dangerous, but indicates that it has to do with the fact that the prisoner is out of the public eye – "unknown and forgotten" – and hence is less likely to be known as someone whose rights should be protected by the community.

Disappearance is worrisome in part because there is the possibility that one has been disappeared permanently by being killed. So, while initially the fear is that one has been indefinitely deprived of one's liberty, part of the fear that one feels is that one is forgotten to such an extent that one will not be missed if one is unjustifiably executed. In Argentina, the mothers of the Plaza de Mayo tried to keep public their disappeared loved ones by carrying pictures of them in all of their demonstrations so that the

---

[4] Jacobo Timmerman, *Prisoner Without a Name, Cell Without a Number*, Toby Talbot (trans.), Madison, WI: University of Wisconsin Press, 2002.
[5] See Carl Wellman's book *Real Rights*, Oxford University Press, 1995.
[6] Blackstone, *Commentaries on the Laws of England*, vol. I, pp. 131–132.

"disappeared" would not actually be forgotten. By displaying their pictures, the mothers fought to keep their sons alive, to prevent their sons from being permanently disappeared. It is in this way that the rights to liberty and life are linked in the concerns about being made to disappear.[7] If one's life and significant liberty can be secretly jeopardized, then it seems that one's other rights will not be secure either.

Yet we have not explained why depriving a person of life or liberty in secret makes it worse than doing so in public view. Blackstone explicitly makes this claim, as would be necessary to defend the pre-eminence of habeas corpus rights over other procedural or even substantive rights. If a person is kept in a highly public prison, rather than in a secret dungeon, why is it less likely that his or her rights would be violated? Why think that it is more likely that a person will be killed in a secret prison than in a non-secret prison? Again, as in the previous section, we are thrown back to the dubious speculations about the psychological states of rulers and what they are likely to be deterred from doing. And Blackstone himself seems to set the stage for such speculation.

But there is another alternative, also suggested by Timmerman as well as the mothers of the Plaza de Mayo, namely that when one is officially forgotten, it is as if one ceases to be a rights-bearer. This is not a matter of psychology and is only loosely related to the fear of being disappeared. Rather, as we will see later, it is something formal, a matter of status, rather than having to do with either the psychology of the political ruler or the subject. I will here begin to explore the connection between the insights about the disappeared and the formal detriment that occurs when one is held in secret and not allowed to be brought into the light of day. One still has rights, in a theoretical sense, but effectively it is as if one did not have them after all.

Rights can be viewed as abstract entities, but even in this mode they are often thought of as claims. And for something to be a claim there must be a rudimentary structure where when one utters various words, there is another person who is required to respond to the claim even if he or she is not required to satisfy it. If one is in a secret prison, where in effect the key to one's cell has been thrown away, there is no one who is required to respond to claims one might make, and in this sense one has no rights, except perhaps in a hortatory or theoretical sense. I suppose

---

[7] See the discussion of this issue in Chapter 7, "Personal Liberty and Security," in Francis Jacobs and Robin White, *The European Convention on Human Rights*, third edn edited by Clare Ovey and Robin White, NY: Oxford University Press, 2002, especially p. 103.

there could be a secret prison where one had the right to make claims and others were required to respond to these claims. But without some kind of public accountability, there is no guarantee that those who are supposed to respond are truly required to do so or have any intention of doing so.

So, I must revise my previous account to say that having effective rights entails that there is someone who is required to respond and that there is a system of holding these individuals accountable. If a person is in a secret prison or is secretly incarcerated in some other way, those who might be required to respond to his or her claims are not subject to public accountability, and hence the people in these prisons are effectively without rights. It is in this sense that they have been forgotten and have disappeared from the community of rights holders. And in this way, the deprivation of the right of habeas corpus could very well result in the effective deprivation of all other rights for the prisoner.

We have not yet explained why others are adversely affected when habeas corpus is denied, but we have begun to see why the prisoner is adversely affected. Yet we have not explained why it is wrong to be deprived of rights. And hence there is another part of the story that must be told, namely what precisely is risked if one loses rights as a result of being deprived of habeas corpus. To understand this additional dimension of our problem, we will turn to our third strategy of understanding the value of habeas corpus, namely in terms of ancillary rights that are related to habeas corpus and that would be put in jeopardy if habeas corpus were to be denied.

5.4 THE TORTURE ARGUMENT

One of the ancillary rights most closely associated with habeas corpus is the right not to be tortured. Initially, as a conceptual matter it is not evident why habeas corpus and torture would indeed be closely linked. In this section I will try to shed some light on this puzzle before setting out my own account of the value of habeas corpus, which will involve aspects of each of the arguments in these three sections. While the right not to be tortured ends up being only ancillary to the right of habeas corpus, it is nonetheless quite important. Indeed, many have argued that torture is the worst thing that people can do to one another and so anything that diminishes the likelihood of torture is of great value.[8] Other ancillary

---

[8] See Henry Shue, "Torture," *Philosophy & Public Affairs*, vol. 7, no. 2, 1978, 124–143.

rights, such as the right not to be excessively deprived of sleep, are also important here.

Torture is vastly unpopular and hence something that would be hard to carry out in any setting other than one of secrecy. There have been secret interrogation centers where the right of habeas corpus has been denied, as has certainly happened within the US. Habeas corpus rights are generally protected within the US, but this has not always stopped torture, although it certainly may have diminished its prevalence. So there is no necessary connection between the denial of habeas corpus and the use of torture, but nonetheless there is a strong correlation. The reason for this again has to do with the lack of accountability in prisons where the right of habeas corpus is denied.

There has been a tendency to shield torturers from public view, as well as public censure and retaliation in the criminal justice histories of many societies. And what better way to shield torturers and their supervisors from public view than not to allow prisoners to be brought into the light of day where the results of torture might be observed? The folk history of habeas, as I said above, has it that one of the things that was looked for when the jailer brought the prisoner out of jail was whether there were marks on his or her body indicating that torture had occurred. Again, this is not definitive because torture does not always leave publicly visible marks, but it often does.

After the fact, torture is not always evident, but the marks on the body will often remain for quite a long time, as will the marks on the demeanor and spirit of the prisoner. Otherwise it is the prisoner's word against that of his or her jailers. But the physical effects of torture "speak for themselves," as is the translation of the legal doctrine of *res ipsa loquitor.* When confronted with such obvious evidence, the denial of the jailer pales completely. So, there is a strong disincentive for prisoners who have been tortured to be allowed into the light of day and a corresponding deterrence of jailers to torture when they realize that their handiwork may be made public because of habeas corpus petitions. One of the things that public scrutiny means is that the most publicly repulsive practices are likely to be diminished. Egomaniacal rulers may not be easily shamed, but jailers who tend to be ordinary people are more likely to experience shame. And in any event, for most people, normal inhibitions seem to be suspended when it is likely that no one will know of one's wrongdoing.

Similarly, other forms of abuse of the prisoner, including the use of techniques that stop short of torture but are nonetheless terrible, such as extreme sleep deprivation, also seem to correlate with lack of protection of habeas corpus rights. As with forms of torture, the effects of these other abuses will often leave marks that will be evident to those who view the prisoner in the light of day. Of course, this does not necessarily mean that such practices will be deterred by the worry about accountability, but there seems to be a tendency in this direction. The more practices that seem to correlate with the kind of lack of accountability that is bred when habeas corpus rights are denied to prisoners, the greater the value of having habeas corpus rights strongly protected in a given society.

Perhaps even more significant than the correlation between a lack of habeas corpus and torture is that between a lack of habeas corpus and summary execution. This is one of the key considerations in the movement against those responsible for the disappeared in Argentina and other countries. Those whose relatives disappeared feared that their relatives were already dead, and those who were held nameless in prisons feared that they could easily be killed and no one would know or seek justice in their behalf. Once dead, they could not seek justice on their own. And if no one knew what had become of them, then no one would act on their behalf to secure justice. In this sense, the prisoners would truly be forgotten, both in life and death, rendered less than human by being denied the dignity of a name, a reputation, and a minimum of respect.

The torture argument is an ancillary argument, not a direct argument for the value of minimalist habeas corpus rights. Indeed, the torture argument turns on certain empirical claims, which I have suggested but not substantiated. The strength of this argument will obviously depend on the strength of the evidence in support of the correlation between a lack of habeas corpus protection and the prevalence of torture I have suggested. Here the various components discussed earlier come together. For we have fear of disappearance as well as the hope of deterrence that are the components of the value of habeas corpus, now linked to other ancillary considerations that make the value stronger yet. The liberties of the prisoner are intimately tied to this one liberty, the right of habeas corpus. And there is a sense, still only inchoate, that if habeas corpus is denied, then the liberties of all have been adversely affected, not just the liberties of the prisoner in question. It is to this topic that I next turn as I set out my own account of the value of minimalist habeas corpus rights derived in part from the considerations we have encountered in the previous sections of this chapter, but now amended in various ways.

5.5 THE RING OF GYGES

In *The Republic*, Plato has Glaucon present the case for the innate self-interestedness of most people. Glaucon describes self-interest as "the motive which all men naturally follow if they are not forcibly restrained by the law and made to respect each other's claims."[9] He then tells the story of the Lydian shepherd who found a gold ring that when turned a certain way made the shepherd invisible to his companions:

He was wearing this ring when he attended the usual meeting of shepherds which reported monthly to the king on the state of his flocks; and as he was sitting there with the others he happened to twist the bezel of the ring toward the inside of his hand. Thereupon he became invisible to his companions, and they began to refer to him as if he had left them. He was astonished, and began fingering the ring again, and turned the bezel outward; whereupon he became visible again. When he saw this he started experimenting with the ring to see if he really had this power, and found that every time he turned the bezel inwards he became invisible, and when he turned it outwards he became visible. Having made this discovery he managed to get himself included in the party that was to report to the king, and when he arrived seduced the queen and with her help attacked and murdered the king and seized the throne.[10]

Later in this section of the text, Glaucon says that the conclusion to draw is: "once give him the power, and he will be the first to use it as fully as he can."[11]

There are several lessons to draw from this parable. First, for several thousand years, philosophers have embraced the idea that if one were invisible, the normal moral constraints would not be operative. This is presumably as true of the Lydian shepherd who could make himself invisible and hence avoid detection of his crimes as of the jailer who can make the prisoner invisible and hence hide the jailer's crimes as well. The second thing to note about the Ring of Gyges example is that, on Glaucon's account, once there is the possibility of making oneself or one's wrongdoing invisible, there is not a human being, no matter how morally upstanding, who can resist the use of this device. Of course, one does not have to be as skeptical about human nature as Glaucon and Adeimantus, and yet still think that it will be very difficult, although not impossible, to resist the allure of being able to commit wrongdoing and get away with it. And the Ring of Gyges then is a parable that applies to our case of the

---

[9] Plato, *The Republic*, 359c, translated by Desmond Lee, second edn, NY: Penguin Books, 1974, p. 105. In a different translation (by Jowett), the motivation to be just is said to turn on whether one is "put to the proof" in terms of "the fear of infamy."
[10] Ibid., 359e–360b.   [11] Ibid., 366d.

jailer who does not have to worry about habeas corpus just as much as it does to the case of the Lydian shepherd.

I wish to use the Ring of Gyges parable to aid us in pulling together a coherent account of the value of habeas corpus. In the first instance, habeas corpus matters because it makes visible wrongdoings that would otherwise be invisible. It is also the case, as we will see, that habeas corpus is important for the maintenance of the rule of law. I will turn to the rule of law issue in a moment, but first I address the issue of the exposure of wrongdoing. There are four main forms of wrongdoing that can be exposed by habeas corpus, even in its minimal form of merely calling for the prisoner to be temporarily brought out of the dungeon to have the charges against him or her publicly proclaimed.

First, there is the wrongdoing of incarcerating someone arbitrarily. This form of wrongdoing can become visible if the prisoner is brought out of the dungeon and there are no charges that can be read against him or her, or where the charges are palpably trumped up. This is instilled in American law as the right of arraignment. Soon after arrest, the prisoner is to be brought before a judge or magistrate and told publicly why he or she is being held. The arraignment is the first stage of the criminal justice process that does not merely involve the police, and it is the first time when the arrested individual may be released if it is determined that the arrest was arbitrary. If arraignment or something equivalent has been skipped, habeas corpus is a simple remedy since it calls for a process that is a kind of stand-in for arraignment.

Second, there is the wrongdoing of having executed the prisoner instead merely of having incarcerated him or her. Again, this form of wrongdoing will be palpable if there is no live body in the name of the prisoner to be brought out of the dungeon. In this sense, habeas corpus makes it virtually impossible for prisoners to become disappeared and forgotten in contravention of their being a person with effective rights. Of course, it does not guarantee that prisoners are not killed while in captivity, only that the wrongdoing involved in summary execution is brought to light. Jailers can claim to have "lost" prisoners only for so long before being exposed as having killed them.

Third, there is the wrongdoing of having tortured the prisoner, a wrongdoing nearly universally recognized as abhorrent. As I indicated above, this form of wrongdoing can be made visible insofar as the marks on the tortured prisoner's body, or on his or her psyche, are still observable. Of course, excuses can be concocted about how the marks were caused, such as by inmates falling down stairs or engaging in self-mutilation. But such excuses again can only mask wrongdoing for a while. Especially in a society with a free press, the questions about how the prisoner became injured will not be easily covered up.

Fourth, there is the wrongdoing of other forms of abuse perpetrated against the prisoner. Habeas corpus will make these abuses visible insofar as there are marks of the abuse on the prisoner's body. If no marks of abuse are present, then in some cases the prisoner will be able nonetheless to voice a complaint against such abuse, or at very least the jailer will worry that the prisoner will give voice to such abuse when brought out of the dungeon. And if there are such marks, then it may be that the wrongful acts that caused them can be brought to the attention of the public. Such wrongful practices as sleep deprivation and waterboarding are not as readily seen on the body of the prisoner, but there are often marks or signs that may reveal the wrongdoing nonetheless.

The Ring of Gyges helps us see how habeas corpus and other procedural rights could prevail against the arbitrary exercise of power. As we have seen, arbitrariness often seems to need the cloak of secrecy and invisibility. Even the benevolent arbitrary exercise of power is highly suspicious and unpopular, both because it is antidemocratic and because of the strong possibility that what was once benevolent can turn malevolent so easily. The Lydian shepherd may use his new power for the good of his people, but if he later chooses to use it for ill, there is no stopping him from doing so. The ruler or jailer who discovers that he or she can render a person invisible from public view may also use this power for wrongdoing, or for hiding wrongdoing, and such abuse of power is at least partially stopped by the anticipation of habeas corpus appeals.

5.6 'THE PRINCIPLE OF VISIBLENESS'

The value of habeas corpus and the other Magna Carta legacy rights concerns what I call the normative principle of visibleness in detention and incarceration. The normative *principle of visibleness*[12] in detention and incarceration is a counter to the secrecy that masks the arbitrary exercise of power in this domain. Habeas corpus stands for the proposition at its most minimal, but also at its most powerful, that no one can be hidden in jail or prison. The reason for this is that such secrecy is too likely to hide mistreatment and abuse. In its first instance, habeas corpus means simply

---

[12] The *OED* lists, as one of the earliest uses of the term visibleness, a sixteenth-century reference to the fact that the Catholic Church did not maintain open procedures.

that the prisoner must be produced. The other rights memorialized in Magna Carta's Chapter 29 (39) spell out what procedures must be in place to deal with a detainee who has now been brought into the light and made visible.

As we saw in Chapter 2, Henry Maine said that "substantive law has at first the look of being gradually secreted in the interstices of procedure."[13] It is fitting that what is secreted in the interstices of the procedural right of habeas corpus is the moral principle against secrecy in confinement. Habeas corpus is in one respect the idea that the body of the prisoner must literally be made publicly visible, but this very rudimentary procedure has very great value. One of the keys is that wrongdoing is rendered visible and is subject to censure and deterrence. The principle of visibleness is simply the normative idea that rulers must make their decisions transparent.

This principle does not guarantee that those who are detained or incarcerated will not be treated wrongly or even that they will be treated fairly, but only that if they are to be treated unfairly, it cannot be done completely in secret. The principle of visibleness is then a protection of security which, as Justice Kennedy said, "subsists, too, in fidelity to freedom's first principles."[14] Security of the person is often a byproduct of habeas corpus; however, as I have indicated, it is not a direct but only an indirect consequence of honoring habeas corpus rights.

Let me cite a recent example. In April 2009, the US District Court for the District of Columbia considered habeas corpus petitions from four detainees at the "Bagram Theatre Internment Facility" at Bagram Air Base in Afghanistan. As of that date, more than 600 detainees were being held in this facility by US forces. What was crucial for Judge Bates was that the US control over Bagram prison "is practically absolute." Even though the Bagram detention facility was much closer to the battlefield than Guantanamo was, Judge Bates was not persuaded that the two cases were all that different. The worry was one of "limitless Executive power," unless oversight was allowed of the sort that was epitomized by granting the habeas corpus petitions of the detainees. So, Bates ruled in the case of *Maqaleh v. Gates* that there should not be loopholes allowed in the rights protection granted to those who are under US custody.[15] As in the

---

[13] Sir Henry Maine, *Dissertations on Early Law and Custom*, NY: Henry Holt and Company, 1886, p. 389.
[14] *Boumediene v. Bush*, 128 S. Ct. 2229, 2256 (2008).
[15] See Kal Raustiala, "Is Bagram the New Guantanamo? Habeas Corpus and *Maqaleh v. Gates*," *ASIL Insights*, vol. 13, no. 8, June 17, 2009.

Guantanamo and Australian cases we will examine later, habeas corpus was the gap-filler in those cases where detainees seemed to be stuck in situations where they could not get their substantive rights to liberty protected in any other way.

The prospect of the revelation of the wrongdoing through even a very rudimentary habeas corpus procedure may act as a deterrent against the wrongdoing occurring at all or against similar wrongdoings occurring in the future. And in this sense, habeas corpus is clearly related to a human good, namely that wrongdoing should not occur. But habeas corpus is indirectly, not directly, related to this good. And it is my view that this is the way that procedural rights are generally related to substantive rights. Procedural rights do not normally have value in themselves, but only as they somehow support substantive rights. There is one clear exception to this idea and that concerns the so-called rule of law.

Merely having some procedural rules that govern human affairs is often thought to be of value insofar as rule by these rules is better than rule by "man." In this sense, rule by rules is definitive of the rule of law and against the kind of arbitrariness that comes when people make decisions unconstrained by rules. Procedural rules have value here because they are constitutive of a norm, not merely because they support some other norm. The norm that these procedural rules constitute is itself a procedure. Procedural rules and rights set out rudimentary procedures; however, their value is not in the procedure itself but in the procedural system they constitute.

As we saw in Chapter 3, procedural rights like habeas corpus have instrumental or derivative value in that they support substantive rights. Procedural rights also have intrinsic value in that they are constitutive of a rule of law that promotes fairness. In this latter sense, procedural rights do not necessarily have content and while they aim at a certain good, that good, fairness, and non-arbitrariness need not have content, unlike the goods that substantive rights aim at, such as property rights or free speech rights, which have content and aim at a human good. Regardless of what is actually being advanced by certain procedures, if one has a procedural right, one has a right that must be respected. It is for this reason that sometimes it appears that procedural rights are trivial. But this is an illusion. Procedural rights ultimately do not derive their value, as we saw in previous chapters, from what it is that they happen to have as their ends. Rather, the key is that procedural rights promote nonarbitrariness and in this way provide a bridge between moral fairness and the bulwark against arbitrariness discussed by Blackstone.

Prior to Magna Carta and for several centuries thereafter, habeas corpus appears to have been mainly discussed as a minimalist right of the sort I have been describing and defending in this chapter. But probably by the time of the Habeas Corpus Act at the end of the seventeenth century, and certainly by the time William Blackstone wrote his *Commentaries on the Laws of England*, habeas corpus was given a wider purview, encompassing at least rudimentary due process and judicial review. And by the middle of the twentieth century in the US, habeas corpus had become so broad as to encompass nearly all aspects of judicial review based on constitutional rights.

In the next chapter I will discuss some of these expansions of habeas corpus, in which habeas corpus will become much more like the epitome of due process that it eventually became in England by the seventeenth century. I will argue that there are very good reasons for some limited expansion of habeas corpus rights beyond the minimalist construal discussed in this chapter, but not necessarily as extensive as is currently true in the US or in some other Western, as well as non-Western, States today.

CHAPTER 6

Due process, judicial review, and expanding habeas corpus

In this chapter I will take up two ways of thinking of habeas corpus that are more expansive than the minimalist or stripped-down version of habeas corpus discussed in the previous chapter. There are various versions of a non-minimalist approach to habeas corpus, including what has come to be seen in the US as the incorporation of the Bill of Rights into the right of habeas corpus. I will be especially interested in this chapter in talking about habeas corpus in the context of judicial review. Habeas corpus as judicial review can come in various forms as well, but what all forms have in common is that habeas corpus would trigger some kind of examination of the situation of the detainee by a court or court official. In the end I shall argue for a limited role for judicial review in our understanding of habeas corpus.

I begin with a section on why the minimalist version may not get quite enough protection to be a true gap-filler on the way toward partially constituting an international rule of law. In the second section I will discuss how habeas corpus can be seen to be constitutive of due process in a somewhat more expansive way than was discussed in the last chapter. In the third section I will discuss a maximalist version of habeas corpus, as epitomized today in the way that US jurisprudence makes habeas corpus virtually synonymous with judicial review of all rights questions that could concern the plaintiff. In the fourth section I will express reservations about having habeas corpus regarded in this expansive way. In the fifth section I discuss the need for at least the idea of habeas corpus as a due process right in global justice.

6.1 PROBLEMS WITH MINIMALIST HABEAS CORPUS

In the last chapter we saw that a minimalist understanding of habeas corpus could merely involve that the detainee is brought out of prison into the light of day and where the charges against him or her are publicly declared. The prisoner could then be simply returned to prison without any determination of whether the charges against him or her did in fact create a prima facie basis for incarceration. At the very least, a more reasonable model of the right of habeas corpus would involve some kind of judicial or quasi-judicial determination that there was such a prima facie basis for the prisoner's continued incarceration. I will explore some of the reasons for this expansion in this section and begin to set out some of the further expansions that have also been called for, only some of which are as patently reasonable as the idea of having a hearing of some sort in addition to having the body produced and the charges against the prisoner read out publicly.

Despite the positive things to be said in favor of being able to offer minimalist habeas petitions or even successive habeas petitions, there is certainly a sense that there should be more to habeas corpus than that, since even Bracton's original construal of habeas corpus seems to make a reference to a somewhat broader right. I here again quote Bracton in his *De Legibus et Consuetudinibus Angliae*:

> that he produce his body ["et nunc praecipietur vicecomiti quod habeat corpus"] on another day by a writ of this kind: The king to the viscount greeting. We enjoin you *before our justiciaries &c.* on such a day the body of A., to answer to B. concerning such a plea.[1]

The key phrase, which I have heretofore skipped over, is "before our justiciaries." The phrase is sufficiently ambiguous that it could mean several different things. But there is one meaning that would fit nicely with a somewhat expanded notion of habeas, beyond merely the minimalist interpretation, and that is that the reading of the public charges must be in the context of some of kind of hearing, before a judicial official, and not merely before the public.

So, I will now proceed to consider this expansion of the domain of habeas corpus so as to allow for some kind of adjudication of the charges, not merely a public reading of them. If habeas corpus were to be expanded this much, then it would at least in part help us out of the "bind" we seem to have been in when the jailer could produce the body of the prisoner, publicly read the charges against him or her, and then simply return the

---

[1] 6 Bracton 474–477, Sir Travis Twiss (ed.), Bracton, *De Legibus et Consuetudinibus Angliae* (London: Longmans, 1883), my italics. I am grateful to Simon O'Connor for discussing this issue with me. See his unpublished M.Phil. thesis for St Andrews University International Relations School, in possession of the author, especially pp. 19–20.

prisoner to the dungeon. While this eventuality can be shown to be not without value, it would surely be much better if some kind of determination could be made about whether there was at least a prima facie plausibility to those charges. As discussed in the previous section, the public reading of the charges could in part help deter the most blatantly implausible charges from being used to support continued incarceration. But there are certainly limits here, and in many cases the public will have a hard time telling whether the charges are indeed "trumped-up." In an era where people were more involved in each other's affairs, because life was more community-focused and communities were considerably smaller, perhaps the public stood a decent chance of ferreting out such abuses, but today this seems highly unlikely. Hence, in general we look to judicial officials to stand in for the rest of us and thereby to make sure that people are not incarcerated on such "trumped-up" charges.

Another infirmity of the minimalist habeas corpus construal is that there is not really much of a procedure here at all, sufficient to call habeas corpus a procedural right. If there is indeed a minimal hearing or other judicial process that is triggered by the habeas petition, then habeas corpus may look less like a protection of substantive rights not to be arbitrarily incarcerated or tortured while in confinement, and more like a straightforward procedural right. Of course, it is also true that the more "procedure" that is required, the harder it will be to sell this as a right that should be recognized internationally, since it will take on the problems of "judicial review" that I will discuss in greater detail in a subsequent section of this chapter. The doctrine of judicial review is highly contentious in domestic settings, and I have every reason to think that it will be even more controversial internationally.

Nonetheless, especially if the extent of judicial review is itself kept to a minimum, the small expansion that I am here considering will make habeas corpus look more like a traditional due process right than before. To say that some minimal hearing will result where some person or persons will determine whether very minimal standards of prima facie plausibility have been met is indeed to focus on procedural aspects of habeas corpus and move us increasingly away from the substantive issues, at least in this one respect. It is also true though that there will have to be some kind of substantive determination of what is the minimal threshold of prima facie plausibility of a charge that can warrant incarceration. I would argue that overall there would be an improvement even if we take into account the addition of this substantive provision. And if I am right, then the slight increase in domain of habeas corpus here will indeed cure one of its clearest infirmities.

6.2 DUE PROCESS OF LAW

Due process of law is often associated with habeas corpus and this has been true since some of the earliest reflections on what habeas corpus stood for, especially as articulated in Magna Carta. I here remind the reader of how Magna Carta was first articulated in the thirteenth century:

No freeman shall be taken or imprisoned or desseised ... or be outlawed or exiled or in any way destroyed, nor will we go upon him nor send upon him, except by the lawful judgment of his peers or by the law of the land.

The phrase "due process" is thought to have been used in one of the early reconstruals of the Magna Carta rights.[2] Indeed, the phrase "by the law of the land" came to be understood as "due process of law" as early as the fourteenth century.

So, from a fairly early point the Magna Carta provision of no arbitrary imprisonment was associated with the idea that arbitrary treatment was to be understood in terms of not following the "law of the land." And as it developed, Magna Carta was actually changed to reflect this fact by the inclusion of the words "in due manner, or by process," as we have seen in an earlier chapter. Historical matters aside for the moment, I will now proceed to defend this idea, again at least in a minimalist way, as a reasonable extension of the very bare bones, minimalist version of habeas corpus discussed in the previous chapter.

According to Hugo Grotius, law can be understood as a "body of rights." Of the rights that are crucial for law is the "right to one's own," especially the right "over oneself."[3] Grotius, and many to follow after him, spoke of these rights as substantive rights to freedom. The rights to freedom or liberty were crucial for marking a society ruled by law from one that was not. Respect for the rights of subjects was crucial for providing law with its moral core. Hugo Grotius was well known for his espousal of a secular version of natural law theory, as was also true for other seventeenth-century theorists.

There is also part of the natural law tradition that saw rights over oneself in terms of the procedural right to be treated before the law in the same way as everyone else, and for the individual's rights not to be unduly

[2] See Mark Freeman's intriguing discussion of the relevance of Magna Carta and due process to the operation of truth commissions, *Truth Commissions and Procedural Fairness*, NY: Cambridge University Press, 2006, especially pp. 109–113.
[3] Hugo Grotius, *De Jure Belli Ac Pacis* (On the Law of War and Peace) (1625), Francis W. Kelsey (trans.), Oxford: Clarendon Press, 1925, p. 35.

restricted before the law. William Blackstone argues that the rights of "personal security, personal liberty, and private property" cannot be secured without what he calls "auxiliary subordinate rights of the subject, which serve principally as barriers to protect and maintain inviolate the great primary rights." And one of the most important is the right of every citizen "of applying to the courts of justice for redress of injuries." According to Blackstone, the "courts of justice must at all times be open to the subject, and the law must be duly administered therein."[4] This is the guiding normative insight behind the idea of due process of law.

As the term indicates, "due process of law" concerns the requirement that laws must follow a certain process, and that process must be what is due to the people in question. I shall discuss this issue as having these two components, that there is a process that governs how law is administered, and that the process in some sense must be what is due to the people who are subject to the law. The process requirement is in many ways the easiest, and fits well with my attempt to defend a somewhat broader right of habeas corpus than the minimalist construal discussed in the previous chapter.

The difficult question is how to understand what process is due to the subjects or citizens of a particular State. Perhaps the simplest idea is that all subjects or citizens stand equally before the law, and the process that is due them is that process that treats them equally before the law, and perhaps that guarantees and safeguards their equal standing before the law. With the exception of societies that distinguish between second-class citizens and the rest of citizens, what is initially due is that people not be demoted to second-class standing by the way the process of law is constructed.

What else is due is that the process in question be one that involves at least a minimum amount of accountability for the officials who are supposed to administer the law. This is a matter of equity, which is different from equality before the law. As indicated above, one of the main reasons for accountability is to curtail or deter abuse by these officials. Mere threat of publicity can do quite a lot, but it is sometimes also necessary to have procedures in place that hold officials to account in a more formal way, by having hearings to which individuals can appeal to bring the officials to answer and where the appeals process can result in penalties for gross misconduct on the part of officials who are supposed to be fairly administering the law.

---

[4] William Blackstone, *Commentaries on the Laws of England* (1765), University of Chicago Press, 1979, vol. I, pp. 136–137.

Due process, at least in the aspect that addresses what is due, is linked to a rudimentary form of judicial review. The subjects or citizens are owed a system of rules that is equally and fairly administered, and this requires that some system of public accountability be established. The most common way to do this is to establish a mechanism whereby an appellate court process or other form of judicial supervision is built into a system of law that instantiates due process. We next explore the forms that judicial review can take and why some of these forms have proven controversial.

6.3 JUDICIAL REVIEW AND HABEAS CORPUS

In the US, judicial review concerns the oversight of the Congress and the Presidency, the elected branches of the US government, by the Judiciary, the only non-elected branch. This oversight may involve ascertaining whether Congressional statutes or Executive orders are unconstitutional in the sense that they violate the rights of US citizens. Judicial review has come to symbolize the veto power of the courts over the other branches of government. Wade Robison has said: "The only way to ensure that those in power do not use that power to deny someone's liberty arbitrarily is to provide a check against such power. No paper guarantee is sufficient."[5]

I begin this section with just a brief response to Robison and others who argue that judicial review is crucial for the efficacy of habeas corpus. While I agree that judicial review can be an especially potent way to bring those in power to do what they should, as I have indicated in other chapters I do not think it is the only way to do so. In part it depends on what rights one hopes to secure against the abridgment by those in power. If we focus on the various forms of abuse discussed in the previous chapter, namely being disappeared or tortured, it is not at all clear that a full-blown separation of powers with proper judicial review is necessary to protect those who are detained or incarcerated from such abuses. Simple methods of rendering visible what jailers are doing can sometimes be quite effective at dissuading jailers from engaging in the type of abuse that habeas corpus has been aimed at. But it is surely true that having a specific judicial body with oversight responsibilities and power to veto the acts of the Executive branch can make things better yet for those who are on the receiving end of such abuses of power.

[5] Wade L. Robison, "The Great Right: Habeas Corpus," in *Coercion and the State*, David A. Reidy and Walter J. Riker (eds.), Dordrecht, The Netherlands: Springer, 2008, p. 165.

So, I am not one of those advocates of judicial review who does not recognize other ways that those in power can be restrained. On the other hand, I am also not in the camp of those who give short shrift to judicial review either. Those who criticize judicial review, such as Larry Kramer and Jeremy Waldron, often draw on the seeming non-democratic or even antidemocratic nature of judicial review.[6] Those who defend judicial review often celebrate the fact that the Judiciary is anti-majoritarian, although not necessarily undemocratic. I want to spend the rest of this section providing a few responses to points made against judicial review by Kramer and other critics of judicial review.

Kramer draws on an analogy between majoritarian decision making and jury nullification – an analogy that I think works much more strongly against Kramer's thesis than for it. Here is his argument:

> The object of judicial supremacy is ... to maximize the Court's authority by inculcating the attitude of deference and submission to its judgments. It is akin to telling jurors that they "must" follow the judges' trial instructions in order to mask the use of the jury's undoubted power of nullification.[7]

Jury nullification is the idea that juries can veto what the judge tells them and decide to rule as they see fit. And while juries clearly have this power, it is one that is not necessarily a good idea to exercise.

When a judge gives instructions to the jury, normally these are instructions about the state of the law. The jury then decides what the facts were and then applies the law, as the judge has declared it, to those facts. So, when the jury nullifies or vetoes the judge's instructions, the jury is putting itself in the position of deciding the law as well as the facts. And yet it is undoubted that the judge knows more about the state of the law than does the average person on the street, the most common way to understand the members of the jury. So, while juries can nullify the judge's instructions, the jury then effectively puts itself above the judge as determiner of the law. Similarly, for members of Congress to override what courts say about the Constitution is in a sense to exercise unwarranted arrogance due to their inferior knowledge.

Jeremy Waldron has responded to an argument of this sort by saying that such an argument "radically underestimates the notion of a right to participate" when a decision affects a person and creates

---

[6] Larry Kramer, *The People Themselves*, NY: Oxford University Press, 2004.
[7] Ibid., p. 233.

duties to which that person is subject.[8] Waldron's powerful arguments against judicial review in his various books on this topic put great emphasis on the political illegitimacy of judicial vetoing of Legislative actions. Like Kramer, Waldron mainly does not concern himself with Executive decisions, focusing instead on Legislative acts, and yet, as we will see later, Executive not Legislative decisions are the ones that are at the core of the kind of judicial review involved in habeas corpus.

Kramer has argued that Congress is responsible to the people in a way that the courts are not and that, as he says:

All the anxiety about Congress is ultimately not so much about legislative institutions or legislators as it is anxiety about *us*, about what we will permit or encourage politically accountable actors to do.[9]

The fact that Congress is politically accountable to the people is supposed to make a difference, but does it? If the vast majority of members of the people are also not trained in law or in the Constitution, why does it matter that they are looking over the shoulders of the members of Congress concerning constitutional questions? Why isn't this like the blind leading the blind? Indeed, it looks like it is an advantage that the courts are not directly accountable to the people, because then we would be back to the idea that unknowledgeable people exercise oversight over those who are knowledgeable.

Kramer then makes matters worse rather than better when at one point he argues that:

there is a qualitative difference between political restraints like bicameralism or a veto and a system of judicial supremacy. It is the difference between checks that are directly responsive to political energy and those that are only indirectly responsive, between checks that explicitly operate from within ordinary politics and those that purport to operate outside and upon it.[10]

But it seems to me that it is just this "political energy" or the operations of "ordinary politics" that is so ill suited to constitutional interpretation. The fact that judges are insulated from ordinary politics, especially its high-energy variety, makes it more likely rather than less likely that judges can look dispassionately on the Constitution and interpret it objectively, or at least quasi-objectively.

---

[8] Jeremy Waldron, "The Core of the Case Against Judicial Review," *Yale Law Journal*, vol. 115, 2006, 1346–1406, especially 1375.
[9] Kramer, *The People Themselves*, p. 242.   [10] Ibid., p. 246.

In any event it is important, I think, to separate the charge of being anti-democratic from the charge of being anti-majoritarian. So, what is the difference? As Kramer notes in the quotation above, there are all kinds of restraints on majoritarian decision making in the US and in other Western societies. Even though the US does not have pure majoritarianism, because of the effects of bicameralism, no one doubts that the US has a democratic form of government. Indeed, a tripartite system of government that has strong checks and balances is often thought to be the hallmark of a democratic government. It is democratic since the people decide, within certain limits, the important questions of the society. But the "limits" are crucially not themselves undemocratic but rather are an intricate part of the democratic system. The courts are clearly un- or even anti-majoritarian, but they can be a crucial part of the democratic system of government.

Ronald Dworkin has argued that it is important that one branch of government sees itself as putting serious checks on the majority, so as to minimize the possible tyranny of that majority. This merely places reasonable limitation on how much of the government is to be decided by majority vote.[11] So, the courts can be anti-majoritarian and yet not undemocratic. Kramer though argues that judges are simply not well placed to be the protectors of minority rights or to act in the name of fairness and justice as moral matters. He addresses an argument of Dworkin directly:

Consider, for example, the argument that judges can reason about questions of political morality "better" because institutional independence insulates them from the grubby self-interest that distorts the thinking of ordinary citizens and politicians ... the argument that this is a good thing runs counter to other epistemic principles – for example, that hard choices are best made by those who have a sufficient stake in the matter to decide responsibly.[12]

Notice here that what Kramer wants is to give priority to decision makers who have a sufficient stake in the matter. But why think that members of Congress, rather than judges, have any greater stake in, say, deciding whether it was unconstitutional for a President to go to war? What exactly is the stake that members of Congress have in this decision? If it is merely worries about being re-elected, this cannot be much of a stake in the constitutionality of a war, especially since, as I argued above, the people who hold Congressional members accountable normally are not

---

[11] See Ronald Dworkin, *Law's Empire*, Cambridge, MA: Harvard University Press, 1986.
[12] Kramer, *The People Themselves*, p. 237.

experts in what the Constitution says, or how it has been interpreted over the last 220 years.

I also wish to try to make quite explicit what it means when, in the Epilogue of his book, Kramer says that the courts should show deference to the elected branches. Think about the debate about the war powers of the President. John Yoo has recently argued, in op-ed pieces and then in a book,[13] that presidential war making power should be seen as unfettered by either Congress or the courts. Think about the decision by the President to hold suspected terrorists indefinitely at Guantanamo Bay, without any significant Congressional oversight, and without even any right of habeas corpus relief. I suppose one could try to justify this by pointing out that Congressional oversight was abrogated when the Congress granted the President the right to take any and all appropriate measures in the war on terrorism.

But it is quite another matter merely for the Executive branch to declare that the Judicial branch has no oversight over the Executive branch's decisions. And what happens when such judicial oversight is stifled by the same Executive branch as was attempted in the Guantanamo habeas corpus cases, as we will see? At least in part, one would hope that the people will hold the President accountable. But what if the President systematically hides what he is doing, perhaps even lying to those people who are supposed to be, in Kramer's view, the very same people who are to hold the President accountable? Here is where we need a separation of powers, not a consolidation of powers.

This brings me to the issue of what to say about judicial overreaching. Being in favor of judicial review is not necessarily to be in favor of an unrestrained Judiciary. And even an activist court is not necessarily an unrestrained court. I would support some insulation from politics when judges do very controversial things that seemingly protect minority rights. But not all actions by the Judiciary are of this sort. And even when the court acts to protect minority rights, we might still want the rights to have some connection to the Constitution.

There are ways to restrain the courts that do not involve nullifying their decisions or trying to engage in court packing to dilute the influence of current judges. Ideally, it seems to me, we would want to restrain the court in a way that does not necessarily leave the court with less oversight of Congress or the President. For ideally what I would advocate is a

[13] John Yoo, *The Powers of War and Peace: The Constitution and Foreign Affairs*, University of Chicago Press, 2005.

separation of powers that gave quite a bit of sway to the Judiciary in rights-protection cases, but did not leave the court unrestrained by the other "elected" branches. Indeed, it seems to me that when the Judiciary is reviewing Executive action, it should have more sway than when reviewing Legislative action, since especially minor members of the Executive, such as jailers, are less closely tied to the will of the people than is the Legislature.

6.4 ASSESSING THE ROLE OF JUDICIAL REVIEW

There is some common ground between a view like Kramer's and one like mine. Kramer, perhaps reluctantly, supports what he calls the New Deal settlement and juxtaposes it to the activism of both left-wing courts like the Warren court and right-wing courts like the Berger or Rehnquist courts. The settlement or compromise was as follows:

the arrangement consisted of a sharp division between constitutional questions regarding the definition or scope of affirmative powers delegated by the Constitution to Congress and the Executive, and constitutional questions pertaining to a broad category of individual rights that limit the form or circumstances in which those powers can be exercised.[14]

I am happy to support, and not nearly as reluctantly as is Kramer, this compromise on judicial review. But such a compromise does not mean that we have to support the idea that the Constitution is "a layman's document not a lawyer's contract."[15] The rejection of extreme popular constitutionalism is not itself a rejection of popular government.

Think again of war issues. The courts surely should not be able to say whether or not the President has the power to make war, with the advice and consent of Congress. But the Court surely should be able to say whether or not the way war is waged has unconstitutionally restricted the rights of certain groups, such as those suspected of terrorism. There are rights that are not to be abrogated except in times of emergency. And the right of habeas corpus review in my view is clearly one such right. Habeas corpus review is, in the somewhat broader view that I am now discussing, merely the means to make sure an individual can challenge his or her incarceration, in times of peace or war, by getting a judicial hearing. Without such a basic judicial mechanism to protect individual rights

[14] Kramer, *The People Themselves*, p. 219.   [15] Ibid.

against the strong popular pressure during wartime, we will be one step closer to a society where the sovereign's word was enough to get a person incarcerated indefinitely. The New Deal settlement is the kind of compromise on judicial review that we should embrace. It allows courts to protect rights, even when the "elected branches" disagree about the precise contours of the protection that is required for subjects and citizens to be fairly treated.

Notice finally that the New Deal compromise restricts the veto power of courts over the acts of Legislatures to that of formal matters, what I have been calling procedural rights, not to matters of substantive right. I support the compromise, although in my full view of these matters I do not believe that all matters of substantive right are off the table for courts. Yet, in international law, restricting judicial review to procedural rights issues is, at least for the foreseeable future, a very good way to proceed, as I will try to explain in the rest of this chapter.

Critics of judicial review point out that in its most robust form, if not in lesser forms, judicial review can allow unelected judges to veto the acts of democratically elected legislators. Indeed, the idea of judicial review, at least in its own maximalist form, is highly unpopular in domestic settings and even more likely to meet stiff resistance at the international level. Even the history of the development of this right appears to many people to betray its undemocratic character. Those who support it say that judicial review is meant to be undemocratic at least in the sense that is anti-majoritarian, in that judicial review protects the rights of minorities against the other branches of government that are supported by majorities.

There is nothing in the US Constitution that requires the kind of extensive judicial review by the courts that has seen a presidential election decided and many duly passed Legislative acts nullified by courts. It was not until the case of *Marbury v. Madison*[16] in 1803 that Chief Justice Marshall announced what is today called the doctrine of judicial review. In many commentators' opinions, the doctrine was simply invented by Marshall, and over the years there has not been a significant effort on the part of the other two branches of the US government to override this unilateral usurpation of power on the part of the Judiciary. Even defenders of the *Marbury* decision recognize that the decision went beyond what had been envisioned for the role of Judiciary in the US Constitution.

---

[16] *Marbury v. Madison*, 5 U.S. 137 (1803).

Defenders claim that judicial review was necessary to guarantee the fairness of the US legal system, but they do not deny that judicial review can be used to overrule what duly elected Legislatures or Executives have been otherwise empowered to do.

It seems to me that judicial review is most problematic, if it is, when it concerns matters of substantive rights rather than procedural rights. If a duly elected Legislature has decided to pass a law concerning substantive rights, and if a flaw is discovered, either in the law itself or in its application, especially in terms of a conflict with the constitution of the State in question, the least controversial remedy is surely to go back to the Legislature and attempt to have the law changed. Concerning matters of substantive rights, majoritarian decision making may not always produce the best results, but it is not clear what forum would produce better results.

When we turn to procedural rights, it is not clear to me that Legislatures are best placed to decide rights matters, especially when there are constitutional principles in play. Indeed, one could argue that judiciaries are best placed to understand and adjudicate procedural issues, and are certainly considerably better than Legislatures. After all, even on a very conservative analysis of what courts should concern themselves with, the setting and application of procedural rules seems relatively uncontroversial. If nothing else, courts are experts on the application of rules, and this is primarily a matter of the interplay of procedural and substantive issues.

In addition, I would argue that when courts override Legislatures on procedural matters, the public is, and should be, generally less bothered than when courts overrule Legislatures on substantive matters. What people tend to care about are substantive issues, and many people do not think much about procedural matters, which is also why procedural rights need greater protection than substantive rights. This is not in itself hugely significant, but it helps explain why the "undemocratic" vetoing of Legislative acts about procedural matters is not as worrisome as when similar things occur concerning Legislative acts about substantive matters. And, as I have suggested, when the Judiciary overrules Executive decisions, especially low-level Executive decisions as is the form that habeas corpus appeals call for, the public is, and should be, less bothered yet. This is because such Executive decisions have not had input from the people who will be subject to them, and hence there is no straightforward overriding of the will of the people by judicial acceptance of habeas corpus petitions challenging detention.

6.5 GLOBAL DUE PROCESS

I favor the idea of somewhat expanding the right of habeas corpus, beyond the minimalist interpretation, to include reference to due process and some rudimentary judicial review. In the current section I will explore what this expanded right might look like in international law. Minimalist habeas corpus is actually harder to work out in the international context than is the somewhat expanded version. Requiring jailers to bring prisoners out into the light of day and publicly proclaim the charges against them is very hard to supervise internationally without some kind of rudimentary hearing also being required along with a rudimentary process of appeal. When the minimal judicial review elements are added, then it is easier to supervise and to make sure that the minimalist process is indeed being followed.

Before looking at the particularities of possible global institutions, let me address the question of what kind of process is due to the inhabitants of the world community. Primarily the question is best seen as involving the type of process that is due for the protection of human rights, the closest we have to civil rights for members of that international community. Given the great variety of States and societies that comprise the international community, part of what is due to members of that international community is that there is some way to guarantee a rough equality before the international law. So, some kind of standardization of treatment, at least at a minimal level, is what would most be due as a matter of global due process. But the form that this standardization would take would not deny all local and regional differences, but would only make sure that a rough equality of procedural rights protections resulted.

Institutionally, it makes sense to look first to the protection of a global right of habeas corpus to the individual States where people reside, and where it is normally the case that human rights protection occurs. So, at one level all that is needed is some kind of international supervisory effort to make sure that States in fact are promoting at least a minimalist right of habeas corpus through domestic institutions. In some cases, as we will see in Chapter 11 where institutional issues are more fully explored, States may fail at this task and then a more robust institution will have to take over for the State at the international level. But in most cases, this kind of direct involvement will not be needed very often since, if the past is any indication of the future, many States will generally protect the rights of their citizens if given sufficient incentive to do so.

I also favor a rudimentary international judicial review, something along the lines of the New Deal compromise described by Kramer. The rudimentary hearing that should be part of my somewhat expanded notion of habeas corpus would have an appeal process that would allow, normally not very often, for the overruling of an Executive action, typically a low-level executive decision of a jailer or a minor government official who has oversight duties concerning actions of a jailer. Of course, this is where things get dicey, since such international judicial review is a direct affront to State sovereignty. In the final paragraphs of this chapter, let me explain why I favor this view and why I think that ultimately it will be something that States will also accept.

The primary reason for a minimal amount of judicial review is for there to be accountability in international law. Let me explain this idea by reference to what occurs at the ICC. This Court is a court of compulsory jurisdiction, at least for those approximately 110 States that as of 2010 had ratified the ICC's Rome Statute. But there are various provisions in the ICC Statute that allow for States to avoid compulsory jurisdiction by taking action on their own. The most significant among these provisions is the principle of complementarity. According to this principle, the Court will only exercise its compulsory jurisdiction if States are unwilling or unable to prosecute the matter in that State's domestic courts. So, in theory, a State may never face the affront to sovereignty that would come by the ICC overseeing and potentially overruling that State's Executive decision.

Indeed, it appears that two things will likely result from the principle of complementarity. First, States will have very strong incentives to set up, or more greatly deploy, rudimentary domestic judicial review. Second, when States fail to do so, it is not such a strong affront to State sovereignty since the State will have chosen to accept international judicial review rather than handle the matter domestically. Of course, there is a serious problem with handling judicial review in this manner, since State consent to the arrangement is required and may not be forthcoming. But this is true of all matters in international law and is not by any means unique to international criminal procedure.

In non-criminal matters, due process also is very important, and this is certainly true in global justice as well as in domestic justice contexts. Mark Freeman has argued that truth commissions, set up as alternatives to criminal proceedings in the aftermath of war and atrocity, are in need of strong due process restraints. As Freeman rightly notes:

In any human rights investigation – judicial, quasi-judicial, or non-judicial – there is a duty on the part of the investigating body to be fair. There is, however, no such thing as a universally applicable standard of fairness ... The challenge is to define parameters and measures of fairness that are appropriate to the particular investigation or proceedings.[17]

One of the key considerations is "the nature and severity of the consequences that may result" from the proceedings.[18] In non-criminal matters, the consequences to the defendant of adverse decisions are generally not as severe as in criminal matters, and so the nature of the due process restraint is different as well.

In all of its aspects, global procedural justice needs to be thought of in due process terms. As I said at the end of Chapter 1, various forms of civil detention, such as occur in detention centers or refugee camps, are equally in need of due process restraints as in criminal arenas of incarceration. As has been recognized at least for several centuries, prisoners of war are also in need of very strict procedural restraints, as are currently found in the Geneva Convention provisions. Wherever justice is an important consideration, issues of due process are bound to arise. Indeed, if it is true that a crucial dimension of justice is fairness, and if fairness is at least partially a matter of due process, then global justice considerations of all sorts should be addressed at least in part in terms of due process as well.

As I will argue later, there is a progressive development of institutions that should be adopted to protect the rights of detainees and prisoners across a wide variety of contexts. In light of the discussions in this current chapter, it could be argued that some form of rudimentary judicial review is also to be recommended, especially when civil proceedings can result in serious consequences such as non-punitive detention. In the US, for instance, immigration violations have landed thousands of people into detention facilities. In other parts of the world, denial of asylum has resulted in hundreds of thousands consigned to refugee camps and many others rendered Stateless. Judicial oversight of such situations is very badly needed. So, one can begin to see that there are larger implications of the discussions in this chapter than might at first meet the eye. Due process and even judicial review is crucial wherever there are detainees or others seriously deprived of basic liberties. And internationally we have a growing need for something like international judicial review as a check on unfair and arbitrary treatment of a non-criminal as well as a criminal nature.

---

[17] Mark Freeman, *Truth Commissions and Procedural Fairness*, Cambridge University Press, 2006, p. 88.   [18] Ibid.

CHAPTER 7

Habeas corpus as jus cogens *in international law*

As we saw in previous chapters, for hundreds of years procedural rights such as habeas corpus have been regarded as fundamental in the Anglo-American system of jurisprudence. In contemporary international law, fundamental norms are called *jus cogens*. *Jus cogens* norms are rights or rules that cannot be derogated even by treaty. In the list that is often given, *jus cogens* norms include norms against aggression, apartheid, slavery, and genocide. All of the entries in this list are substantive rights. In this chapter I will argue that some procedural rights, crucial for the functioning of criminal proceedings, such as habeas corpus, should also have the status of *jus cogens* norms.

I will begin by explaining what it means for a right to have *jus cogens* status. And I will follow this with a defense of having procedural rights like habeas corpus added to the list of *jus cogens* norms. I will then rehearse some of the debates about the *jus cogens* status of procedural rights in the European Commission on Human Rights. At the end of this chapter I will look at the attempts to deal with the abuses at Guantanamo by the American Commission on Human Rights, and by the US and Australian courts, as a way to understand why there needs to be a stronger support for habeas corpus than is today provided by regional courts. Procedural rights can have the status of gap-fillers in international criminal law, making it possible to cover much more abuse than can be captured under prohibitions against specific substantive rights violations. I also consider a significant objection to my view.

7.1 THE IDEA OF 'JUS COGENS' NORMS

Conceptually, *jus cogens* norms share much in common with garden variety universally binding norms as well as with norms that are imbedded in the conscience of the world community. I will begin by exploring these connections before explaining why I think that there can be procedural as well as substantive norms that fit the *jus cogens* mold. The general idea is that *jus cogens* norms are "peremptory norms of general international law."[1] Unlike almost everything else in international law, States cannot opt out of their obligations to these norms and cannot exempt one another by multi-lateral or bi-lateral treaties. *Jus cogens* norms are not consensual norms relying on the agreement of States for their validity; rather, they are non-consensual. While the definition of these norms is clear enough, the underlying rationale and conceptual justification for them is somewhat elusive.

The question of the source of such norms is problematic since the entire international legal system seems to be grounded in consent of the States, not in anything intrinsically binding. In "Peremptory Norms as International Public Order," Orakhelashvili argues that the source of *jus cogens* norms must be in morality. He then surveys the main categories of *jus cogens* norms in an attempt to show that they are instrumental in supporting the moral norm of public order in the international arena.[2] I will argue that *jus cogens* norms are instrumental in supporting a broader norm than public order, namely something like Mill's harm principle, as well as intrinsically valuable as partially constituting the rule of law. But I agree with Orakhelashvili that the ultimate source of *jus cogens*, given its universal scope, is morality.

The main idea of *jus cogens* norms is that certain norms are "compelling law," "law known to be binding" or "universal norms." In international law this idea derives from the Vienna Convention on the Law of Treaties (VCLT) and various cases before the International Court of Justice and other tribunals. Article 54 of the Vienna Convention speaks of "peremptory norms of general international law."[3] Examples include prohibitions of the use of force, genocide, war crimes, crimes against humanity, slavery, apartheid, or torture, among others. *Jus cogens* norms are often thought to be equivalent to constitutional principles of international law, to an international bill of rights, or they are said to constitute the highest in a norms hierarchy. These norms are the most serious challenge to State sovereignty because they bind regardless of what States do or whether States think they are so bound. *Jus cogens* norms are especially problematic since they supposedly give rise to obligations *erga omnes* (on all States)

---

[1] Vienna Convention on Law of Treaties, May 23, 1969, U.N.T.S 331, 8 International Legal Materials 679 (1969), Article 53.
[2] Alexander Orakhelashvili, *Peremptory Norms in International Law*, Oxford University Press, 2006.
[3] Ibid.

including obligations of universal jurisdiction (where all States are required or at least permitted to enforce these norms).

There are a variety of proposed sources of *jus cogens* norms but each has serious conceptual problems. The VCLT declared that some norms were "accepted and recognized by the international community of States as a whole from which no derogation is permitted and which can be modified only by a subsequent norm of general international law having the same character." So, the Vienna Convention seems to see *jus cogens* norms as voluntarist due to requirements of "acceptance."

But what of States that have not accepted or recognized *jus cogens* norms? This is called the problem of the persistent objector. And why couldn't States un-accept such *jus cogens* norms at a later date? Here we see starkly the problem of how to get voluntarist norms to become universal. Another proposed source of *jus cogens* norms is in treaties – *jus cogens* norms arise from the express acts of States. Such a view is clearly voluntarist and hence has the same problems as one interpretation of the language of the VCLT. Here again we can ask why one would think that treaties can create norms that supersede treaties.

Non-consent-based sources of *jus cogens* norms most frequently refer to custom – that is, the longstanding tradition of acceptance of certain *jus cogens* norms. But why think that custom can ground universal norms and most importantly what about counter customs as seem to exist for each of the proposed examples of *jus cogens* norms? In addition, there are "natural law" or reason-based sources of *jus cogens* norms. Here what makes some norms acceptable to all is that they have certain characteristics that make them acceptable, so it is not acceptance but the character of the substance of the norm. Such views are clearly non-voluntarist and hence could be seen as universal. But we still need to figure out what is the source of natural law or at least what sorts of characteristics make norms clearly known to be binding.[4]

Most recently, Evan Criddle and Evan Fox-Decent have proposed a "fiduciary theory" where vulnerability generates *jus cogens* duties on the part of those who have made one vulnerable and can offer protection.[5] But, as the authors acknowledge, considerable work needs to be done to explain why only some vulnerabilities generate such duties and not

[4] For more discussion on the debates about the sources of *jus cogens* norms, see my book *Crimes Against Humanity: A Normative Account*, NY: Cambridge University Press, 2005, Chapters 2 and 3.
[5] Evan J. Criddle and Evan Fox-Decent, "A Fiduciary Theory of Jus Cogens," *Yale Journal of International Law*, vol. 34, Summer 2009, 331–387.

vulnerability due to a denial of any one of the entire list of rights listed in the UDHR. And, not fully addressed by Criddle and Fox-Decent, why think that fiduciary as opposed to less strenuous duties are generated? Criddle and Fox-Decent offer a series of conditions that they argue will allow for *jus cogens* norms to achieve specificity, such as that these norms must have as their object the good of the people and treat persons as moral equals, and supply equal security.[6] I have argued that it is the last of these conditions that is the most important, as will become clear.

My view is most similar to the fiduciary theory. I have previously argued that States have the capacity to act against their citizens and that, when this occurs, States have violated their prime duty, which is to maintain the safety of the people. Because of the vulnerability of the people to the consolidated power of the State, the State has special obligations to the people. It is indeed consistent with such a view to see *jus cogens* norms as stipulating the specific duties that States have that arise from the common vulnerabilities of the citizens. These duties are best characterized, as I will explain later, as falling under a general prohibition of doing harm to these citizens. I have characterized the duties that soldiers have to prisoners of war in fiduciary terms, but have worried about whether the better category of duties is not one of stewardship duties. Stewardship duties differ from fiduciary duties in that the steward is supposed to place the interests of the vulnerable one in at least as high a position as his or her own, whereas the fiduciary is supposed to treat the interests of the vulnerable as the highest, even higher than his or her own interests.[7]

Focusing on the vulnerabilities of citizens in the face of State power, and on duties rather than rights, can allow for a grounding of *jus cogens* norms that explains why these norms are such a challenge to State sovereignty. Yet such a focus also shows States that their actions of violating *jus cogens* norms actually undercut the sovereignty they wish to retain. By violating *jus cogens* norms and rendering citizens significantly less secure, States also render themselves less secure. In this sense, *jus cogens* norms are merely a reminder to States of what they need to do to secure their sovereignty by maintaining the only foundational duty that they have, to secure the *salus populi*, the safety of the people.

---

[6] Ibid., 354–356.

[7] See my discussion of this issue in my book *War Crimes and Just War*, NY: Cambridge University Press, 2007, especially Chapter 7.

In the *Barcelona Traction* case, the International Court of Justice (ICJ) held that:

such obligations derive, for example, in contemporary international law, from the outlawing of acts of aggression, and of genocide, as also from the principles and rules concerning basic human rights of the human person, including protection from slavery and racial discrimination. Some of the corresponding rights of protection have entered into the body of general international law ... others are conferred by international instruments of a universal or quasi-universal character.[8]

There is some controversy about whether *jus cogens* norms are universal or could in some sense be regional, but it makes the most sense out of the vast majority of discussions of *jus cogens* norms to think that they have universal binding force. It is theoretically possible that norms could be only regionally binding and yet have peremptory status. Think of the norm against capital punishment. Such a norm could be a norm of overridingly binding status, as it is among the Member States of the European Union, and yet not have binding force within North America. But if these norms are to be principles of "general international law," it is hard to understand them as general rather than specific if these norms are restricted geographically. At the very least it is not elegant, but rather messy, to have international norms that are binding on all in the strongest possible terms and yet not binding at all in certain regions of the world. But it is not utterly implausible that this would be so.

The least messy way to view *jus cogens* norms is if they are universally binding internationally. Think of the substantive *jus cogens* norms against apartheid, slavery, and genocide. While there have been multi-lateral treaties on these topics, with the vast majority of States in the world ratifying these treaties, it is also true that even those few States which have not signed on do not deny that these norms are universally binding. The fact that these States consent to these norms does not seem itself to be the source of their validity since even if many States withdrew their consent, the norms against aggression, apartheid, slavery, and genocide would seemingly still have universally binding status. But if these norms are universally binding and also not based on consent, then of course there is a need to explain what exactly they are grounded in. And in the case of the four norms mentioned above (against aggression, apartheid, slavery, and genocide) there is an obvious candidate: the moral principle against the

---

[8] *Case Concerning the Barcelona Traction, Light, and Power Co., Limited*, Second Phase, *Belgium v. Spain*, 1970 ICJ, 3, 1970 WL 1.

infliction of serious harm, especially to life or liberty, a variation on John Stuart Mill's famous "harm principle."

If there are to be general principles of international law that are binding on all States and that are not grounded in consent, then something as relatively uncontroversial as the harm principle may indeed supply the normative grounding. One way to understand *jus cogens* norms then is that they protect individuals globally from serious abridgements to life or liberty. International law is especially concerned to protect these rights when their abuse is widespread or where there is some systematic attack on them, as in the case of government-sponsored action.[9] Guantanamo exemplified the kind of abuse in both respects that the world community should concern itself with. Yet the abridgement was not necessarily arbitrary imprisonment but the lack of procedural safeguards such as habeas corpus that are related to arbitrary imprisonment.

Some attention will have to be given to the problem of specifying *jus cogens* norms in such a way that there is not an endless proliferation of such norms. And here the idea of such norms attaining a certain level of seriousness is the key. In answer to this problem I would support something like Henry Shue's strategy for paring down the long list of rights in the UDHR by specifying only those rights that are "basic."[10] Similarly I would argue that certain liberties are basic in that their security is the key to any minimally reasonable human life.

If protection of liberty is the key, then procedural safeguards that protect liberty should also have great weight attached to them. The first and least controversial category of *jus cogens* norms is that against aggression, since the use of force is explicitly contrary to the Charter of the UN. Waging aggressive war normally causes great disruptions of rights to liberty as well as to life. What has remained controversial is how best to define aggression.[11] The second category that is now well accepted concerns the prohibition on engaging in substantive international crimes, especially genocide and crimes against humanity, as well as certain especially heinous violations of the rules of war. The prohibitions on piracy and slavery are also relatively uncontroversial examples of *jus cogens* norms. The prohibition on torture can also fit under this rubric, although it seems that States violate this norm nearly as often as they affirm it,

---

[9] See my discussion of this issue in *Crimes Against Humanity: A Normative Account*, NY: Cambridge University Press, 2005.
[10] Henry Shue, *Basic Rights*, Princeton University Press, 1980.
[11] See my book *Aggression and Crimes Against Peace*, NY: Cambridge University Press, 2008.

including even the very same States that ratified the torture treaty. All of these acts are easily characterized as falling under a harm principle that focuses on serious harms or harms to basic liberties.[12]

One question to ask is whether non-substantive norms could also have *jus cogens* status. I propose that it is just as important that serious harm be condemned as that serious unfairness also be condemned. And if serious violations of fairness are to be candidates for *jus cogens* norms, along with substantive infliction of harm, then the door is open for procedural rights to have *jus cogens* status along with substantive rights. And I would then propose that habeas corpus should be at the top of the candidate list for *jus cogens* status. Procedural rights can also be defended not in instrumental but in intrinsic terms. In this latter respect, the way that certain procedural norms constitute a rule of law is crucially relevant. But the rule of law does not appear to be easily incorporated under the harm principle. We could think of the rule of law as advancing substantive liberties or we could think of it as having value in itself, but then we would have to expand slightly the idea of harm to include fairness concerns.

7.2 'JUS COGENS' AND EQUITY

It is not well recognized, but *jus cogens* norms are in many ways similar to equity as it has developed in the Anglo-American legal system. In this section I will explore this issue before turning to the practical question of how *jus cogens* should be instantiated in the international legal system. There is a narrow use of the term equity in international law, as it relates to the settlement of disputes over the continental shelf and other boundary disputes between States. But there is also a much wider use of the term equity in the expression of Article 38(2) of the ICJ's statute, which has been interpreted to mean the ability to create new legal relations by international courts.[13] I will concern myself with a use of the concept of equity that lies in between these two, but is still fairly broad, and which, in my opinion, best represents the longstanding use of this concept in Anglo-

---

[12] I here follow H. Waldock, a special rapporteur for the International Law Commission, who tried to provide a categorization scheme for *jus cogens* norms in 1963. See the summary of his position in Lauri Hannikainen, *Peremptory Norms (Jus Cogens) in International Law*, Helsinki: Finnish Lawyers Publishing Company, 1988, pp. 158–159.

[13] See Hersch Lauterpacht, *The Development of International Law by the International Court*, Oxford University Press, 1958, p. 213; and Thomas Franck, *Fairness in International Law and Institutions*, Oxford University Press, 1995, p. 54.

American jurisprudence. Equity is here a principle for fairly deciding cases but is itself still rule-based and is not merely synonymous with judicial discretion. Thomas Franck has referred to this particular conception of equity as "broadly conceived equity."[14]

In the Anglo-American system, equity is associated with fundamental fairness: the conscience of the king and later the conscience of the republic. Equity has been a clear way to deal with unfairness in an otherwise proper legal proceeding, and when the laws are either silent or ambiguous. Indeed, since at least the time of Thomas More, the first lay official in England to be Lord Chancellor and to expand the reach of equitable relief, equity has been seen as the bridge between morality and legality in a system of law.

In his classic work *Commentaries on Equity Jurisprudence*, Justice Joseph Story sketches the broad nature of equity:

> In the most general sense, we are accustomed to call that equity, which in human transactions, is founded in natural justice, in honesty and right, and which properly arises *ex aequo et bono*. In this sense it answers precisely to the definition of justice, or natural law, as given by Justinian ... Now it would be a great mistake to suppose that equity, as administered in England, embraced a jurisdiction as wide and extensive as that which arises from the principles of natural justice above stated ... But there is a more limited sense in which the term is often used, and which has the sanction of jurists in ancient, as well as in modern times ... Thus Aristotle has defined the very nature of equity to be the correction of the law ...[15]

Indeed, Aristotle said that equity is outside of legal justice, since it is a correction of it, but is also better than legal justice and is one of the most important considerations of law.[16]

Jus cogens norms and equitable principles are similar in several important respects, especially concerning procedural *jus cogens*. In the following paragraphs I will explore three ways in which the principle of equity and procedural *jus cogens* norms are indeed similar. And I will indicate that these two concepts are complementary, indeed mutually supporting, ideas.

First, and most importantly, *jus cogens* norms and principles of equity are grounded in morality, especially in the moral norm of fairness. In my

---

[14] Franck, ibid., pp. 65–75.
[15] Joseph Story, *Commentaries on Equity Jurisprudence* (1834), London: Stevens and Hayes, 1884, pp. 1–3.
[16] Aristotle, *Nicomachean Ethics*, Book V, Ch. 10, 1137b10.

book *Crimes Against Humanity: A Normative Account*, I began to sketch an argument for understanding the prohibitions on aggression, apartheid, slavery, and genocide that form the core of the *jus cogens* norms in terms of foundational moral norms for the international legal system. I argued that humans, as a contingent matter of how they are, have no basis for obeying law if they are not secured in their persons and property by the sovereign. I left open the question of whether security is a norm of universal scope or merely a quasi-universal norm, based only on what we have known humans to be like. All that matters is that there is a philosophical basis for universal or quasi-universal norms, grounded in basic human rights, upon which the norms of international law might rest.[17]

My conception of *jus cogens* norms is grounded in moral minimalism. What is most appealing about moral minimalism is that it explains the nearly universal recognition of such norms as self-preservation and self-defense. The drive for self-preservation is indeed a feature of humans, at least as we know them now and as they have been known. Of course, there are situations where self-preservation is overcome by other motivations. But societies are not structured on such exceptional cases. Rather, there is a general recognition of the importance of minimal moral maxims that support self-preservation and that give weight to something like the Millian harm principle. And such a basis could very plausibly explain the appeal of the idea of *jus cogens* norms. In addition, *jus cogens* norms seem to provide a minimal moral fairness in how people must interact with each other as fellow humans deserving of minimal respect. In this sense, at least minimally, there is a merging of morality and legality.

Second, procedural *jus cogens* norms and principles of equity are corrections of the law in terms of justice. Equity is a matter of justice, especially natural justice, which can be understood in terms of correcting the occasional mismatch between law's generality and the specificity of cases. Unfairness can creep into an otherwise fair system of law when unanticipated cases arise that seem technically to fit under a given law but where injustice would result. Similarly, I conceive procedural *jus cogens* norms as gap-fillers that are necessary for the application of law to make sense in terms of fairness both because of law's generality and because of possible gaps in the application of law due to the character of new types of cases. Procedural *jus cogens* norms, like habeas corpus rights, will fill gaps in the way that equity often does in domestic legal contexts.

---

[17] May, *Crimes Against Humanity*, Chapter 2.

Third, procedural *jus cogens* norms and the principle of equity do not allow for unlimited discretion but seek to provide rule-based corrective mechanisms for the application of law that might result in specific forms of unfairness. In the case of both broadly conceived equity and also procedural *jus cogens* norms, judges are not left with unlimited discretion. There are rules that govern how both equity and *jus cogens* norms are to operate, restricting discretion but allowing for it in a limited way. In particular, the procedural rights will specify both what practices have to be adhered to and also what sort of case the rights can be applied to. In this way equity can be both rule-bound and also morally foundational. Indeed, *jus cogens* norms, when understood on this model of equity, will have the kind of foundational status that will also breed stability, since judges will not be left all at sea in deciding hard cases.

When equity is understood as broadly conceived but still rule-bound, it will be a basis for significant gap-filling on the way toward a genuine international rule of law. And the kind of problems that later I will identify at Guantanamo and Christmas Island will perhaps not recur. But there is obviously no guarantee. For that to occur, there would have to be a much stronger conception of equity or procedural *jus cogens* than I have defended here. What is lost when very broad discretion is given to judges to correct for distributive injustice is the very stability and order that the rule of law is centered on. Thomas Franck has put this point well: "Fairness . . . accommodates a deeply popular belief that for a system of rules to be fair, it must be firmly rooted in a framework of formal requirements about how rules are made, interpreted, and applied."[18] When judges are merely given discretion to decide on what is fair, this popular belief is undermined. Only when there is an institution with a clear set of rules do we then have an international rule of law that is deserving of respect in that it accommodates this popular belief.

Christian Tomuschat, a respected international legal theorist, talks of *jus cogens* norms as the most fundamental norms of international law and describes them as "rules of conduct which proscribe certain attacks on a number of particularly cherished goods of the international community."[19] Democracy and the rule of law are goods, even if not the sort of goods that are typically listed as important human goods, such as health

---

[18] Franck, *Fairness in International Law and Institutions*, pp. 7–8.
[19] Christian Tomuschat, "Concluding Remarks," in *The Fundamental Rules of the International Legal Order: Jus Cogens and Obligations Erga Omnes*, Christian Tomuschat and Jean-Marc Thouvenin (eds.), Leiden: Martinus Nijhof, 2006, p. 430.

and well-being. Rather than goods of bodily integrity, for instance, the rule of law is a good of fairness. Indeed, fairness is cherished by the international community, as is true of all communities. Insofar as it is an important good, the rule of law should be promoted, as should those things that are constitutive of it, such as habeas corpus.

One author has summarized the state of procedural rights in terms of the idea of internationally recognized *jus cogens* norms as follows:

> in addition to the substantive rights expressly declared to be non-derogable, a number of procedural rights, which are instrumental to the effective protection of non-derogable rights, must also be respected in all circumstances. Among them is the right to have access to the domestic courts for violations of non-derogable rights, and the right of habeas corpus. Some fundamental aspects of the right to fair trial are also generally considered as non-derogable.[20]

I would only add that some procedural rights, such as habeas corpus, should be seen as *jus cogens* even if not strongly instrumental in this way. The intrinsic value of habeas corpus also needs to be recognized.

If there is to be an international rule of law, certain core rights will have to be protected against abuse wherever in the world that abuse occurs. A good example is the failure of the US government to provide core procedural rights at the prison in Guantanamo Bay, Cuba, as well as the failure of the Australian government to protect the habeas corpus rights of refugees in the infamous Christmas Island case. If human rights are to be protected globally and if there is to be a system of international criminal law, protecting such procedural rights as habeas corpus across the world is crucial. Yet the protection afforded at the moment is weak, as we will see.

7.3 ARBITRARY INCARCERATION IN EUROPEAN HUMAN RIGHTS LAW

The European Convention on Human Rights has two articles that concern similar matters to that of habeas corpus but neither, in my view, provides the same fundamental protection as habeas corpus. Articles 5(3) and 5(4) declare that:

(3) Everyone arrested or detained in accordance with the provisions of paragraph (1)(c) of this article shall be promptly brought before a

---

[20] Silvia Borelli, "Casting Light on the Legal Black Hole: International Law and Detentions Abroad in the 'War on Terror,'" *International Review of the Red Cross*, vol. 87, no. 857, March 2005, 39–86, p. 55.

judge or other officer authorized by law to exercise judicial power and shall be entitled to trial within a reasonable time or to release pending trial. Release may be conditioned by guarantees to appear for trial.

(4) Everyone who is deprived of his liberty by arrest or detention shall be entitled to take proceedings by which the lawfulness of his detention shall be decided speedily by a court and his release ordered if the detention is not lawful.

In some respects, the article seems to cover more than habeas corpus does. For the focus here is on getting a judge or court to review the case for the arrest or detention of the prisoner, whereas habeas corpus, at least in its stripped-down version, does not necessarily involve review by a judge or court, but only the pubic reading of the charges against the prisoner. But there are several gaps in these two sections of Article 5 that an international right of habeas corpus could fill.

First, Article 5(3) only refers to arrest or detention in accordance with (1)(c), which only relates to:

the lawful arrest or detention of a person effected for the purpose of bringing him before the competent legal authority on reasonable suspicion of having committed an offense or when it is reasonably considered necessary to prevent his committing an offense or fleeing after having done so.

Hence, Article 5(3) does not apply to the full gamut of reasons for which one might find oneself incarcerated or detained. Indeed, it does not concern any post-conviction detention, or a wide range of detentions for public health or safety reasons.

Second, Article 5(4) does concern these additional bases of detention or arrest, since it applies to "everyone arrested or detained." But the focus of this provision is quite a bit narrower than even the stripped-down version of habeas corpus, where historically the prisoner had only to be brought out of the dungeon and have the charges against him or her publicly declared. For the prisoner can only challenge the lawfulness of the detention. In many cases there are other important bases of challenging detention. This section of Article 5 would not sweep so widely as to include prisoners who wish to challenge abuse or secret confinement if there is no serious question of the lawfulness of their detention in the first place. Those who have been tortured or made to disappear would not be able to petition to be brought into the light of public scrutiny by employing this provision.

It could be argued that torture and other forms of cruelty, as well as death, of a prisoner are covered in other provisions of the European

Convention on Human Rights. Article 2 of the Convention says that
"Everyone's right to life shall be protected by law." And Article 3 declares
that "No one shall be subjected to torture or to inhuman or degrading
treatment or punishment." A combination of these articles plus the
provisions of Article 5 quoted above, it might be argued, could still cover
the cases I have indicated to be in need of protection that would be
covered by a habeas corpus right.

Generally speaking, habeas corpus covers more and also less than
does the kind of "judicial review" that is called for by Article 5(4) of
the European Convention. This fact has been recognized by the
European Court of Human Rights, which has been given the task
of interpreting the European Convention. In the case of *X v. United
Kingdom*, the Court ruled that the habeas corpus proceedings available
in England did not meet the requirements of the provisions of Article
5(4). The Court declared that having satisfied a habeas corpus procedure was "not sufficient for a continued confinement," finding that
"Article 5(4) required an appropriate procedure allowing a court to
examine whether the prisoner should continue to be incarcerated."
A broad-based "judicial" review is the key to Article 5(4), not the kind
of attention to the jailer that is the hallmark of habeas corpus
proceedings.[21]

Article 5(2) seems to come closest to the stripped-down version of
habeas corpus when it declares that: "Everyone who is arrested shall be
informed promptly, in language which he understands, of the reasons
for his arrest and of any charge against him." But notice two things that
limit this right more than habeas corpus is normally limited. First, this
right only concerns arrest and seemingly does not concern forms of
confinement that occur well after arrest and preliminary charges have
been read, or where no formal arrest occurred at all, as in some refugee
cases. Second, there is no provision here for the public reading of the
charges against the prisoner, but the article could be satisfied by a secret
reading of these charges where the only one present is the prisoner and
his or her jailer, thereby defeating one of the main purposes of habeas
corpus.

While it may be that the sum total of provisions in Article 5 of the
European Convention on Human Rights covers what habeas corpus

---

[21] *X. v. United Kingdom*, Judgment No. 46, European Court of Human Rights (5.11.1981) pp. 56–58,
quoted in J. E. S. Fawcett, *The Application of the European Convention on Human Rights*, NY:
Oxford University Press, 1987, pp. 120–121.

covers, and I doubt that this is true, as I have indicated above, nonetheless, there are critics of the Convention who argue that its lack of clarity about such matters is a major problem. Jacobs and White contend that given the importance of the right to liberty it is "regrettable that the text of Article 5 of the convention is rather confused and unclear." In addition, they point out that there are rather large lacunas in the protections offered by Article 5, including the fact that "as it now stands States are free to deprive asylum-seekers of their liberty as long as deportation proceedings are in progress." And they conclude their chapter on Article 5 by saying: "The extent to which States are required to take action to prevent unlawful detention by third parties – either within national jurisdiction or extraterritorially – is another area where clarification from the court would be welcome."[22] Such a conclusion is especially apt in the light of the controversy over Guantanamo detainees. I next turn to the way that Guantanamo was handled by the Inter-American Court of Human Rights.

7.4 THE INTER-AMERICAN COMMISSION ON HUMAN RIGHTS

After September 11, 2001, the US and its allies arrested hundreds of supposed enemies of the US in Afghanistan. Starting in January 2002, many of those arrested were transferred to a prison at Guantanamo Bay. The detainees were held in captivity without access to legal counsel and without even having their names released or the charges against them publicly proclaimed. One administration official said that the principal motivation for transfer to Guantanamo was that it was "the legal equivalent of outer space." And a British judge referred to Guantanamo detainees as existing in a US-created "legal black hole."[23]

The Bush administration claimed that it was fighting an asymmetrical war, where the enemy fighters did not recognize the rules of war. The Bush administration thus referred to these fighters as illegal combatants, and for this reason did not feel constrained by the Geneva Conventions and the other rules of war in terms of how these fighters were treated. In addition, because the fighters were being held at Guantanamo, Cuba, not technically on American soil, the administration argued that the fighters also had no US Constitutional rights either. And for this reason, the

---

[22] Francis Jacobs and Robin White, *The European Convention on Human Rights*, third edn edited by Clare Ovey and Robin White, NY: Oxford University Press, 2002, p. 138.
[23] Borelli, "Casting Light on the Legal Black Hole," note 22, p. 45, and note 6, p. 41.

administration claimed that these fighters should not have habeas corpus rights recognized. In support of all of this, the administration also argued that it was acting pursuant to the highest value that any US administration should follow, namely keeping Americans safe by detaining enemies of the US.[24]

In 2002 the Inter-American Commission on Human Rights (IACHR) considered a petition from some of the detainees at Guantanamo who argued that their habeas corpus rights had been violated. On March 22 of that year the Commission issued "precautionary measures in favor of the detainees being held by the United States at Guantanamo Bay, Cuba." The Commission "decided to request that the United States take urgent measures necessary to have the legal status of the detainees at Guantanamo Bay determined by a competent tribunal." The US disputed the Commission's jurisdiction. The Commission rejected the US's objections and maintained its request. The matter was never resolved as the "Commission did not subsequently receive any information indicating that its request for precautionary measures had been complied with." But despite the IACHR reiterating its concern about the Guantanamo detainees each year for seven years after its initial issuing of precautionary measures, there is little evidence that the US changed its behavior or policies.

The habeas corpus petitions of several Guantanamo detainees were also filed in US courts. Initially, in *Rasul v. Bush*, 542 U.S. 466 (2004) the US Supreme Court ruled that habeas corpus petitions could be filed by these detainees. Some lower courts affirmed and other courts denied their appeals. Congress then passed the Detainee Treatment Act of 2005 attempting to strip Guantanamo detainees of habeas corpus rights. In *Hamdan v. Rumsfeld*, 548 U.S. 557 (2006) the US Supreme Court reaffirmed the importance of habeas corpus and ruled that the Detainee Treatment Act was not relevant to cases already pending before it. Congress then passed the Military Commissions Act of 2006, stripping habeas and other judicial appeals from all Guantanamo detainees regardless of whether their cases were pending before US courts or not. In *Boumedienne v. Bush*, 128 S. Ct. 2229 (2008), a deeply divided US Supreme Court ruled that the Military Commissions Act was unconstitutional because of its denial of the fundamental right of habeas corpus as an instrument of the protection of individual liberty and the rule of law.

---

[24] John Yoo, *The Powers of War and Peace: The Constitution and Foreign Affairs*, University of Chicago Press, 2005. See also Victoria Toensing, "KSM Deserves Military Justice," *The Wall Street Journal*, Tuesday, March 2, 2010, p. A23.

What is most significant, as a matter of international law, is that the Inter-American Commission did not feel it could take stronger measures against the US in the Guantanamo case. Indeed, even after it became clear that the US would ignore the Commission's Precautionary Measures, the Commission did not seek further measures to protect the Guantanamo detainees, who the Commission admitted were at grave risk. It is striking that there has never been a decision of the IACHR against the US on this issue, or anything stronger from the Commission than the "request" that was articulated above. So, while it is true that the IACHR at least took up the issue of the deprivation of rights of the Guantanamo detainees, the result is quite far from minimally satisfactory – calling into question the ability of at least this particular regional human rights commission, if not the entire structure of human rights commissions, to protect procedural rights such as those of habeas corpus.

The Inter-American Human Rights Commission and Court are the bodies that are supposed to interpret and enforce the Organization of American States's Declaration of the Rights and Duties of Man. Article XXV of the Declaration states:

No person may be deprived of his liberty except in the cases and according to the procedures established by preexisting law … Every individual who has been deprived of his liberty has the right to have the legality of his detention ascertained without delay by a court, and the right to be tried without undue delay, or, otherwise to be released. He also has the right to humane treatment during the time he is in custody.

The Guantanamo Precautionary Measures were based on the Commission's interpretation and application of this article from the American Declaration of the Rights and Duties of Man.

The Commission could have tried to apply the relevant portions of a different and more stringent document, the American Convention on Human Rights. But since the US was not a party to the American Convention, the IACHR chose to apply the older American Declaration to the petition brought by several human rights groups within the US on behalf of the Guantanamo detainees. At least in part, this strategy was fueled by a concern that no one should fall between the cracks of human rights protection within the Americas. The various OAS bodies, especially the IACHR and the Inter-American Court of Human Rights have an excellent track record of redressing human rights abuses, especially in Latin America. And the American Declaration has proved to be especially useful concerning putative abuses by some countries that did not sign the

American Convention on Human Rights but did agree to the Declaration at the time of the signing of the OAS Charter.[25]

The American Declaration's treatment of arbitrary incarceration is a shorter version of the European Convention's treatment of arbitrary incarceration. And like the European Convention, the OAS Declaration does not quite capture the same ideas as those of habeas corpus. Both documents focus on the need for judicial review to ascertain whether the detention is illegal. But neither one of these documents refers to a right that the prisoner has that must be responded to by his or her jailer. Yet this is highly significant both for the status of the right and for the kind of things that would follow from pressing one's rights claim. Judicial review is one way to have the legality of the incarceration tested. But for certain kinds of case, it is far more efficacious that a particular person has to answer for the deprivation of liberty, and if that person is the jailer, it is even more efficacious.

Nonetheless, the IACHR was not able adequately to respond to the claims of the Guantanamo detainees. A similar sort of worry concerns non-refoulement. There were repeated findings that non-refoulement, or the right of non-return of refugees if they are likely to be harmed, was an absolute right, especially strongly voiced in the Commission's 2005 finding in respect to the practice of moving Guantanamo detainees to third-party countries like Egypt. Despite these findings as well as warnings, there was continuing credible evidence that the detainees were still being subjected to torture. What is curious is that if the treatment of the Guantanamo detainees was so clearly a violation of the OAS Declaration, why was something stronger not attempted as a response to the US's failure to respond to the initial request? And here is one of the problems with regional enforcement of human rights norms – the most powerful regional players will not be subject to the sanctions in the same way that the smaller players are. Of course, especially in the case of the US, this is sometimes also true at the global level.

In thinking about how to make procedural matters become as significant as substantive matters, we need to think about the norms that are acknowledged in these areas. Concerning substantive rights, the most important are afforded the status of *jus cogens*, norms which a State cannot derogate even by an explicit act of treaty or other law making. In my view

---

[25] See Brian D. Tittemore, "Guantanamo Bay and the Precautionary Measures of the Inter-American Commission on Human Rights: A Case for International Oversight in the Struggle against Terrorism," *Human Rights Law Review*, vol. 6, no. 2, July 2006, 378–402.

it is time to consider adding certain procedural rights to the list of *jus cogens* norms in international law. I will next say a bit about cases in Australia before considering a significant objection to the idea of *jus cogens* in global justice.

7.5 DAVID HICKS AND THE 'MV TAMPA'

In this section I will discuss two recent Australian cases where habeas corpus rights failed to be protected by domestic courts, and also where international protection seems to have been needed. In Australia the writ of habeas corpus has been similarly lauded as it was in the UK since Magna Carta and in the US where habeas corpus is the only right listed in the main body of the 1789 US Constitution. As early as 1824, the Australian Attorney-General, Joseph Gellibrand said, habeas is a "glorious bulwark of our constitution." In 1966 the International Commission of Jurists (Australian Section) declared: "the effectiveness of the writ of habeas corpus, as an essential bastion of personal liberty, should not be diminished."[26] And in 1993, one of the leading human rights jurists, Michael Kirby, called habeas corpus "that ancient and still precious remedy."

Yet there is only one book dealing with Australian habeas corpus in the Australian National University's law library. In this book the authors declare that "the writ has been all but ignored in Australasian legal writing," and in practice the writ is often treated in a "dismissive" way.[27] According to the authors, the heyday of habeas corpus in Australia was in the early part of the twentieth century: "Many of the habeas corpus cases in Australia during the 20th century arose out of the operation of the notorious dictation test."[28] "The legal rule was that an immigration officer could require an immigrant to take a dictation test in any European language."[29] If the immigrant failed the test, then he or she could be convicted of the offense of being a "prohibited immigrant" and incarcerated or sent out of the country. Those convicted of such an offense filed habeas corpus petitions, and it appears that Parliament acted to try to restrict habeas corpus in general to prevent this remedy to the "Whites Only" immigration laws in Australia.

---

[26] See Law Reform Commission, Report 1 (1966) – Application for Writs of Habeas Corpus and Procedure to be Adopted, September 26, 1966.
[27] David Clark and Gerard McCoy, *Habeas Corpus: Australia, New Zealand, The South Pacific,* Sydney: Federation Press, 2000, pp. 7–8.
[28] Ibid., p. 9.   [29] Ibid. p. 10.

In both of the recent cases I wish to examine, habeas corpus writs were sought in Australia in very high-profile cases of individuals who were being detained. As in the US case I examined, once the Australian domestic courts turned down the habeas corpus petition, the individuals had no recourse, since there is no international body that has the authority to hear appeals concerning habeas corpus. While the cases each offer interesting technical questions about how to understand habeas corpus, especially concerning the understanding of what constitutes detention and what counts as having the power to end detention, it appears that politics intervened to render habeas corpus mute just when it was needed most. I will explain the circumstances of the habeas corpus appeals in each of these cases.

To continue with the Guantanamo story from above, it is noteworthy that one of the Guantanamo detainees was an Australian citizen. David Hicks had been captured in Afghanistan in late 2001 and transported to Guantanamo in January 2002.[30] After several charges against Hicks were dropped, in 2006 the Australian government indicated that it would seek repatriation of Hicks unless charges against him were forthcoming. To cut a long story short, on March 27, 2007 Hicks was eventually charged with "providing material support for terrorism" and he submitted a guilty plea to this charge. The Australian government indicated that it would not seek to request Hicks's release. Lawyers for Hicks then commenced habeas corpus proceedings in the Australian Federal Court for Hicks's release and repatriation. Even though he was outside Australian territory, Hicks argued that the Australian government had a duty to protect his basic rights.

Hicks had been one of the petitioners whose case was ultimately heard by the US Supreme Court as *Rasul v. Bush* in 2002. His petition before the Australian Federal Court was also heard, as *Hicks v. Ruddick* [2007] FCA 299 (March 8). In the latter case, Justice Brian J. Tamberlin sided with Hicks and called for an expedited hearing to determine whether there was a prima facie case for Hicks's continued detention at Guantanamo. While this appeared to be a victory for Hicks and generally for the efficacy of habeas corpus in Australia, political considerations intervened and Hicks was transferred from Guantanamo to a prison in Australia where he served most of his sentence. In responding to several technical issues that arose, the Australian Federal Court seemed to restrict the right of habeas corpus quite a bit further than has been true in either the UK or the US, despite the similarity in rhetoric lauding the right.

---

[30] See Stephen Tully, "Australian Detainee Pleads Guilty before the First Military Commission," *ASIL Insights*, vol. 11, issue 11, April 23, 2007.

In a second Australian case, a group of refugees had been rescued from their sinking boat by the Norwegian ship, the *MV Tampa*. The Norwegian ship tried to make port at Christmas Island, part of the territorial immigration zone of Australia. On August 26, 2001 the ship and its rescuees were detained off the coast of Christmas Island by the Australian navy and were prevented from landing on Christmas Island, which was then a port from which Australian asylum could be initiated. It was alleged that several people on board required immediate medical attention that could not be provided at sea by the *MV Tampa*. But the main issue was that the Australian government did not want these rescuees to claim asylum in Australia.

On the basis of being detained on the *MV Tampa* by Australian forces, the rescuees applied for habeas corpus relief. Initially, their petition for habeas corpus was accepted by Justice North of the Australian Federal Court in *Minister for Immigration and Multicultural Affairs & Ors v. Eric Vadarlis* (*Ruddock v. Vadarlis* [2001] FCA 1329). But on appeal a bank of three Federal Court Justices, with the Chief Justice dissenting, ultimately rejected the habeas corpus appeal. The main ground for rejecting the habeas corpus petition was the claim that the acts of the Australian government did not constitute restraint or detention. The "actions of the government had been incidental to preventing the rescued from landing on Australian territory, 'where they had no right to go.'"[31] These last words were delivered by Justice French, who now sits as the Chief Justice of the High Court of Australia, arguably the most powerful jurist in Australia today.

In analyzing the *Tampa* case, Ernst Willheim presents the case as a failure of law:

> International law relating to asylum seekers rescued at sea is sadly lacking in clarity. Maritime law did not confer on Captain Rinnan or on Norway any legal rights in relation to discharge of rescued passengers. Nor did maritime law impose on Australia or Indonesia any specific duty to receive these passengers. There is urgent need for IMO and UNHCR to work in cooperation to develop agreed principles to cover disembarkation of asylum seekers at sea.

Willheim highlights how non-refoulement also failed to offer this protection in the current way these rights are protected in international law.

In both of these Australian cases, habeas corpus was petitioned, and at least initially the Justices of the Australian Federal Court granted the writ

---

[31] See the analysis of the ruling in Erika Feller, Volker Turk, and Frances Nicholson, *Refugee Protection in International Law*, NY: Cambridge University Press, pp. 230–232.

of habeas corpus. But in the first case the granting of the writ was overridden by political considerations, and in the second case the writ was then disallowed on appeal. There have been very few other habeas corpus cases in Australia in recent years, at least none that has been at such a high-profile level. It is curious that habeas corpus has been ignored or dismissed, although the lack of success of obtaining the writ in these high-profile cases is surely one reason why habeas corpus is not seen as an important remedy today in Australia, or at least not as much as it is in the US, where all of the people on death row, along with all of the people at Guantanamo, use the petition for the writ to try to provide a remedy for their claims of being arbitrarily incarcerated.

7.6 AN OBJECTION

I wish next to consider an objection to the idea of a global *jus cogens* norm concerning habeas corpus defended in this chapter. The objection is that the standard way of thinking of *jus cogens* norms is actually highly problematic since it tends to reify what are already existing biases within international and even domestic systems of law. Hilary Charlesworth and Christine Chinkin in "The Gender of *Jus Cogens*" offer several criticisms of *jus cogens* in international law. The one most relevant for my study is:

International law is almost exclusively addressed to the public or official activity of States, which are not held responsible for the "private" activities of their nationals or those within their jurisdiction.[32]

Focusing on individual detention, as habeas corpus does, looks initially like part of this problem since it is the relationship between the jailer, as representing the State, and an individual detainee that has been the focus of the right. But if detention is given a wider purview, perhaps including those rescuees on ships that are being prevented from entering territorial waters, even though the focus is still on official action, it would include many more women than merely focusing on those who have been formally incarcerated. In addition, perhaps other procedural rights could be of similar importance to habeas corpus. Prohibitions on sex discrimination, for instance, are at least as much procedural as substantive, as much a focus on substantive liberty as on formal fairness

---

[32] Hilary Charlesworth and Christine Chinkin, "The Gender of *Jus Cogens*," *Human Rights Quarterly*, vol. 15, 1993, 63–76, reprinted in Larry May and Jeff Brown (eds.), *Philosophy of Law: Classic and Contemporary Readings*, Oxford: Wiley/Blackwell, 2010, pp. 610–619.

before the law. Focusing on procedural rights does not necessarily give priority to civil and political over social and economic rights. Indeed, procedural rights do not seem to favor the interests of men over women.

Yet it still seems to be a good idea to think about how to make sure that procedural rights are not hijacked by issues that do not affect women much. And we need to be sure that the procedural rights orientation does not diminish the importance of "private" life considerations. On one level, habeas corpus and the other Magna Carta legacy rights do not seem to be focused on private life issues at all. But there is a sense in which having these procedural rights in the background can help protect a whole range of substantive rights. In particular, in protecting procedural rights there is as a result a significant increase in visibility and account-ability. And the visibility and accountability does not merely fall on jailers.

Some government officials, especially the police, can play a large role in protecting people in private as well as public sectors. Consider family violence issues. The police often can be enlisted to help women and children at risk of violence in the home. Having procedures in place that make police practices visible will make it harder than normal for the police to shirk their duties to protect women and children in abusive private settings. And the increase in accountability that a focus on pro-cedural rights can generate will also make it easier to hold the police department's feet to the fire if that is needed to get such protection to be more effectively administered.

It is true that my focus in this study has primarily been on those who are languishing in prison or who have been rendered Stateless, rather than on those who are bereft of supportive families. Although, even here, displaced persons are often quite likely to be women, despite the fact that women are not typically found on the battlefield or in prisons in the same numbers as men. Mark Janus talks of *jus cogens* as including "pacta sunt servanda"[33] which would be another example of procedural *jus cogens* that may not fall prey to the important criticism that Charlesworth and Chinkin have mounted, since all people are equally affected if treaties are not enforced.

Throughout this section I have argued that habeas corpus should receive the same protection as other rights recognized as *jus cogens* in

[33] Mark Janis, "The Nature of *Jus Cogens*," *Connecticut Journal of International Law*, vol. 3, 1988, 359–363, reprinted in *Philosophy of Law: Classic and Contemporary Readings*, pp. 184–186.

international law. The crises that developed at Guantanamo Bay and Christmas Island could have been averted if there was such protection recognized in international law today. For this to occur, an international court or other institution must be charged with hearing habeas corpus petitions, and such an institution should be just as strongly supported as is the ICC that deals with substantive rather than procedural issues. As we move increasingly toward a system of international law that embodies an international rule of law, it is vitally important that there be an institution that gives voice to remedying the gap-filled nature of international human rights protection. In later chapters I will examine alternatives to such a world court, such as international administrative rules as well as expanded roles for international human rights commissions and councils, but I remain convinced of the importance, at least in the long run, of such an international court to protect basic procedural rights. In the next part of the book I turn to other Magna Carta legacy rights, the protection of which could partially constitute an international rule of law.

PART III

Deportation, outlawry, and trial by jury

CHAPTER 8

Collective punishment and mass confinement

This chapter will act as a bridge between discussions of habeas corpus on the one hand and the other Magna Carta legacy rights on the other hand. Due process rights are normally discussed in the context of particular prisoners who are in detention while awaiting trial or who have been sentenced. But some refugee camps should also be treated as forms of detention, even incarceration. And the detention or confinement is itself especially problematic given its link to collective punishment. In such cases those procedural rights that have been recognized as fundamental since the time of Magna Carta are in need of special protection not commonly recognized. In this chapter I want to consider the relationship between collective responsibility and collective punishment by considering mass confinements of such people as those in detention while waiting extradition and those people who are forced into refugee camps.

Collective responsibility plays a prominent role in the supposed justification of detention imposed upon groups when some of its members pose security threats and it is hard to sort out who poses serious threats versus those who merely might do so. The US used this rationale for incarcerating large numbers of people found on the "battlefield" in Afghanistan and for sending them to prison in Guantanamo. And when the civil war in the Sudan reached a certain tipping point, large numbers of people were punished by being forced into refugee camps. I examine both sorts of arguments, finding them to be seriously flawed. I will look to the debates in the Just War tradition and contemporary international law for guidance.

In the first section I consider the idea of collective responsibility and its relation to collective punishment. In the second section I look at the Just War tradition, where collective punishment was initially accepted but later rejected, especially by Grotius and his followers in international law, where most but not all forms of collective punishment are now condemned. In the third section I discuss the conflict between security issues and the protection of rights of those who are confined or incarcerated, offering a compromise proposal. In the fourth section I argue against collective punishment involving confinement in light of considerations of equity. In the fifth section I respond to several objections to my view, most significantly the challenge that if one is critical of collective punishment, one must also be critical of collective responsibility.

8.1 COLLECTIVE RESPONSIBILITY AND PUNISHMENT

Over the last sixty years, collective responsibility has gained limited, if grudging, acceptance in theoretical circles.[1] At least in part, this is because of the recognition that in some ways collective responsibility has become a fixture of our normal moral discourse to such an extent that when we speak of corporations or armies as responsible for various consequences, this is so common that we do not even think that we are employing moral terms in any way that is especially problematic. Conceptions such as those of corporate responsibility even assume that some members will be held responsible for what other members have done – perhaps the hallmark of what was considered so objectionable about collective responsibility in the past. Of course, there have always been acceptable cases of vicarious responsibility, such as parents being held responsible for the actions of their children. But only recently did theorists begin to see the large range of cases involving institutions and other large groups where collective responsibility did not look all that objectionable after all.

One of the main insights in recent years is that many of the most important social consequences are a product of the acts of multiple actors acting in concert. When we try to stick to the task of assigning responsibility only to what each person has done on his or her own, we fail to understand and account for the source of these social consequences. At the very least, we need to take account of how each person influences others, perhaps only in very subtle ways. In addition, we need to realize that social consequences often result from the combination of efforts that could not have succeeded except for the organization as well as the direction that some of the members have provided to the joint effort.[2] Once all of this is recognized, certain forms of collective

---

[1] See Larry May and Stacey Hoffman (eds.), *Collective Responsibility: Five Decades of Debate in Theoretical and Applied Ethics*, Savage, MD: Rowman & Littlefield, 1991.
[2] See the excellent treatment of this subject in Mark Osiel, *Making Sense of Mass Atrocity*, NY: Cambridge University Press, 2009.

responsibility can be seen as plausible in ways that make the vast majority of the historical literature's harsh condemnation of collective responsibility nearly incomprehensible. And so the following question arises: if collective responsibility has been accepted, why is collective punishment still roundly condemned?

There are several forms of what might be called collective punishment, where individuals are punished for what others did:

1. punishing all the members of a group for what has involved every member of the group;
2. punishing all the members of a group for what only some members of the group have done, where it is difficult to figure out who did what;
3. punishing all of the members of a group for what only some members of the group have done, even though it is known which members did what;
4. punishing one member, or some members, of a group for what some other members of the group have done;
5. punishing the institution or organization that contains the group without punishing any individual member.

Only some of these forms of collective punishment involve punishing some for what others have done.

In the first category, when all of the members of a group have together engaged in a wrongful act, punishing all of the members of a group seems the most plausible of all of the forms of collective punishment. What is unclear is whether this is best understood as full-blown collective punishment. It is possible still to assign punishment based on what each has contributed even as all members are punished. But if all are assigned exactly the same punishment or penalty, even as it is known that their contributions were different, this is more problematic, although if there is an agreement to do the collective act on the part of all, it may not be implausible to punish all in the same way.

In the second category, punishing all for what some have done but where it is unknown who did what, there is a kind of practical plausibility here, but not one upon which to generalize. The plausibility here is merely due to the contingent fact that it is unknown who did what and that some should be punished for deterrent or retributive reasons. If and when it could be known what each contributed, it would be fairer to punish only those members of a group who contributed to a harm, and to do so based on their contributions. So, it is only fair to punish all members due to the contingent fact of lack of knowledge about who did what. And the contingent plausibility of this form of collective punishment will not affect other forms.

In the third category, a classic case of collective punishment, I will argue in subsequent sections that fairness is so offended by such punishment as to make it prima facie unjustifiable in all circumstances, and where the prima facie unjustifiability is only overridden perhaps where the group was so cohesive that what one member did was agreed to by all of the other members. Even though prima facie unjustifiable, there may be some circumstances where other values are at stake that outweigh the prima facie unjustifiability of engaging in this form of collective punishment. Although we must be very careful here since it is so easy to abuse this category. In Chapter 12 I will take up the problem of security as it butts up against fairness and rights issues in such cases.

In the fourth category, punishing some for what was known to be done by others, I can see no plausibility for this form of punishment, unless there are special ties between the members where one member has taken on responsibility for what the other members of a group are doing, such as in parent/child or employer/employee relations. But if the only ties are those that form the group into a group in the first place, fairness seems to dictate that we should punish based on contribution. However, perhaps punishment can exceed exact contribution in those cases where all conspired to act together, even though only some members actually acted.

Finally, I suppose there might be forms of collective punishment, at least in theory, which involve punishing a group without punishing any of the members. The case that is often cited is that of punishing a State or corporation, perhaps by very heavy fines. While possible, it is nearly always likely that what appear to be non-distributive forms of punishment will turn out to be distributive forms, since the members will suffer whenever their group is made to suffer, thereby raising fairness issues again, since only some members contributed to the wrong.

In thinking about the justifiability of collective punishment, one also needs to think about the wide range of sanctions that can be meted out under the label of collective punishment, including:

1. putting individuals in jail or prison after judicial proceedings;
2. putting individuals in jail or prison without judicial proceedings;
3. confining individuals in prisons for the protection of society;
4. confining individuals in refugee camps for entering a State illegally;
5. issuing monetary fines to individuals;
6. barring individuals from the exercise of some of their minor freedoms.

Historically, and in contemporary discussion, when significant abridgments of liberty (1–4) are the type of sanction employed, it is harder to justify the collective punishment than if monetary fines or types of minor infringement of liberty (5–6) are the sanctions.

While some of the types of collective sanction seem reasonable, the same difficulties faced by justifying collective responsibility afflict collective punishment. If it is minor infringement on liberty that follows from the attribution of collective responsibility, then perhaps the idea of collective sanctioning can still seem acceptable. But when we turn to meting out criminal punishment to some for what others have done, the old worries seem to return in intensified form. There is an increased concern, for instance, for the fairness of putting some people in jail for what other people have done. Criminal punishment is almost always the kind of test case that causes one to pause in sanctioning some for what others have done. The one exception seems to be those individuals who were the ringmasters of great atrocities like genocide, where there is nearly universal condemnation for how they influenced others and where it seems acceptable to employ criminal punishment even though what the leaders are punished for is what those they should have restrained did.

Collective punishment is not necessarily exhausted by the idea that some can be punished for what others have done. There is an even more difficult type of collective punishment that follows on the heels of a type of collective responsibility that is itself not nearly so reviled. The general idea is that if it is true that a group of people is causally responsible for a wrongful consequence, then the entire group should be held responsible. To many people this makes more sense than trying to figure out who played what role, since it was the combination of acts not the singular roles that caused the harm. In addition, as we will see, it seems to matter if all somehow agreed with the harm that was being done by their group. Indeed, the recent debate about Israel's attack on Gaza raises this issue since arguably the people of Gaza voted Hamas into power knowing that Hamas would act violently toward Israel. Recently, in both philosophical and legal debates, the idea of collective punishment as a way to deal with groups whose members entered voluntarily knowing what the group was likely to do was defended and even applauded.

Another wrinkle to the debates about collective punishment concerns cases where it is clear that a single person was causally responsible for a given harm, but where it is thought that deterrence, or some other social goal like retaliation, demands punishing the entire group that that person belongs to, rather than merely the one who is causally responsible. Views have changed over the centuries. There is quite a bit of support for this idea in centuries gone by, then we have a strong reaction against such practices in the late nineteenth and early twentieth centuries, followed by a recent return to acceptability of this type of collective punishment in very recent years. In what follows I will be largely interested in this last case of collective punishment, although I will occasionally also discuss other cases.

My thesis is that the recent turn toward collective punishment as a means of deterrence or retaliation is unsupportable, although there are cases where it looks more plausible than in other cases, especially where the cases are mixed with other considerations such as the inability to tell who really was causally responsible, or at least who was the most causally responsible for a harm, or where people agreed to a given wrong even if they did not contribute to it. In the next section I will look for guidance in addressing our issues from those who have historically considered them over the years and those who struggle with them practically as a matter of international law.

8.2 THE JUST WAR TRADITION AND INTERNATIONAL LAW

For those of us who have defended collective responsibility, one of the most difficult cases concerns collective punishment as a justification for war or the tactics of war.[3] Most contemporary theorists to consider this issue are opposed to any form of collective punishment as a just cause for war.[4] But in the Just War tradition, if a State committed a wrong, the State as a collectivity was thought to deserve to experience retaliatory punishment, and hence there is a sense that this would be a justified form of collective punishment. War can be justified as a means of punishment since just cause focuses on wrongs, and punishment is about the proper response to wrongs committed, whether by individuals or by States. Indeed, if there is no likelihood that a State that commits a wrong will get the punishment it deserves by any other means, war has seemed to be justified as a means to mete out such just deserts to an aggressive State and its people.

Writing in the early sixteenth century, Francisco Vitoria expresses this doctrine well when he quotes Aquinas as having said: "for a just war 'there

---

[3] See my books *The Morality of Groups*, University of Notre Dame Press, 1987; and *Sharing Responsibility*, University of Chicago Press, 1992.
[4] See Kenneth W. Kemp, "Punishment as Just Cause for War," *Public Affairs Quarterly*, vol. 10, no. 4, October 1996, 335–353.

must be a just cause, namely, they who are attacked for some fault must deserve the attack.'" Vitoria then quotes Augustine as having said "It is involved in the definition of a just war that some wrong is being avenged, as where a people or state is to be punished for neglect to exact amends from its citizens for their wrongdoing or to restore what has been wrongfully taken." Here it is clear that Vitoria is advocating war as a means collectively to punish a people or State. Vitoria summarizes the 300-year tradition since Aquinas as follows:

Where, then, no wrong has previously been committed ... there is no cause for just war. This is the received opinion of all the doctors, not only of the theologians, but also of the jurists ... and I know of no doctor whose opinion is to the contrary.[5]

Up to Vitoria's time, in the early part of the sixteenth century, war was largely thought to be justified as retribution or retaliation for wrongs done.

But in the seventeeth century things changed. Hugo Grotius, for instance, says that "guilt attaches to the individuals who have agreed to the crime, not to those who have been overmastered by the votes of others."[6] In discussing the sharing of punishment, Grotius says that individuals who have not consented to the "wrong done by the community" cannot be punished.[7] On the Grotian account, for war to be just, it must be for the common good, not merely to avenge a wrong done to a specific State or individual.[8] While Grotius is seemingly not sure how best to characterize the issue, he is sure that war is just when it is waged to deter or repair wrongdoing. But retaliation which achieves neither of these goals is much more problematic.[9]

If a war is fought to punish a State for wrongdoing, there is quite a bit of support for the justifiability of this war in the Just War tradition, especially if aimed at deterrence. But if war is fought to punish a people that constitute part of the population of a State, problems are soon recognized, even though it is very unclear how a war could be waged to punish a State without also to a certain extent punishing various parts of the population of that State. And here is the crux of the problem concerning collective

---

[5] Francisco Vitoria, *De Indis et de Ivre Belli Relectiones* (*Reflections on the Indians and on the Laws of War*) (1557), John Pawley Bate (trans.) and Ernest Nys (ed.), Washington, DC: Carnegie Institution, 1917, Section II, para. 11, pp. 143–144.

[6] Hugo Grotius, *De Jure Belli Ac Pacis* (On the Law of War and Peace) (1625), Francis W. Kelsey (trans.), Oxford: Clarendon Press, 1925, p. 535.

[7] Ibid., p. 544.   [8] Ibid., pp. 482, 502–503, and elsewhere.   [9] See ibid., p. 462.

punishment. Collective punishment can be understood on the model of collective responsibility as involving either distributed or non-distributed liability. If one thinks of punishing the State for its wrongdoing, one tends to think of non-distributive responsibility, and this may indeed be accomplished in some cases if there are assets of the State that when lost do not harm the populace of the State.

Yet in most cases of collective punishment of a State, what in fact happens is that punishing the State is a form of distributive collective liability in that the populace will bear the weight of the punishment, not truly the State itself. And then we run afoul of the Grotian dictum that punishment needs to be assigned only to those individuals who have done wrong, or at least agreed to its having been done.

Let us now turn to considerations of international law for more guidance on our topic. In the various formulations of the laws of war, it appears that prior to the first Hague Peace Conference of 1899, collective punishment as a rationale for waging war and for various tactics during war was considered legal. Even the famous rules set out to govern the conduct of Union soldiers during the US Civil War seem to allow collective punishment on the battlefield. The Lieber Code stipulated that: "The citizen or native of a hostile country is thus an enemy, as one of the constituents of the hostile state or nation, and as such is subjected to the hardships of war."[10] And while other provisions of the Lieber Code placed restrictions on acts of retaliation and revenge, the general idea that the members of a population could be subject to the hardships of war merely because they were part of a State that had done wrong was not disputed.

At the end of the nineteenth century, though, the consensus in international law seemed to have shifted quite dramatically. Article 50 of the Hague Regulations, adopted at the Hague Peace Conference of 1899, provides that: "No general penalty, pecuniary or otherwise, can be inflicted upon a population on account of the acts of individuals for which they can not be regarded as jointly and severally responsible."[11]

Yet, despite the fact that many significant statements of a similar sort were incorporated into sources of international law, collective punishment continued as a practice through both World Wars, especially on the part

---

[10] Lieber Code, Instructions for the Government of the Armies of the United States in the Field, General Orders No. 100 (1863), Article 21.
[11] See Shane Darcy, *Collective Responsibility and Accountability under International Law*, Leiden: Transnational Publishers, 2007, p. 17.

of Germany. In 1939, during the Second World War, Von Neurath, Reich Protector for Bohemia and Moravia, declared that "the responsibility for all acts of sabotage is attributed not only to individual perpetrators but to the entire Czech population."[12] And as late as 1948, an Italian Military Tribunal declared that the expression "collectively responsible" refers to "an exceptional rule in occupied territory when the normal proceedings have not led to positive results. In substance, collective responsibility may arise where it has appeared impossible to establish who was or who were the culprits."[13]

There is also quite a difference in the recent international law debates if the subject is whether fines can be extracted as a collective punishment, as opposed to the more common forms of physical assault and abuse that is inflicted on the battlefield or the restrictions to basic liberties when prisoners are being held in captivity. The Hague Conventions seem to rule out even monetary fines, but the actual practice appears to be that monetary fines were treated quite differently than physical force as a form of collective punishment. Collective punishment during war meted out as a kind of tax is seen as not nearly as noxious as collective punishment meted out in terms of killing or jailing.[14]

There is one controversial kind of collective punishment that seems to be accepted in international law in some form, namely what is sometimes called "protective retribution." This appears to be the only form of collective punishment not tied to deterrence that is recognized in international law, but this also is somewhat misleading. While the punishment must be proportional to what was inflicted, the salient consideration is that the purpose is to coerce "the law-breaking party to cease its violative conduct."[15] So, this form of collective punishment is actually closer to deterrence than retribution, despite its name. And when retaliation seems to have limited deterrent objectives, even if there is a deterrent objective, proportionality considerations come to the fore and make it much harder for the practice to be justified in international law. Yet many of the practices that seem to be based on self-protection are only loosely so based, with retaliation instead being the main objective. Pure collective retaliation, even when somewhat "protective," is simply and properly condemned in international law.

---

[12] International Military Tribunal (Nuremberg) Judgment and Sentences 1 October 1946.
[13] *In re Kappler, Italy, Military Tribunal of Rome, 20 July 1948, Case no. 151.*
[14] See James Gardner, "Community Fines and Collective Responsibility," *American Journal of International Law*, vol. 11, no. 3, 1917, 511–537.
[15] *Oxford Manual on the Laws of War*, 1880.

Indeed, the very idea of collective punishment, either as a retributive rationale for initiating war or as a rationale for using certain tactics during war, has been roundly condemned by most international agreements since 1899. One of the strongest such statements comes from the International Law Association, which declared in 1921 that "Collective punishments shall not be imposed on account of the misconduct of individuals . . ."[16] War is simply too serious a matter to be justified by such questionable rationales as collective punishment. Contemporary international law adopts the Grotian maxim that punishment should only be inflicted for what the individual person has done or agreed to.

8.3 COLLECTIVE LIABILITY AND CONFINEMENT

Detention is much less severe than war, and so one might think that collective punishment directed at confinement or detention rather than war would be easier to justify. And this is indeed the case, but it is not as helpful in cases like Guantanamo as one might think. There are two reasons that collective detention as a form of collective punishment has been much easier to justify than full-scale wars based on the rationale of collective punishment. First of all, loss of liberty in detention is not as serious as loss of life in war. Second, security considerations are much less problematic in the justification of collective detention than war. But there are other problems with collective detention that nonetheless make it very hard to justify, as we have seen to be generally true of collective punishment.

The two kinds of collective detention cases I am most interested in are, first, those who are in detention centers such as Guantanamo Bay who were picked up on the battlefield, for which little evidence exists to link them individually to crimes, but who are claimed to be a threat to the US, which is holding them. And, second, I am interested in people who are Stateless and currently occupying refugee and displaced person camps, who were forced to flee from their home countries, and yet who have not been accepted into the host countries where the camps are established. Considering such cases helps us to see why it is somewhat easier to justify collective detention than collective punishment in war, but also why such cases are nonetheless very problematic.

These two groups of detention cases are similar in that the people detained are not treated in terms of what these individuals have done

---

[16] International Law Association, declaration of 1921.

or even as deserving of rights protection – indeed, the point of the punishment is to deprive these individuals of the protection of their rights. Non-collective detention may deprive people of their rights as well, but collective detention almost always does so, since when whole groups are detained there will inevitably be different degrees of culpability among the group members, where very often some members will have no culpability at all, except perhaps for the loosest of complicity. Indeed, there is good reason to believe that most of the people held at Guantanamo did not do anything to warrant their detention.[17] And those held in refugee camps generally did not individually do much wrong to warrant their detention.

Refugee detention centers are good examples of detention that is seemingly justified, if at all, by collective liability. The people who are so detained, since they have not been detained because of what they have personally done, are in a never-never land concerning the protection of their individual rights. Collective punishment schemes that diminish the importance of determining whether a given person is indeed guilty have been at the center of the problem of collective detentions. So, even though collective detention may be easier to justify than collective liability rationales for war, collective detention should also be roundly condemned.

There is a rationale for detention, even for collective detention, that is similar to that for anticipatory self-defense in cases of justified war. Here a concern for security could propel one to round up all those who are judged to be dangerous to the State and to detain them until the threat to the State has abated. Indeed, even the right of habeas corpus, sometimes seen as the most significant of all rights in the Anglo-American legal system, can be suspended when security considerations warrant it, as is also true for another Magna Carta legacy right, non-refoulement.

Habeas corpus, since before the time of Magna Carta, was identified with protecting rights of those most vulnerable. In the US Constitution only one right is listed in the main body, not in the first ten amendments, of this document. Article 5, section 2 states:

The Privilege of the Writ of Habeas Corpus shall not be suspended, unless when in Cases of Rebellion or Invasion the public Safety may require it.

---

[17] In a recent article it was claimed that more than ninety percent of the 779 men held at Guantanamo were originally captured for suspicious reasons. See Jacob Sulum, *Reason Magazine*, January 21, 2009, pp. 1–2.

This clause of the US Constitution is most commonly referred to as "the suspension clause" rather than the "habeas corpus rights clause," referring to its justifiable abridgement in emergency situations rather than to its protected status in normal times.

One of the first expressions of the idea of non-refoulement, that individuals cannot be sent to countries that are likely to torture or kill them, is in Article 33 of the 1951 Refugee Convention:

1. No Contracting State shall expel or return (*"refouler"*) a refugee in any manner whatsoever to the frontiers of territories where his life or freedom would be threatened on account of his race, religion, nationality, membership of a particular social group or political opinion.

But the Convention goes on to specify security exceptions:

2. The benefit of the present provision may not, however, be claimed by a refugee whom there are reasonable grounds for regarding as a danger to the security of the country in which he is, or who, having been convicted by a final judgment of a particularly serious crime, constitutes a danger to that community.

So, like habeas corpus, non-refoulement can be abridged when security concerns warrant it. Yet neither the US Constitution nor the Refugee Convention gives clear criteria for when such abridgement can legitimately occur. And as we will see, it is this gap that has allowed for abuse to occur that further underlies the need for truly global protection of these rights.

Government officials often use emergency situations to reframe the relationship between security and rights in their desired direction long after the crisis is over.[18] Such maneuvers are unfair in that they exploit the crisis in ways that readjust the security/rights divide initially portrayed as a one-time response to an emergency crisis in ways that the overall population would not find acceptable once the crisis was over. Indeed, as we will see in the next section, such rights violations are violations of equity.

8.4 REFUGEE DETENTION AND EQUITY

Collective confinement and detention is problematic in nearly every case because it violates the Grotian maxim that people should only be punished for what they have done or agreed to. Some forms of collective

---

[18] See Oren Gross and Fionnuala Ni Aolain, *Law in Times of Crisis: Emergency Powers in Theory and Practice*, NY: Cambridge University Press, 2006. See also Michael Gross, *Moral Dilemmas of Modern War: Torture, Assassination, and Blackmail in an Age of Asymmetric Conflict*, NY: Cambridge University Press, 2010.

punishment may be justifiable on the Grotian maxim if all of the members of the group supported each other in performing a wrongful collective action. And it may even be possible to justify collective punishment if there was a democratic process that led to a wrongful collective action. But these possible rationales will not succeed in justifying mass confinement of those who did not engage in collective action but who were treated as a group simply because of similarities of behavior, such as all being found in the same place where wrongful behavior was occurring. For here there is a lack of either action or agreement in a wrongful collective action. If these situations can be justified at all, it will be only on the grounds of security considerations.

Yet, as I will argue in detail in Chapter 12, it will be difficult to justify mass confinement on security grounds. And in any event, the possibility of abuse of the security rationale makes it especially important that strong procedural constraints be in place. I wish to stress again the special importance of Magna Carta legacy procedural rights in providing these constraints and protections from abuse by States. In my view, cases like that of the Guantanamo detainees highlight just the problem that is faced when States seemingly abuse their power to arrest en masse and detain people who do not satisfy the Grotian maxim.

One category of people most in need of protection from the abuses of collective punishment are those refugees who have been forced to flee their home States because of war or the wrongful behavior of these home States, and who have not been accepted as subjects or citizens of the State in which they find themselves. The refugee camps of the world are largely centers of "detention" if that term is used a bit more broadly than normal, where the inhabitants are also practically right-less in that no State is willing to protect them from the most severe of human rights threats, including the threat of death, rape, torture, and other serious harm.[19] While these people are recognized as Stateless, and there are international treaties that afford them rights protection, there are too many gaps here.

One of the reasons for the problem of rights enforcement in refugee camps is that some of the people in these camps are people who are considered a current threat or who have a criminal past, even though the

---

[19] Amnesty International, in a 2009 report, cited a "dramatic increase" in detention of immigrants where such detentions have increased three-fold in just over a dozen years. *Amnesty International Report on United States Immigration Detentions* (2009), reported in *International Law in Brief,* ASIL, April 17, 2009, pp. 2–3.

overwhelming majority of these people are innocent men, women, and children. But the fact that there are some miscreants in these camps has given some host States the ability to claim that it does not have to protect any of the rights of these refugees who are detained since collectively they pose a threat to the safety or security of that State. Worse yet, it has sometimes given the host State what it believes is a right to attack the people in the refugee camps on the grounds of collective punishment. So, there is a clear issue here that needs to be addressed by something like a court of equity or a similar international institution that can redress these rights abridgements.

In the discussion of the application of the Geneva Conventions, the International Committee of the Red Cross Commentary authors state that the clear intention of the Geneva Conventions drafters was that the Geneva Conventions would not have gaps such that some people would not be protected during war.[20] I will here make a similar argument for the gapless reach of international law concerning those who are forced to suffer in the aftermath of war or atrocity. It should not matter whether one is in a refugee camp or on the soil of one's home State in terms of whether human rights protection can be claimed, assuming that the basis of the claim is a good one. And in general there should not be some people whose State protects their rights and other people who are practically rendered rightless because no State will protect their rights.

Equity is the category in which gap-filling is discussed. In the current condition of world affairs, where States dominate, most human rights protection occurs at the State level. But there are various gaps in human rights protection since States mainly care about protecting the rights of their own citizens, but States rarely care about non-citizens. Equity is offended when there are gaps, especially in human rights protection. But many have thought that such gaps in human rights protection can be justified if security is threatened, especially in situations where it is unclear who is truly dangerous and who is not within a group of people who are being considered for detention.

Detention for security reasons does not only occur collectively, for there is an increasing use of protective detention for those convicted of sex offenses, and who have served their sentences, but who are thought likely to commit sex offenses again if released back into the general population. Here, as in cases of collective detention not based on the

---

[20] See *Commentary on Geneva Convention IV*, Jean S. Pictet (ed.), Geneva: International Committee for the Red Cross, 1958, p. 51.

conviction of each person for what he or she has done, there is a very serious failure in terms of equity. It is true that collective detention treats the members of a certain group equally, in that all are detained who seem to constitute a similar threat or risk. But equity is not the same as equality. The appropriate question to ask is whether the treatment is just as a matter of fairness.

The problems with the case of refugee detention arise because of the patently unfair way that the "punishments" of detention are inflicted. Once in detention or confinement, people are punished for being associated with others who are either high-risk or who have actually committed serious wrongs. Some of the people in detention may deserve severe punishment, but many of the detainees do not, and so it is patently unfair to treat them all "equally," in the sense of disregarding relevant differences. As Aristotle first recognized, equity is a correction of normally functioning justice. And equity clearly calls for the application of the Grotian maxim that people should only be punished if they have done wrong or agreed in some way to the wrong being done.

My point is that if human rights have meaning, it is that people have significant rights merely by being members of the human or world community. This is the only fully justifiable collective membership that should matter morally where basic rights are at stake. When a person is deprived of human rights protection by falling through the cracks of the regime of international rights protection, that person is practically rendered not fully human. Collective detention in most cases treats a human person not as a responsible agent but merely as a means to someone else's end. When this is done to deter the person being detained, in some cases it can be justifiable. But in most cases, where the intent is not deterrence of this individual but of others, collective detention violates the underlying principle behind human rights. And even when detention is for emergency situations, the burden must remain on the detainer to prove that the detention is necessary and is not a mere pretext for long-term retaliation for unproven offenses or security threats, in a similar way to the justifications for supposedly protective retribution as a just cause for war.

Eight hundred years have elapsed between Magna Carta and Guantanamo. But the principles enunciated in Magna Carta, especially concerning arbitrary imprisonment, outlawry, or exile, are still relevant, especially as a stop to practices of collective confinement and detention, as a form of collective punishment. And in a similar vein, war cannot be justified by reference to collective responsibility and punishment either – except in the cases of deterrent or self-defensive war. But in those cases it is misleading to talk of collective punishment, especially of "protective retribution" when what is really at stake is simple deterrence of those who have already caused harm and are likely to do so in the future. And it can be similarly problematic to talk of "protective detention" since it is often merely a euphemism for what is really collective detention in violation of deep-rooted principles of equity.

8.5 OBJECTIONS

In this last section I will consider five objections to the view I have set out in this chapter. The first objection to consider is that I have set myself up for a serious challenge by suggesting that States have duties to refugees who are no longer on their soil, thereby suggesting a set of cosmopolitan duties that could sweep so far as to swamp the resources of most States. Once refugees are indeed in refugee camps outside a State's borders, it is a mistake to think that the State continues to have significant obligations to them. And in any event it will be very difficult to make sure that some States are not unduly penalized for having lots of their citizens become refugees, especially those States that already have trouble supplying needed resources to those who remain within their borders.

My response is to acknowledge this as a serious problem to be addressed. One strategy of response is to argue that only those States that have caused their citizens to become displaced refugees by acting wrongly toward them are those that have strong duties to protect the rights of these refugees, even though they are no longer on the soil of the State in question. Merely because a State's citizens have left or even fled due to no fault of the State in question does not bring forth obligations on the State to protect these refugees. But in many refugee camps the refugees have been forced to leave their home States either by being subject to rendition or by being persecuted to the point where they see no other option but to flee. In these cases it makes sense to see the home State as having a continuing obligation, under international law, to protect the rights of these refugees.

A second objection to consider is that I have overstated what happens when rights protection is not granted to a person. Surely it is too strong to say that a person loses his or her rights, and becomes rightless, when his or her home State does not protect a person's rights. Indeed, it is hard even to make the point that one has been treated badly if having rights is conditional on them being protected. It seems conceptually and normatively better to separate completely the having of rights from the protecting of those rights. Even the claim that one has practically lost one's rights risks the misleading impression that human rights can indeed be lost when protection of rights is not efficacious.

I certainly do not want to suggest that a person literally ceases to be a human if his or her human rights are not protected. But there is nonetheless such a significant loss here that it does make sense to speak of a person being not treated as fully human in terms of the respect that should be afforded when rights are not protected. Having rights is both a normative and an empirical matter. As an empirical matter, having rights entails that one is in a position to make claims and those claims are recognized as ones that need to be responded to. It is true that rights are also normative in the sense that they are hortatory – setting out a status that should be respected and where this normative status is independent of whether one is so respected. But it is a mistake to think that having rights in general can be practically divorced from being in a position to make claims that are recognized.

A third objection is that my security rights compromise does not give States enough leeway to protect their citizens from attacks, especially in our age of asymmetrical warfare and terrorism. In asymmetrical warfare, where one side in a war is either not a State or does not recognize the normal rules of war, non-rogue States have to be able to protect themselves in ways that would otherwise be regarded as violating the rules of war. If these rules are not abridged in such conflicts, non-rogue States will be rendered hostage to the rules that only they are following and not sufficiently able to protect their populations from those rogue States that are not following the rules.

I have tried very hard to give States some leeway in the way that I view the security/rights compromise.[21] But I am not willing to grant to States more ground than I have, since I would risk undercutting the rights of those who are deemed to be security threats. It is too easy for States to claim that a person represents such a threat as a way to remove those whose only threat is to the political leadership's attempt to curtail dissent. It is important not to sacrifice the very ideals upon which support for non-rogue States has been built, by allowing States to get a pass when they violate their own highest ideals. In any event, I have not advocated an absolutist approach in these regards since I allow for some forms of

---

[21] See Charlie Savage, "Senator Proposes Deal on Handling of Detainees," *The New York Times*, March 4, 2010, p. A20.

compromise, as we will see in Chapter 12, thereby giving States the ability to protect themselves as long as doing so does not undermine the ideals the State should hold dear.

A fourth objection is that I have stretched too far the idea of confinement and detention in including cases of those in refugee camps. We should restrict the idea of detention to those who are forcibly under the guard of the State rather than those who are living in a camp that they can leave, even if it might cause hardship to do so. It is important, so the objection would run, to keep our strong condemnation of detention and confinement only for those who have been subject to imprisonment at the hands of the State, rather than to dilute the idea by including marginally similar cases of those in refugee camps. Refugee rights should be protected, but they should not be assimilated to rights of those who are citizens or residents of a State.

Detention and confinement are terms that admit of several meanings. Detention normally implies that one is being restrained, and confinement similarly has the normal implication that one is forcibly prohibited from leaving. But in both cases there are also meanings of the term that imply restrictions that are moral rather than physical, as when one is restrained by rules. In urging that we think of some refugee camps as centers of detention or confinement, I am thinking of those camps where fear or economic circumstance confines the refugees, and where these factors act to confine just as efficaciously as if there were bars and guards at the door. What becomes crucial is how these circumstances were created. If a State is responsible for creating these conditions, just as a State is responsible for creating the conditions of imprisonment, then it may be appropriate to talk of the cases in similar terms.

A final objection is to wonder how someone, such as me, who has strongly supported notions of collective responsibility can nonetheless strongly condemn collective punishment. How can one support collective responsibility without supporting what seems naturally to follow from such support, namely support for collective punishment? Is it even conceptually possible, or normatively plausible, for there to be responsibility without punishment? It is hard not to draw the inference that if I condemn collective punishment, I would have to abandon my previous support for collective responsibility.

In this chapter I have not condemned all forms of collective punishment; indeed, the issuing of fines or barring individuals in the exercise of some of their non-basic freedoms seems to me, in some cases, to be appropriately directed at members of a group, especially when it is very hard to tell who is a threat and who is not. What I have objected to is the deprivation of basic freedoms that comes from incarceration as well as other forms of detention and confinement directed at the members of a group. So, I can support collective responsibility that has as its consequence moral blame or various forms of legal sanction including penalties and non-basic liberty deprivation. And while my earlier strong support for collective responsibility will surely be somewhat weakened by these considerations about collective punishment in this chapter, I can still support collective responsibility nonetheless.

Throughout this chapter I have been motivated by the Grotian maxim that no one should be deprived of basic liberties unless that person has done something that is wrongful or creates a threat. Collective responsibility can still make sense practically even when it is associated with restricted kinds of collective penalization. As Mark Drumbl has argued, members of groups so penalized "could be permitted to avoid footing the bill, or foot less of the bill than others, by affirmatively demonstrating what they did to prevent genocide or oppose the State,"[22] for instance. But subjecting people to mass confinement based on what others have done is simply not morally acceptable, except in the most extreme emergency. The mass detention centers and refugee camps of the world are insupportable unless they conform to the Grotian maxim. Thus, what has been recognized as true about the use of war as a vehicle for collective punishment should also be true of the use of mass confinement.

---

[22] Mark Drumbl, *Atrocity, Punishment, and International Law*, NY: Cambridge University Press, 2007, p. 204.

CHAPTER 9

Non-refoulement and rendition

In this chapter I will focus on rights connected to deportation and extradition, and especially to rendition and non-refoulement, as well as certain other equity considerations that are recognized but are not currently enforced internationally in an effective way. As we gradually incorporate the Magna Carta legacy rights into international law, we will move increasingly toward an international rule of law and toward at least piecemeal cosmopolitanism.

Non-refoulement and habeas corpus are related in an interesting way only hinted at in the previous chapter. Habeas corpus, among other things, protects those who have been imprisoned or otherwise detained from being tortured or abused while in custody. Non-refoulement protects people who are residing in one country from being sent to another country where they will be tortured or abused. There are two principal ways that abuse of those who are under the control of a State takes place: either by secreting someone within the State's own prison or detention system, or by sending the person to another State's prison or detention system. Put in other terms, either a State abuses an individual in terms of basic human rights by dirtying its own hands or it passes the individual to another State known for using its own dirty hands in such abuses. Part of the challenge of this chapter is to explain why it is just as bad normatively whether one causes abuse in one or the other of these two ways.

In the first section I will discuss the problem of dirty hands and expand the discussion to cover what I call the problem of "vicarious dirty hands." In the second section I will explain what non-refoulement is and what its value is. I will also argue that non-refoulement is primarily a procedural right, just as is true of habeas corpus. In the third section I will argue that non-refoulement should be granted *jus cogens* status in international law, recognizing it as a foundational procedural right. In the fourth section I will argue for expanding the scope of non-refoulement in international law to cover cases where the harm that people would face in being deported to another State is not based on membership in a protected group. And finally I will consider some objections to granting the right of non-refoulement *jus cogens* status.

9.1 THE PROBLEM OF "VICARIOUS DIRTY HANDS"

The problem of dirty hands is that in politics it is sometimes the case that in order to accomplish a morally good objective, it is necessary to employ tactics that are morally bad. The idea behind the problem of dirty hands is that people do not like being caught in such moral quandaries; they are happier if they can achieve good without doing bad. Sometimes people try to respond to a dirty hands problem by attempting to accomplish good by having others do their morally bad, or "dirty," work for them. Refoulement and rendition are aimed at just this kind of solution to the dirty hands problem but then fall into what I call the problem of "vicarious dirty hands," the problem of knowingly enabling or allowing others to do one's dirty work so that one can remain personally with clean hands.

There is a controversy about whether there is a problem with dirty hands and what the extent of this problem is. Some theorists have argued that the good that can be done may be such that it simply overrides whatever bad is involved in the tactics one needs to use to accomplish the good results for one's political community. Michael Slote argues that in some cases the good does override the bad, but that in other cases it may not be the fault of the person nonetheless. In his view, we simply do not live in "a morally good world" and that we need to realize that while this is "sad" it is not necessarily the fault of the person who must make tragic choices.[1]

Kai Nielsen argues that there is no way to resolve these problems except to try to do what is the lesser evil. Both of the options are evil and so there is no sense that the choice is between doing good versus doing evil. But there is a sense of doing what is right that can be consistent with doing evil. Nielsen sees this as a matter of ascertaining what, all things considered, is the morally best thing to do in a given situation. If we do what is the right thing to do in a given circumstance, namely the lesser wrong or

---

[1] Michael Slote, "Dirty Hands in Ordinary Life," in *Cruelty and Deception: The Controversy Over Dirty Hands in Politics*, Paul Reynard and David P. Shugarman (eds.), Peterborough, ONT: Broadview Press, 2000, pp. 27–41. Slote's position is similar to that of Michael Walzer in his essay "Political Action: The Problem of Dirty Hands," *Philosophy & Public Affairs*, vol. 2, no. 2, 1973, 160–180.

evil, we do what we ought to do. In this sense, he argues, there really is no problem of dirty hands.[2]

But many thinkers who have considered this topic are bothered by the seeming necessity of having to do wrong in order to accomplish often very important goods. Many theorists see the situation as one of tragedy that belies a deep problem either about the nature of morality or about the relationship between the way the world is and the way morality is conceptualized. Many have tried to find ways out of the dilemma so that either morality, as an absolute or near absolute system of rules, is saved or so that individuals do not feel guilty for having been forced to make tragic choices. Indeed, the scholarly reaction mirrors the reaction outside of the academy and has fueled interest in strategies that might resolve the dilemma in some way.

To resolve the dilemma, it seems that the obvious strategy is to get someone else to do the work that is needed in order to accomplish the political community's good. And this is indeed precisely what happens in cases where one State extradites a prisoner to another State where it is predicted that the prisoner will now be tortured so as to get the information needed to secure a community good in the first State. But, as I will argue, this is only an apparent resolution of the dilemma, since all that is accomplished is that the wrong is now attributable to the first State vicariously rather than directly, and there is little moral difference between these two types of attribution of wrong.

The specific dilemma that concerns rendition and refoulement is that legitimate and morally compelling security considerations sometimes seem to require that a certain person be deported or harshly interrogated, and yet to accomplish this task the person's own safety and right not to be harmed may be put in jeopardy. Or to put it in terms where there is no good alternative: either the State must jeopardize the security rights of its own people or it must jeopardize the security rights of the detainee or prisoner. By deporting the detainee or prisoner to a target State, the end can be accomplished without the State leaders of the home State getting their hands dirty. This solution is clever, but still involves a variation of the problem of dirty hands, the problem of "vicarious dirty hands."

"Vicarious dirty hands" problems are a subspecies of the problem we have been examining. I will explain why vicarious dirty hands problems

---

[2] Kai Nielsen, "There is No Dilemma of Dirty Hands," in Reynard and Shugarman, ibid., pp. 139–155.

are especially troubling morally. The main issue here is that one person or entity enlists another person or entity and encourages that person to do what the first person knows or believes to be wrong and, in addition, in doing so, the second person does do what is morally wrong. Encouraging others to do what is wrong is itself a species of wrongdoing, so at least initially what seems clear is that the strategy of employing rendition or refoulement does not evade the problem of doing wrong to accomplish good. And there is another problem that is also generated, making vicarious dirty hands problems even more problematic than one might think.

Crucially, the first person feels entitled not to feel guilt for what the second person has done, even though the second person has done so with the encouragement of the first person. In this sense, the first person does not feel the moral emotions that would in the future operate to inhibit such actions, even if the first person continues to believe that in the current case what he or she did was in some sense justified. In dilemmatic situations what is crucial is that one not deny the moral emotions that tug against both of the alternatives one is faced with. Even as a person must choose one of these alternatives, it is important that there be a moral remainder, such as felt guilt, to remind the person that something important has been lost or sacrificed by making the choice. Such a moral remainder, then, in a sense, operates to remind the person that something was sacrificed that should not be sacrificed in the future if it can be avoided. The problem with vicarious dirty hands is that the person is encouraged not to accept the moral remainder.[3]

In effect, the problem of vicarious dirty hands is that a person is encouraged to have what the existentialists call bad faith, that is, to train oneself systematically to deny what is truly morally important. And because of this, the vicarious dirty hands problem is worse than the original dirty hands problem. Insofar as refoulement and rendition can be characterized as having the problem of vicarious dirty hands, they are also even worse than if the prisoner or detainee had been mistreated directly. I next turn to a description of non-refoulement and its status in international law before returning to moral issues, especially an argument for thinking that non-refoulement should be afforded fundamental or *jus cogens* status in a system of international law.

---

[3] See my discussion of some of these issues in my essay "Metaphysical Guilt and Moral Taint," in my book *Sharing Responsibility*, University of Chicago Press, 1992.

9.2 WHAT IS NON-REFOULEMENT?

One of the first expressions of the idea of non-refoulement is in Article 33 of the 1951 Refugee Convention:

1. No Contracting State shall expel or return ("*refouler*") a refugee in any manner whatsoever to the frontiers of territories where his life or freedom would be threatened on account of his race, religion, nationality, membership of a particular social group or political opinion.

2. The benefit of the present provision may not, however, be claimed by a refugee whom there are reasonable grounds for regarding as a danger to the security of the country in which he is, or who, having been convicted by a final judgment of a particularly serious crime, constitutes a danger to that community.

There are many limitations of this construal of the non-refoulement right, not the least of which is that it is restricted to refugees. Refugees are defined narrowly in international law only to include those who:

have a well-founded fear of being persecuted for reasons of race, religion, nationality, membership of a particular social group or political opinion, is outside the country of his nationality and is unable or, owing to such fear, is unwilling to avail himself of the protection of that country, or who not having a nationality and being outside the country of his former habitual residence as a result of such events, is unable, or owing to such fear, unwilling to return to it.[4]

Thus, the definition of non-refoulement, which relies on the concept of refugee, is limited to only threats based on several group characteristics. In addition, the grounds for disallowing the benefit are quite broad and it is highly likely that refugees and non-refugees alike who are being detained will be subject to abuse in the name of expanded national security interests. As Hathaway notes, "the intention to establish a broadly applicable duty of non-refoulement was qualified during the final phase of the drafting process in order to accommodate critical public order and national security concerns which may arise during a 'mass influx.'" It became clear that non-refoulement was not recognized as absolute or *jus cogens* by the drafters of the Refugee Convention.[5] And yet it is in just

---

[4] Convention Relating to the Status of Refugees (1951), Article I.A(2).
[5] James C. Hathaway, *The Rights of Refugees under International Law*, Cambridge University Press, 2005, pp. 355–356.

such cases of mass influx of refugees when non-refoulement is most in need of protection.

The 1984 Torture Convention has a simpler and more far-reaching statement on non-refoulement:

1. No State Party shall expel, return ("*refouler*") or extradite a person to another State where there are substantial grounds for believing that he would be in danger of being subject to torture.
2. For the purpose of determining whether there are such grounds, the competent authorities shall take into account all relevant considerations including, where applicable, the existence in the State concerned of a consistent pattern of gross, flagrant or mass violations of human rights.

Here, though, the prohibition on refoulement is restricted to the case where the person might be subject to torture. But a general account of non-refoulement would not be so restricted.

Lauterpacht and Bethlehem argue that in international *treaty* law there is not "a sufficiently clear consensus opposed to exceptions to non-refoulement to warrant reading the 1951 Convention without them."[6] But they then go on to argue that there is sufficient basis in international *customary* law to understand the principle of non-refoulement as allowing of no limitation or exception.[7] In addition, other commentators have pointed out that "procedural protections in expulsion proceedings" extend "only to non-citizens 'lawfully within the territory' of a State party" according to the International Covenant on Civil and Political Rights.[8]

My sense is that a normatively defensible general non-refoulement provision would combine the best aspects of each of these treaties, and the customary consensus, as follows:

1. No State shall expel, return ("*refouler*") or extradite a person to another State where there are substantial grounds for believing that his or her life or freedom would be significantly jeopardized.
2. For the purposes of determining whether such grounds exist, it will be relevant whether the potential harm to be suffered is the result of a lawfully executed final judgment of an authoritative tribunal, or

---

[6] Elihu Lauterpacht and Daniel Bethlehem, "The Scope and Content of the Principle of Non-refoulement: Opinion," in *Refugee Protection in International Law*, Erika Feller, Volker Turk, and Frances Nicholson (eds.), NY: Cambridge University Press, 2003, pp. 87–181, especially p. 132.
[7] Ibid., p. 163.
[8] See David Weissbrodt, *The Human Rights of Non-Citizens*, Oxford University Press, 2008, p. 61.

whether there are good grounds for thinking that the person is a threat to the State in which he or she currently is.

If we were to adopt this proposal, then there would be a sufficiently broad understanding of non-refoulement to allow such a right to be very important in the overall protection of human rights globally, and specifically global procedural justice.

Non-refoulement is a basic procedural right that clearly protects substantive rights to life and liberty. Like habeas corpus, non-refoulement is also a procedural right that partially constitutes a rule of law. Governments should not be able to throw people in jail and should be accountable for the treatment of the detainees under their care, but similar considerations should apply if detainees are transferred to the care of another government. Unless the right is one that extends to how other States act toward the detainee, it will be too easy for States simply to transfer detainees to States where it is known that harm is likely to be done to the detainee. And this will allow States to get the same results as if the transferring State had harmed the detainee itself, but without getting its hands dirty. What is needed is a clear procedural provision that calls for any transfer to be scrutinized to determine if the transfer is likely to lead to such harm. In this way, light will be cast on the transferring State's actions, not allowing the transferring State to escape the charge of dirty hands.

It might be objected that non-refoulement is not truly a procedural right, or what might be called a right to a procedure, but rather a right to an outcome, making it much more like a substantive right than a procedural right. Non-refoulement does not actually guarantee that anyone will be sent to a particular State, but only that there is a procedure that disallows sending the detainee to a State that is likely to harm him or her. In this way, non-refoulement both aims at a certain result and also at a certain process, that detainees be treated fairly and not subjected to the kind of arbitrary treatment that is often the epitome of abuse of Executive prerogative – namely, sending people out of one State to States where they will be treated in ways that they are forbidden to be treated at home. As I indicated in earlier chapters, when a right aims at fairness and non-arbitrariness, it should be conceived as procedural, at least in part.

In Chapter 3 I addressed the distinction between procedural and substantive rights, arguing that the best strategy was to see procedural rights as especially weighty rules that primarily aim at fairness and especially at formal fairness. There are two aspects to the right of non-refoulement. The first is that it protects the substantive right that people should not have life or liberty jeopardized by being deported. The second is that fundamental fairness should be extended to those who are detainees or prisoners within a given State. Here, as in the case of habeas corpus, the fairness concerns a particular procedure that is to be followed in deportations.

In many ways non-refoulement is even more of a mixed right than is habeas corpus. While there is a specific procedure indicated in this right, there is also explicit mention of particular human goods that are to be served by these procedures. So, in determining whether non-refoulement is to be thought of as primarily a procedural right, two questions must be answered: first, which of the two aspects of this right dominates over the other? And, second, we need to ask does non-refoulement's procedural aspect convey the most significant part of its value?

Initially, non-refoulement is a harder case in this respect than is habeas corpus. Habeas corpus also has multiple aspects, but they all seem to be directed at fairness, whether fairness is broadly or narrowly construed. There are substantive rights that are related to habeas corpus, but only as a contingent matter. Whereas in the case of non-refoulement there are substantive rights that are mentioned in the description of the right and that play a constitutive, not merely contingent, role in the right itself.

Yet I believe that non-refoulement should be seen as primarily a procedural right and only secondarily as a substantive right. Primarily, non-refoulement sets a minimal limit on deportation and extradition proceedings, and hence becomes part of these procedures. When a right sets a limit on procedures, there is good reason to see that right as at least in part procedural as well. The secondary component of non-refoulement is nearly as important to this mixed right, but on balance I think that the right should be seen as primarily procedural, especially when understood in connection to habeas corpus and the other Magna Carta legacy rights, insofar as these rights taken together form a core of procedural protections against arbitrariness and abuse.

Let me just say a few words about the idea of rendition, which is closely allied with non-refoulement. As part of the larger reaction to September 11, the US sent some detainees to Guantanamo, and other detainees were transferred to States where it is commonly believed that torture and other abusive treatment is widely practiced. This practice was known as extraordinary rendition. Rendition involves the transfer of a person from one State to another. Extraordinary rendition involves the extra-judicial transfer of a person from one State's jurisdiction to another. In this sense, non-refoulement is a species of rendition. Non-refoulement may involve transfers that are either by judicial or extra-judicial means. The distinctive feature of non-refoulement as a species of rendition is that the transfer puts the transferred person's life or liberty in jeopardy.

It has seemed obvious to many people that the recent US policy of extraordinary rendition is grossly unfair. It was clear that basic rights had been violated and that most people would have condemned this action. It seems that the US government was aware that this would be the reaction, given that the US government would not publicly admit what it was doing and that it tried to hide the practice from public view. As we have seen, the principle of visibleness is often violated in such circumstances when governments try to avoid the appearance of arbitrariness and unfairness so as to avoid controversy on the part of the populace.

Non-refoulement is a principle that articulates a basic procedural right that is closely connected with habeas corpus and the other Magna Carta legacy rights in constituting a minimal international rule of law. When these Magna Carta legacy rights are fully protected, there will not be holes or gaps in the protection of substantive human rights and there will not be gaps in the system of rights that people can count on to stand in the way of arbitrariness and unfairness on the part of State officials and other State representatives.

9.3 NON-REFOULEMENT AS A 'JUS COGENS' NORM

In general there is probably not sufficient agreement and State practice at the moment to think that such an understanding of non-refoulement has achieved international customary law status. Indeed, the multi-lateral treaties that concern non-refoulement discuss a quite restricted version of this right. It is my view, though, that a good case can be made for expanding the right and for considering it to be a fundamental procedural right in international law. In this section of the chapter I will argue that there are reasons for thinking that such a right should be seen as *jus cogens*, for similar reasons to those that I discussed in Chapter 7 where I argued that habeas corpus should be seen as *jus cogens*.

I have previously argued that *jus cogens* norms are the foundational norms of the international legal system. They are norms that are essentially moral and come to have legal status because they are compelling, so that no derogation from them is possible in order still to have a system of international legal norms that is worthy of support. I will here try to make the case for thinking that non-refoulement is a crucial procedural right that should have significant international protection. Along the way I will also explain why I think of non-refoulement as on the same level as the right of habeas corpus, just as seems to have been true at the time of Magna Carta.

Magna Carta says that no freeman shall be "exiled or in any way destroyed ... except by the lawful judgment of his peers." Exile is different from non-refoulement in that it means that one is simply sent out of one's country, whereas non-refoulement means that one not be sent to a country where one is likely to be harmed. But it appears that there might have been a linkage between exile and being destroyed in that the words "or in any way destroyed" after "exiled" seem to indicate that the kind of exile contemplated was that which put one's life in jeopardy. Whether there is good historical evidence for this or not, I will proceed in what I regard as the spirit of Magna Carta and speak of non-refoulement as the right today that best captures what underlies one of the rights that Magna Carta enshrines.

Non-refoulement, even less than habeas corpus, rarely turns up on the lists of *jus cogens* norms. Lauterpacht and Bethlehem point out that the non-derogable character of non-refoulement has been recognized by two sources, but conclude that the most one can say is that non-refoulement is "acquiring the character" of a peremptory norm.[9] Indeed, there is some support for seeing non-refoulement as a fundamental customary procedural right. The European Court of Human Rights has interpreted Article 3 of the European Convention on Human Rights as prohibiting non-refoulement. Article 3 states: "No one shall be subject to torture or to inhuman or degrading treatment or punishment."

In the European Court's 1989 *Soering* judgment, non-refoulement was said to be a fundamental component of the prohibitions of Article 3. In fact, the Court held that the European Convention intends to bar not only actual but potential breaches:

It is not normal for the Convention institutions to pronounce on the existence or otherwise of potential violations of the Convention. However, where an applicant claims that a decision to extradite him, if implemented, be contrary to Article 3 by reason of its foreseeable consequences in the requesting country, a departure from this principle is necessary, in view of the serious and irreparable

---

[9] Lauterpacht and Bethlehem, "Scope and Content," p. 107.

nature of the suffering risked, in order to ensure the efffectiveness of the safeguard provided in that Article.[10]

In the ICTY's *Furundzija* judgment, the European Court's *Soering* ruling was said to be "authoritative" across all of international law.[11]

And then in the 1997 *Chahal* decision, the position of the European Court of Human Rights was made crystal clear in paragraph 79 of its decision:[12]

> Article 3 enshrines one of the most fundamental values of democratic society. The court is well aware of the immense difficulties faced by States in modern times in protecting their communities from terrorist violence. However, even in these circumstances, the Convention prohibits in absolute terms torture or inhuman or degrading treatment or punishment, irrespective of the victim's conduct. Unlike most of the substantive clauses of the Convention and of Protocols Nos. 1 and 4, Article 3 makes no provision for exceptions and no derogation from it is permissible . . .

The use of the terminology of "no derogation" signals that the European Court sees the prohibition on torture as having the main component normally associated with *jus cogens* norms, being non-derogable.

In paragraph 80 of the *Chahal* opinion, an explicit connection is made between the prohibition on torture and that of refoulement:

> The prohibition provided in Article 3 against ill-treatment is equally absolute in expulsion cases. Thus, whenever substantial grounds have been shown for believing that an individual would face the real risk of being subjected to treatment contrary to Article 3 if removed to another state, the responsibility of the Contracting State to safeguard him or her against such treatment is engaged in the event of expulsion. In these circumstances, the activities of the individual in question, however undesirable or dangerous, cannot be a material consideration.

As Lauterpacht and Bethlehem point out, the "conclusions of the European Court on this matter are echoed by the UN Human Rights Committee in its General Comment No. 20 (1992) on the interpretation and application of Article 7 of the ICCPR."[13] The same fundamental status afforded to the prohibition on torture is also afforded to non-refoulement. Recently, the European Court of Human Rights, in *Saadi v. Italy*, February 28, 2008,

---

[10] *Soering v. United Kingdom*, 11 European Court of Human Rights (ser. A) (1989), para. 90.

[11] *Prosecutor v. Anto Furundzjia*, International Tribunal for Yugoslavia, Trial Chamber Judgment, Case No. IT-95–17/1-T, 10 December 1998, para. 148.

[12] *Chahal v. United Kingdom*, 108 ILR 385 (1997). For an important commentary on the *Soering* and *Chahal* cases, see John Dugard and Christine Van den Wyngaert, "Reconciling Extradition with Human Rights," *The American Journal of International Law*, vol. 92, no. 2, April 1998, 187–212.

[13] Lauterpacht and Bethlehem, "Scope and Content," p. 157.

reaffirmed the *Chahal* decision and did not "permit states to balance the security threat the person poses against the likelihood he will be mistreated if transferred."[14]

Jus cogens norms generally trace their lineage back to the Vienna Convention on Treaties. Article 54 of the Vienna Convention states:

A treaty is void if, at the time of its conclusion, it conflicts with a peremptory norm of general international law. For the purpose of the present Convention, a peremptory norm of general international law is a norm accepted and recognized by the international community of states as a whole as a norm from which no derogation is permitted and which can only be modified by a subsequent norm of general international law having the same character.[15]

Notice the distinctive use of the language of "no derogation" and then remember the use of the same terminology in the European Court's decision about non-refoulement. On this basis, at least in the European context, there are certain legal grounds for thinking that non-refoulement has *jus cogens* status.

And the ICTY has also made it clear, in a controversial opinion, that non-refoulement, or at least that part concerning torture, is also a *jus cogens* norm across international law:

the prohibition on torture is a peremptory norm or *jus cogens*. This prohibition is so extensive that States are even barred from expelling, returning, or extraditing a person to another State where there are substantial grounds for believing that the person would be in danger of being subjected to torture.[16]

And the ICTY underlined this fact when it said that the international community has decided to outlaw torture across the board. The ICTY held: "No legal loopholes have been left."[17] While controversial, I strongly support the move to characterize all forms of non-refoulement as *jus cogens*.

I will next offer normative reasons in support of the *jus cogens* status of non-refoulement. The main normative arguments are two: first, that non-refoulement is absolutely necessary for the protection of substantive rights that themselves have *jus cogens* status, such as the prohibition on torture, and, second, that non-refoulement is one of the procedural cornerstones

---

[14] Ashley Deeks, "*Saadi v. Italy*: ILM Introductory Note," 47 ILM 542 (2008), reprinted in *Newsletter of the American Society of International Law*, July/September 2008, p. 8.

[15] Vienna Convention on the Law of Treaties, Article 54.

[16] *Prosecutor v. Anto Furundzjia*, International Tribunal for Yugoslavia, Trial Chamber Judgment, Case No. IT-95–17/1-T, 10 December 1998, para. 144.

[17] Ibid., para. 146.

of the prohibition on arbitrariness, a prohibition that is crucial for the maintenance of the rule of law. And while this latter consideration is not normally given *jus cogens* status, it is fairly easy to see why it should be given that status, as I will show.

In order to prevent a State from torturing or otherwise employing inhumane treatment against one of its citizens or subjects, it is crucial that the State not be allowed to "contract out" the torture or inhumane treatment to another State that is either less democratic or at least less inhibited to employ torture or inhumane treatment. Normatively, insofar as preventing torture and other forms of inhumane treatment is a rock-solid *jus cogens* substantive norm, then so should be any procedural right that is necessary for the protection of the *jus cogens* substantive right. What is necessary for the protection of a fundamental right must also be seen as fundamental, at least in some sense of that term, and hence *jus cogens* as well.

To see why procedural rights in particular should be seen as *jus cogens*, one needs to remember my earlier discussion of Fuller's conception of procedural natural law in Chapter 4. Some norms are essential for there to be laws, or systems of laws, at all. In the domestic context it is not controversial that laws must be clear and publicly accessible to be laws. It is not always recognized that the same characteristics must be manifest at the international level. In addition, there are some procedures that are uniquely important for a system of international law that is largely treaty-based. As several commentators have pointed out, most notably Mark Janis, the least controversial of all procedural rights that have *jus cogens* status in international law is the principle of *pacta sunt servanda*.[18] For treaties to be the cornerstone of international legal obligation, there must be a prior principle recognized as valid independently of treaty obligations, namely the principle that treaties must be kept.

Some procedural norms are pure and some are of mixed origin. *Pacta sunt servanda* is a pure procedural *jus cogens* norm. As I have indicated, habeas corpus and non-refoulement are mixed principles, incorporating procedural and substantive provisions. These provisions protect the integrity of any system of norms that lays claim to be a system of law. As I have indicated, one of the main ways that this is accomplished is in exposing

---

[18] Mark Janis, "The Nature of *Jus Cogens*," *Connecticut Journal of International Law*, vol. 3, 1988, pp. 359–363, reprinted in Larry May and Jeff Brown (eds.), *Philosophy of Law: Classic and Contemporary Readings*, Oxford: Wiley/Blackwell, 2010, pp. 184–186.

attempts by a State to "contract out" torture or other forms of inhumane treatment so that unfairness is accomplished, just not by the State's own dirty hands.

There is a possible misuse of the principle of non-refoulement that calls for a short comment before concluding our discussion of this right in international law. Some States have used non-refoulement as a reason for why those who are being detained after having been denied immigration status still languish in prisons. The detainees are kept in detention indefinitely supposedly because there is no State to which the detainees can be sent without violating non-refoulement. Yet surely non-refoulement is meant to protect people from human rights abuse, not to act as a rationalization for States arbitrarily to incarcerate, and abuse the rights of, individuals.

There is an unfortunate tendency of some States to manipulate or abuse human rights principles for their own benefit. This has become more common with the rise of terrorism and the response to this threat on the part of many States. So, it is true that States have used the Convention on Trafficking as a vehicle to stop illegal immigrants from entering their countries, even though the point of the Convention was to protect women and children from being trafficked into sexual slavery and other forms of abuse. As it has gotten harder to gain illegal entry into States, due to counter-terrorism measures, more and more use is made of traffickers with sinister reputations of abuse as a desperate act for those forced to gain illegal entry. The attempt to stop such persons from operating is not necessarily an ignoble goal, although it can be if States have no good reasons to prevent certain people from crossing their borders. But it is nonetheless an abuse to take a human rights principle, articulated in a multi-lateral treaty, and put it to a use that it was never intended to have and that is not in keeping even with the spirit of the treaty.

It is because of the possibility that States will abuse the principle of non-refoulement that I propose that non-refoulement be protected as an international right, where some type of international court or other institution would oversee the correct application of the principle, as well as stamp out abuse of the principle. For all of the reasons advanced in this section, giving non-refoulement *jus cogens* status is normatively desirable and legally plausible. Of course, *jus cogens* status remains highly controversial in international law. But what should not be controversial is that non-refoulement is, and should be, a fundamental principle of a system of international law.

9.4 EXPANDING THE SCOPE OF NON-REFOULEMENT

I wish next to consider whether it might make sense to think of non-refoulement in an expanded way from the way it is often characterized. I will here be especially concerned about expanding non-refoulement to include cases of economic deprivation and displacement. When people are forced to be exiled in other States, where they will be forced to live in horrible refugee camps, there is a sense that non-refoulement has also been violated by their home States. And while it is often true that other rights have been violated, such as occur when creating the conditions that forced them to leave their home States in the first place, there is also a sense that non-refoulement, or some similar anti-rendition principle, has been violated as well, as I will argue in this section.

Consider the example of sending people who have a disease to a State where it is known that there is not sufficient treatment for those with that disease. Recently in the UK, a Labour MP, Neil Gerrard, criticized his own party's government for "permitting the deportation of people diagnosed in the UK with HIV to countries where they may not get the drugs they need to stay alive."[19] Such State action is relevant to the debate about whether *jus cogens* is a sexist concept in international law, especially whether the application of *jus cogens* status to procedural rights would fall prey to this objection. I would argue that non-refoulement should also be given a wide enough status as *jus cogens* to cover such cases. I wish only to note how procedural rights can affect not only those who are in prison or in risk of loss of civil and political rights, but can also affect social and economic rights that have impact broadly across the globe, not merely for one gender group. This is yet another way to respond to the worries of Charlesworth and Chinkin discussed in Chapter 7. My view is that non-refoulement should be expanded to include many forms of rendition, such as the case just discussed.

Earlier I suggested that there is some reason to think that historically the right not to be arbitrarily deported was meant to cover cases of being exiled so as to be deprived of basic rights. In addition, it is now relevant to consider that Magna Carta's Chapter 29 (39) also speaks of the right not to be "desseised." This term meant the dispossession of one's property. The very next right in Magna Carta is the right not to be exiled. It is possible that there was thought to be a connection between these rights

---

[19] Sarah Boseley, "Britain is Criticized for Deporting HIV Patients," *The Guardian*, Monday, December 1, 2008, p. 1.

that might help us in our expansion of the domain of non-refoulement. For one way to dispossess a person of property is to exile that person to a place where the person's property rights would not be respected. Indeed, most forms of exile dispossess a person.

In addition, as we think of cases where people are deported to a refugee camp in another State, we should also recognize the widespread rape and child abuse in many such camps as a violation, on the part of the deporting State, of non-refoulement or other related rendition prohibitions. Yet, today, unless rape is seen as a form of torture and engaged in for political reasons, it is hard to get such a situation to fit under the existing definitions of non-refoulement. This very narrow construal of non-refoulement seems unjustified. If a person is being sent out of a country where the known result is that basic rights are violated, why should it matter whether this is done out of political motivations or not? I suppose it is slightly more worrisome if it is done for political reasons. And when we consider a broader array of reasons, some of these will not be as straightforwardly problematic as those done for political motivations. But the underlying wrongness of the rendition or refoulement does not seem to turn on the character of the motivations. I have argued in other places that we should not confuse intention with motivation.[20] Once again I would urge that motivational considerations not be given pride of place in the wrongness of acts.

The underlying moral principle of the right of non-refoulement, and the larger rubric of rendition cases that non-refoulement falls under, is that no one should be forced to go to a State where his or her basic human rights are likely to be jeopardized. The current way that the right of non-refoulement is characterized does not fit well with this underlying rationale and can only be made to fit if there is an expansion of the domain of cases that fit under non-refoulement. There is no reason in principle to restrict cases of non-refoulement to ones that involve group-based deprivation of individual rights. Such a case might be made if we are talking about criminal prosecution, as I argued in my book *Crimes Against Humanity: A Normative Account*. But when the sanctions are directed primarily at States rather than prison sentences for individuals, I see no good reason to restrict the scope of non-refoulement in this way, except the obvious practical one that concerns how the terms of the various multi-lateral treaties have actually been drafted.

---

[20] See *Genocide: A Normative Account*, NY: Cambridge University Press, 2010, Chapter 8.

I propose that if a State deports someone into a refugee camp, where basic rights to life or liberty are put in jeopardy, it is prima facie grounds for thinking that the State has violated non-refoulement or has engaged in some other form of illegal rendition. And I further propose that in other cases the right of non-refoulement not be restricted to the threat of group-based harms in the States where the individual is to be deported. Such expansions of the right of non-refoulement will make this right better able to engage in the kind of gap-filling that I have argued above to be the moral basis of such international procedural rights. As I indicated in the first section of this chapter, the upshot of my specific proposal is that non-refoulement concerns the prohibition on any deportation or extradition that would be likely to jeopardize life or freedom of the person to be exiled.

9.5 OBJECTIONS

In this section I wish to consider two objections to my proposal. The first objection is that it will be very hard to set up international institutions that would effectively protect a global right of non-refoulement. If we think again about the US response to September 11, we quickly see how easy it was for the US to engage in nearly undetectable extraordinary rendition. If a State engages in judicially authorized rendition, it is easy to monitor, but these cases have for obvious reasons been quite rare. Far more frequently States that violate non-refoulement do so in a clandestine way. It is hard enough, this objection would continue, to stop abuses of habeas corpus since typically there is some paper trail that leads up to the initial incarceration or detention. But rendition and refoulement are often aimed at avoiding just this public judicial process, making it very hard to figure out what sort of monitoring institution could be effective.

One idea is to set up a global court of equity, as I will argue below. A world court of equity is a partial solution to the problem identified above. For a court to exercise supervisory status, it must be informed of the possibility of an abuse of the principle of non-refoulement in the first place. Here it might be a good idea to allow those who are not themselves materially affected by State action to have some kind of standing to initiate court proceedings. So, one ancillary procedural proposal would be to weaken the normal Anglo-American provision on standing, perhaps adopting what appears to be the right in India of media members or other friends of the court to inform the appellate court about possible abuses and to trigger a judicial investigation even if no one directly concerned is bringing a complaint.[21] This is especially important if a State has coerced or incarcerated all of those who could under normal circumstances make such a complaint.

A second idea is to move toward the prosecution of State leaders or other sanctions against States that violate non-refoulement by engaging in deportation of individuals to countries where they will be tortured or otherwise harmed, or who engage in the extraordinary rendition of prisoners of war or others captured on the battlefield. There are international instruments that recognize the right of non-refoulement, but they have not often been enforced, as was true at Guantanamo. In my view, what is needed is for an international court or other institution to have this as part of its subject-matter jurisdiction as a way to protect some of the most vulnerable of people, those who are currently Stateless. I would extend non-refoulement further than it is recognized now, so that all people who are imprisoned or detained are under its authority. Even though it is hard to enforce, all it will take would be a few cases to act as a deterrent on the rest, or most of the rest of the cases.

The second objection is that in calling for an expansion of *jus cogens* norms I have violated the first prerequisite of a good legal system, the idea that new law-making itself be regulated by strong procedural requirements. Merely to propose that international law be augmented without going through anything like the established mechanisms for law-creation in international law looks itself to be a serious violation of procedural norms and the international rule of law.[22] If customs are to be manufactured, or general principles constructed out of whole cloth, the very hope that international law can become less infirm will be dashed.

I agree with this objection insofar as it concerns the stretching of custom to construct universal norms, even against those States that have a well-established record of dissenting from the custom or of forming a counter-custom.[23] But there is much more leeway concerning how to understand the sources of general principles of international law than concerning how to interpret the sources of international customary norms. Indeed, the ICJ lists the following account of general principles of international law, saying only that: "c. the general principles of law [are] recognized by civilized

[21] See Jeremy Cooper, "Poverty and Constitutional Justice: The Indian Experience," *Mercer Law Review*, vol. 44, 1993, 611–635, reprinted in *Philosophy of Law: Classic and Contemporary Readings*, Larry May and Jeff Brown (eds.), Oxford: Wiley/Blackwell, 2010, pp. 569–584.
[22] See Eibe Riedel, "Standards and Sources: Farewell to the Exclusivity of the Sources Triad in International Law?" *European Journal of International Law*, vol. 2, no. 1, 1991, 58–84.
[23] See my discussion of this point in *Crimes Against Humanity: A Normative Account*, NY: Cambridge University Press, 2005, Chapter 3.

nations."[24] Here it looks like the only requirement is that general principles must be recognized as such by all or most States.

Some interpreters have linked this third source of international law with the fourth: "d. subject to the provisions of Article 59, judicial decisions and the teachings of the most highly qualified publicists of the various nations . . . [are] subsidiary means for the determination of rules of law." In this case it looks like judicial decisions and even the writings of legal scholars could uncover or create general principles of international law. It seems as if these principles would have to be recognized as well, but it does not seem that there is a problem with such norms originating in some other way.

And others have suggested that general principles might also be linked to "2. This provision shall not prejudice the power of the Court to decide a case *ex aequo et bono*, if the parties agree thereto." Here another possible route to general principles of international law would be that they are considered initially to be required by what is understood as the fair and the good. Again it also looks like these "moral" principles would then have to be recognized by all or most States to become general principles of international law. I have argued that this is indeed a good way to think about general principles of international law and also *jus cogens* norms. Universal moral principles are what undergird most domestic constitutions and there is reason to think of the foundation of international law in similar moral terms.

What all of this seems to indicate is that adding new general principles is not especially problematic as long as the principles are indeed recognized by all or most States after their initial articulation as principles laid down by judicial opinions, the writings of legal scholars, or even the moral principles of an international society. Adding general principles that have *jus cogens* status would thus seem no more difficult or problematic than adding any other general principles of international law based on the ICJ statute which is itself commonly recognized today as providing the core sources of international law.

James Hathaway begins his wonderful book on refugees with a pessimistic note:

In far too many cases, refugees in less developed states have been detained, socially marginalized, left physically at risk, or effectively denied the ability to meet even their most basic needs . . . Instead of a universal and comprehensive system of human rights law, the present reality is instead a patchwork of standards.[25]

---

[24] United Nation's Charter, Article 39.1.c.
[25] Hathaway, *The Rights of Refugees*, pp. 3 and 6.

In the Epilogue to his book, Hathaway catalogs some of the problems with the existing system of refugee rights protection. He singles out two factors: the lack of oversight and enforcement by international institutions and the lack of political will on the part of States. These two factors come together when he concludes that:

The vital role played by the UNHCR [UN High Commissioner for Refugees] does not amount to a transparent system to ensure accountability by states . . . the legal duty to protect refugees is understood to be neither in the national interest of most states, nor a fairly apportioned collective responsibility. It is therefore resisted.[26]

I agree with Hathaway that the key to protecting rights of refugees, as well as those who find themselves deported or extradited, in international law is to make it clearer why States will benefit from such protection and especially how an international regime of protection will indeed be fair in terms of collective responsibility, as I have argued in previous chapters.

In this chapter I have tried to indicate how a system of transparent norms that follow in line with Magna Carta legacy rights, especially non-refoulement, can aid in creating a transparent system of oversight for refugee rights. And I have indicated how non-refugees also need to be protected when States attempt to transfer them to other States where they are likely to be harmed. The right of non-refoulement is primarily a procedural right that protects the Magna Carta legacy right not to be arbitrarily exiled and also protects against practices that jeopardize the life or liberty interests of the person to be exiled, deported, or extradited. Indeed, seen in this light, non-refoulement is at least as important as habeas corpus for those who are detained.

Such procedural rights as non-refoulement should be considered as *jus cogens* in international law, just as should be true of other Magna Carta legacy procedural rights, as well as all basic rights for that matter. If this occurs, one more way in which international law is infirm will be addressed and at least potentially cured. In the next chapter I will explore the other Magna Carta legacy rights and will be especially concerned to see if there is a coherent set of these rights that could be the basis for an international rule of law that will aid further in curing the current infirmities caused by gaps in international law. In that respect I will outline what it means to have a right to be subject to international law in such a way so that one's status as "human" is protected.

[26] Ibid., pp. 993 and 1000.

CHAPTER 10

The right to be subject to international law

A major problem that non-citizens continue to face is arbitrary detention. Although arbitrary detention is prohibited under the International Covenant on Civil and Political Rights, non-citizens – especially asylum seekers, undocumented immigrants, and victims of trafficking – continue to be placed in detention for indefinite periods.[1]

Magna Carta was slightly amended in 1225 to include, after "desseised," the words "of any free tenement or of his liberties or free customs." When added to the idea of outlawry already in the original version of Magna Carta, this was understood to mean also the right not to be deprived of citizenship rights.[2] As we move slowly toward an international legal order, the key rights will be something like the right to be a subject of international law, and the right not to be allowed to lose one's rights as a "citizen of the world." Related to these rights is the idea, also from Magna Carta, that something like trial by a jury of one's peers is crucial for the protection of all of one's other rights. I am not proposing that the category of "world citizen" is yet established in practice today, but only that as we move toward such a global order there are various procedural rights that will need to be secured to guarantee to all persons the equal protection of international law. The positive right to be subject to international law, or the negative right not to be excluded from the protection of international law, is of the highest priority for the progressive development of something like global citizenship rights that correspond to human rights.

The idea explored in this chapter is for international courts or other institutions to step in and offer relief when detainees have been allowed to slip between the cracks of extant legal systems or rights-enforcement

---

[1] David Weissbrodt, *The Human Rights of Non-Citizens*, Oxford University Press, 2008, pp. 3–4.
[2] See Faith Thompson, *Magna Carta – Its Role in the Making of the English Constitution 1300–1629*, Minneapolis, MN: University of Minnesota Press, 1948, p. 68.

regimes. In addition, I would also argue that something like trial by jury in criminal matters should be an acknowledged international right, which can be overridden only in rare cases. And this is probably the most controversial of the four proposals to adopt Magna Carta's procedural rights that I have previously put on the table, for there have not yet been major international instruments that have recognized trial by jury as a requirement of criminal proceedings. This was one of the lynchpins of the evolving Magna Carta doctrine. The right to trial by a jury by one's peers is crucial for justice, or so it was thought over time as procedural justice developed in England in the centuries after Magna Carta. Yet today there are no international jury trials, so this right is a long way from being recognized and enforced, although the recently decided US Supreme Court decision in *Boumediene* seems to be on the road to recognizing this right.[3]

In this chapter I will first examine the idea of being an outlaw or a Stateless person as someone who is effectively rightless. Second, I will explain what it means to be rendered an outlaw in international law. I will argue that each human person has a right not to be outlawed in this way. Third, I will connect the right not be outlawed to something like the right to trial by a jury of one's peers. I will acknowledge that in some cases it is very difficult to allow for such a right in international law, but nonetheless argue that the cases where the right to jury is denied should be few. Fourth, I will argue that once these rights are recognized, we will have progressed quite far toward a full version of the international rule of law. Finally, I will address an objection to my proposal for seeing the world peopled by global citizens. In addressing this objection, I outline my general normative view which falls some-where between a State-centric and an individual-centric position about global justice.

10.1 THE CONCEPTS OF OUTLAWRY AND STATELESSNESS

The term "outlaw" literally refers to the status of being outside the law. At the time of Magna Carta, a person could escape from the sanctions of the State by leaving its jurisdiction, which meant going to the parts of England where the king's armies did not reach. But there is a more

---

[3] *Boumediene v. Bush*, 128 S. Ct. 2229, 2256 (2008). Kennedy cites Harlan's concurring opinion in *Reid* as criticizing *Ross* in wondering "whether jury trial should be deemed a necessary condition of the exercise of Congress' power to provide for the trial of Americans overseas."

interesting way to become an outlaw, namely by being made into an outlaw by the king's act of stripping a person of his or her effective citizenship rights and forcing him or her out of the protective jurisdiction of the king's law. And among the things that this meant was that a person was no longer able to petition to have a jury of his or her peers determine if he or she had been properly deprived of rights or wronged in other ways. Outlaws could be killed without risk of State sanction, but none-theless became folk heroes in England and many other societies emerging out of feudalism.[4]

The somewhat mythical "Robin Hood" story illustrates both senses of being an outlaw. He is said to have escaped the king's sanctions, perhaps at the time of Magna Carta itself in the early thirteenth century or somewhat later, by retreating into Sherwood Forest where the king's men could not easily get to him. But it is also alleged, on his behalf, that the king, perhaps either Edward or John, improperly issued sanctions against Robin Hood and thereby forced him into outlaw status.[5] What I am interested in is the latter type of case, although I recognize that sometimes it is difficult to sort out the causes of a person's becoming an outlaw. In this sense, there is a close parallel between Robin Hood and the detainees at Guantanamo who were forced out of the protection of all legal systems.

The term outlaw today is more commonly used to refer to those who spurn the legal requirements of civilized societies, who voluntarily choose not to conform to legal standards. Robin Hood may have been a case in point, although as I said it is not clear. In any event, historically, pirates are those who have often been declared to be outlaws, in the sense of having placed themselves outside of the obligations of the law. In this sense, it is also true that the "outlaw" status is often claimed to trigger a kind of reaction, both domestically and internationally, not to respect the rights of these people who are outside the law. In other works I have argued that this is a grave mistake.[6]

I would like to revive the older idea of an outlaw as someone who has been forced outside of the protection of the law, and to reserve the term bandit for those, like pirates, who have voluntarily chosen to be outside of the protection and obligation of the law. One of the least commented on

[4] See, E. J. Hobsbawm, *Bandits*, London: Pelican Books, 1972 [1969].
[5] See R. B. Dobson and John Taylor, *The Rymes of Robin Hood: An Introduction to the English Outlaw*, London: Sutton Publishing, 1977.
[6] See Larry May, *War Crimes and Just War*, NY: Cambridge University Press, 2007, Chapter 14; and Larry May, *Aggression and Crimes Against Peace*, NY: Cambridge University Press, 2008, Chapter 15.

sections of Magna Carta was the right not to be made an outlaw as one of the rights that was to be protected by the king. This right was clearly related to the right not to be exiled. Indeed, both of these ideas, exile and outlawry, are attempts by the leaders of the State to remove a citizen or subject from the protection of the laws into a realm, whether it be outside the territorial borders of the State or outside the domestic reach of the State. It might be thought that today, becoming an outlaw is not much of a problem because there are no longer places within States that are not subject to the legal protection of the State. Yet, as we have seen, Guantanamo Bay and Bagram Air Base are examples today, as are the detention centers for those who are unsuccessful asylum seekers, as well as many of those in refugee camps.

In the remainder of this section I will briefly explore the reasons for thinking that there is a right not to be arbitrarily made into an outlaw. The most important point here is that when one is placed outside of the protection of the State, one has effectively lost one's rights as a member of that State, whether subject, citizen, or resident. To render someone an outlaw is most significantly to render ineffective that person's civil rights. There is a sense in which a person never really loses rights merely when they are not protected. But rights have little meaning except as hortatory unless there is a political body that recognizes that it must respond when claims are made on the basis of one's rights.

In the case of human rights it is even clearer that one cannot literally lose one's rights, since they are premised on being a member of the human community. But, as in the case of civil rights, if no State or other institution protects these rights, then it is as if one has indeed lost these rights. Being made an outlaw is then equivalent to being deprived of the right to be subject to a legal regime where one's other rights are protected or at least given uptake, or recognized, by some institution in the claims one makes. And this is simply one of the very worst things that can happen to a person, nearly equivalent to ceasing to be a person altogether.

Conceptually, it is not necessary that a person be a citizen of a particular State in order to be effectively a rights-bearer. This is especially true if we are talking of legal rights rather than moral rights. But even in the case of legal rights, a person who is Stateless could still be a rights-bearer if there is some political entity other than a State that the person is a citizen of. If there were to be a world government that had the ability to grant world citizenship status to those who are not formally citizens of any national State, then people could be legal rights-bearers even though they were not citizens of any national State.

In my view, rights-bearers must have some political institution to which they can appeal if their rights are not respected or their rights-claims are not heard. James Hathaway has summarized the issue in respect to refugees: "Refugee status is a categorical designation that reflects a unique ethical and consequential legal entitlement to make claim on the international community."[7] To have international rights, such as the right to be protected as a refugee, means being able to make claims against the international community, since refugees are seeking national citizenship status but currently lack it.

For purposes of analytic clarity, we can distinguish between de jure and de facto Statelessness. People who are de jure Stateless literally have no official citizenship in any national State, having either lost their official citizenship status or never having been granted such status. People who are de facto Stateless may be people who have left their country of habitual residence in order to seek asylum, or who have lost their citizenship papers, or who are attempting to return to their country of habitual residence but are blocked from doing so. Such people are de facto Stateless since it may be true that they formally are citizens of a State, but that they cannot exercise their rights as citizens for various reasons (perhaps because they are detained in another State) and are thereby effectively rendered Stateless.

Being a person, a moral subject, is to occupy the status of having both rights and duties – indeed, there is a sense that the rights and duties correlate with each other, so that if one has obligations without also having rights, one has ceased to be a full moral subject. This harkens back to our much earlier discussion, in Chapter 5, of how those who are languishing in prison had no hope of getting out. In such cases the jailer has no accountability for the treatment of the prisoner, who has "disappeared" as a person and may as well be dead. Of course, these people have the benefit of not having actually died, but as far as their rights go, it is very much as if they have indeed died. The disappeared are just one of many contemporary cases of being made an outlaw. And, as we will explore in the next section, such cases are a major affront to the idea of human rights and to the international, as well domestic, rule of law.

Outlawry is not often discussed anymore, but I believe that a return to this idea can help illuminate what is especially problematic about States

---

[7] James Hathaway, "Forced Migration Studies: Could We Agree to Just Date?" *Journal of Refugee Studies*, vol. 20, 2007, 352. See also the discussion of this issue in *Refugees, Asylum Seekers, and the Rule of Law*, Susan Keebone (ed.), Cambridge University Press, 2009, especially pp. 304–308.

that hold detainees in indefinite duration, effectively depriving them of rights of subjects or citizens. Such actions are very much like exiling or deporting someone, but doing so in such a way that the detainee remains within the territory of the State. This is precisely what it meant in late-medieval England to force a person to be an outlaw. I will draw on the insights about this idea from English history to discuss this idea's modern-day equivalent in international law.

10.2 OUTLAWRY AND STATELESSNESS IN INTERNATIONAL LAW

The term outlaw does not have a technical definition in international law. Perhaps the closest idea is that of being an outlaw or rogue State, namely a State that does not subscribe to the main provisions of international law. There are two other popular meanings of individuals who are outlaws that are also not technical usages in international law. First, a person could be an outlaw in the sense that he or she is Stateless. As a Stateless individual, and hence without the protection of the laws of any State, the person is both outside the laws of States and also to a certain extent outside international law, insofar as international law is formed by the agreements of States. Second, a person could be an outlaw in the sense of being expelled from a State and not allowed to enter any other State, perhaps destined to remain in the high seas, and hence not in the territory of any State, perhaps like those on the *Tampa* discussed in Chapter 7. In this latter sense, a person can be an outlaw in international law in the same way that Robin Hood was an outlaw in Sherwood Forest in the thirteenth century.

Currently, there are many people who are Stateless and in that sense they are the modern equivalent of outlaws. Some of these people are in refugee camps, having been expelled from their home country but now not recognized as members of the State in which they reside. Some of the people are in detention centers in countries like the US and Australia, having arrived on the soil of these countries but then having been denied asylum. With no State willing to accept them, they are placed into detention centers (often some of the most gruesome prisons) to wait for some State to accept them or their asylum decisions to be overturned on appeal.

In the current regime of international law, one is not necessarily unprotected if one is Stateless, but it certainly is harder for one's rights to be protected without some sort of membership or citizenship status in an existing State. Various treaties have attempted to protect those who are Stateless, including many who would otherwise be outlaws. The Geneva

Conventions tried to protect all those who suffered from the ravages of war, including those who had become displaced from their original States. The Refugee Convention and the Convention on the Elimination of all Forms of Racial Discrimination singled out displaced persons for special protection. And the Convention Relating to the Status of Stateless Persons, which was modelled on the Refugee Convention, is quite explicit in setting out a regime to protect the rights of Stateless persons. But, as I will argue later, these various regimes suffer from the fact that there is no international institution to which people can appeal when they are deprived of what the regimes are supposed to secure.

There is one class of outlaws that has remained virtually unprotected, namely those who have been expelled from the protection of law because of their alleged illegal activities or the danger they pose to the State in question. Indeed, the Stateless Persons Convention explicitly rules out the application of the treaty to those who "have committed a serious non-political crime outside the country of their residence prior to their admission to that country."[8] This is a major gap in the protection of human rights and especially of procedural rights.

Those who are not citizens of a given State and have been detained within that State, and whose detention is for an indefinite period of time, are some of the clearest cases of individuals who fall through the cracks of the system of protection afforded by States. These people may not be strictly "Stateless" in a de jure sense. Yet, since there has been no deter-mination that their asylum status may not be revived or that there might not be a State that can be found to accept them, they may be de facto Stateless. If a State offers security reasons for not granting asylum or for not transporting the person to another State, the person in question is in a kind of limbo, and the major international instruments on Statelessness do not seem to recognize these people as needing protection.

Another category of people who have recognized protection, although not enough, are refugees. There is a specific provision of the Refugee treaty that should govern some of these matters, but also seemingly has a gap. The problem relates to the interplay of rights protection and security issues. As Matthew Gibney puts it, there is a clash of perspectives here that is hard to reconcile:

In the first, the view of the person forced from his country, to be a refugee is to be "lost." The refugee is forced to eke out an existence in a place where the social

---

[8] Stateless Persons Convention, Article 1.2 (iii)(b).

and political markers that enable orientation in the world are alien and difficult to decode. In the second, the perspective of the receiving country, the refugee is an interloper, someone from whom any request is "impertinent," or . . . "shameless." He is a person who, betrayed by his own state, is forced to rely on the sufferance of others.[9]

From this clash of perspectives it is hard to see how to proceed without some kind of adjudicatory board that could decide whether the rights of the refugee or the interests of the State should prevail. I discuss this security issue in Chapter 12. Suffice it here to say that if to be a refugee one must cross into a given State, then it is in the interests of some if not many States to keep potential refugees from ever getting that foothold on their claimed rights.

When a person is deprived of human rights protection by falling through the cracks of the regime of international rights protection, that person is effectively rendered not fully human. I will expand on this idea later in this chapter and I will also address the fourth and most controversial of the Magna Carta legacy rights, trial by a jury of one's peers, and connect this right to the right not to be outlawed. Before addressing that topic, let me briefly discuss what is meant by my claim that individuals should be subject to international law.

10.3 BEING A SUBJECT OF INTERNATIONAL LAW

There are of course two meanings of the term "subject" in the expression "subject to international law." People are subject to a legal regime when they have obligations to obey the legal rules of that regime. And people are also subject to a legal regime when they have legal rights that are enforced in that regime. In the Stateless Persons Convention, the obligations are listed first, before the lengthy discussion of rights. I believe that this is no accident since, like all multilateral treaties, the drafters wanted to make it as appealing to States as they could. As in matters of corporate governance generally, those in control of corporate power have looked for a linking of rights with responsibilities. And the international domain is no exception here, with global leaders as well as national leaders all looking for a way to bind people to arrangements that increase security as well as rights globally.

---

[9] Matthew J. Gibney, "'A Thousand Little Guantanamos': Western States and Measures to Prevent the Arrival of Refugees," in *Displacement, Asylum, and Migration*, Kate E. Tunstall (ed.), Oxford University Press, 2006, p. 139. See also Melissa Lane, "Response to Matthew J. Gibney, 'A Thousand Little Guantanamos,'" in *Displacement, Asylum, and Displacement*, pp. 171–172.

As international law becomes less infirm and more like domestic legal systems, there need to be procedures that guarantee that individuals are subject to international law in both senses of the term "subject." There are currently significant impediments to recognizing that all persons are subject to international law in both of these ways. Not the least of these impediments is that international law relies heavily on States to enforce the provisions of international law. States are sometimes quite reluctant to enforce international law when it conflicts with domestic law or where its enforcement is against one of its own nationals, especially high-ranking political and military leaders who are its nationals. And because of this reluctance, especially when the State in question also does not feel bound to protect the rights of the individual in question as a matter of domestic law, the individual ends up being effectively rightless.

Think again of people who are truly Stateless in that they have been forced out of their home State and have not been accepted as subjects or citizens of another State, perhaps now eking out a bare existence in a refugee camp on the border of their previous home State. David Miller has argued that no one has a right to become a member of a particular State.[10] But what if one is now denied membership in any State? One could agree with Miller that no State has an obligation to accept this person and still feel that the person has the right to be subject to some legal order. So that if no State will grant the person citizenship, then at the very least the person needs to have minimal citizenship rights protection extended in some sense by the international community.

Miller argues that States have the right to decide who can become its subjects or citizens. And this is important both for national identity and for meeting national responsibilities. In this work I will not take a stand on whether Miller is correct about this or not, although I would disagree with him about a number of aspects of his position and its supporting arguments. But even Miller would have to admit that in some cases the State's complicity in the Statelessness of a person could affect whether that State has obligations to the Stateless person. But the very difficult case is when no State thinks it has special obligations to a given Stateless person, and yet the rights of the person call for some kind of protection. My view is that if the international protection of human rights was not so infirm, it might make sense in the way that Miller suggests that no State has an obligation to protect this person's rights, but that the

---

[10] David Miller, *National Responsibility and Global Justice*, NY: Oxford University Press, 2007, Chapter 8.

person is not effectively rightless since the international community does have such an obligation.

For international law to recognize that all humans are subjects of international law, in terms of looking to international law for protection of their rights, the most obvious thing to do, and what I have proposed throughout this work, is for there to be a special international court or other institution that looks to the protection of procedural rights that would indeed guarantee that all people are subjects before the law and have access to the equal protection of the international law. Indeed, the somewhat expanded notion of the rights of detainees that I defended above called for there to be minimal due process in the sense that everyone was recognized as equal before the law. The idea is that everyone should be seen as equal before international law as well, as in a sense citizens or subjects of the world. But, as we will see, some have challenged this idea, arguing that it is utopian to talk of there being a category of citizenship of the world.

10.4 TRIAL BY JURY

The most controversial of all of the rights I have discussed in this book is the right to trial by a jury of one's peers. At the moment such a right is not recognized in international law and is generally not offered in international tribunals. Instead, even trial courts at the international level are staffed by panels of judges. And, in addition, trial by jury is the least like a procedural right of all of the rights I have discussed. Yet, as I will argue in this section, trial by jury is intimately related to the procedural rights discussed in this book, as has been true since Magna Carta where a rudimentary idea of trial by jury was one of the four rights enshrined in the famous Chapter 29 (39). And in my view there was good reason to have trial by jury linked to the other rights we have been discussing, especially the right to be subject to law.

One might think of Magna Carta's reference to trial by a jury of one's peers as equivalent to what that idea means today. But this is a mistake – rather, it is the way that this right developed, especially in the seventeenth century, that is like the right today. At the time of Magna Carta, trial by jury in its modern sense was not what was at stake. What the barons sought to secure was the practice "known as *recognitio* or *inquisitio*, which was introduced into England by the Normans and was simply the practice of obtaining information on local affairs from the sworn testimony of local men." It is true that very soon thereafter the information was then institutionalized as the basis of the initial indictment, and that another group of men was then asked to render a verdict in place of trial by ordeal. But according to many historians, what the barons called for at Magna Carta is not the same institution as what we now call trial by jury.[11] The idea, though, of having a group of men decide the legitimacy of the indictment and also the verdict is clearly related to the *inquisitio* that was indeed one of the main rights of Magna Carta. And it is still historically uncontested that such a right had influence on the emerging right of trial by jury that has come down to us today.

In an excellent study of trial by jury, Michael Hill and David Winkler describe a long-term project on juries that sought input from scholars across the globe. Here is one of their conclusions:

History apart, there appear to be two principal justifications for having juries:

- They are independent decision-makers.
- They respect society in the disposition of criminal cases and, as such, they satisfy one (at least) of the socio-political imperatives ... [that] government is "by the people."[12]

Hill and Winkler argue that jury trials can be defended in terms of fair trials, although they acknowledge that there may be other ways to achieve fair trials and that various societies in the past seemed to achieve fair trials without the institution of the jury trial as we understand it today in Western societies.

There are serious costs in a jury system – and "Practitioners working in an existing jury trial system ignore the cost argument at their (and the system's) peril."[13] As the Dutch have seen, in some cases efficiency can be maintained and cost can better be contained when professional judges make decisions rather than lay juries.[14] And professional judges are much less likely to disregard the law and engage in "nullification" than are lay juries. In addition, in societies without a history of trial by jury, the legitimacy of verdicts is far more likely to be recognized by the public if juries are not employed. And there has never been a system that relied exclusively on juries in any event, giving rise to the idea that at very least juries are not in and of themselves stable enough to sustain fair trials.

In my view, despite its potential pitfalls, trail by jury is worth defending at the international level. In the long history of Anglo-American

---

[11] William Sharp McKechnie, *Magna Carta: A Commentary on the Great Charter of King John*, Glasgow: John Maclehose and Sons, 1914, pp. 134–138.

[12] Michael Hill and David Winkler, "Juries: How Do They Work? Do We Want Them?" *Criminal Law Forum*, vol. 11, no. 4, 2000, 397–443, especially 411.

[13] Ibid., 412.   [14] Ibid., 413–414.

jurisprudence from Magna Carta until today, the right to trial by jury has been seen as highly significant in the general protection of the law that should be afforded to all persons who fall under the law's jurisdiction. At least in part, this is because trial by a jury of one's peers is likely to be less subject to political manipulation and abuse than trial by a "jury" of social and political elite judges. Underlying this position is the idea that there is more of a commonality of interest between a person and his peer group than between elites and persons standing in the dock.

Commonality of interest between those who risk conviction and those who convict is important in trials so that those risking conviction have the sense that the proceedings have been fair ones. Of course, those who share commonalities of interest can be unfair to one another. But the kind of unfairness that comes from people having unreasonable expectations or not knowing the normal expectations of people in a particular society can be blunted by making sure that people from the same society as the accused are in the group that decides on conviction. Even judges that come from the same region as the accused do not necessarily have commonality of interest since such commonalities are a function of socio-economic status as well as region.

Trial by a jury of one's peers also gives expression to the idea that those who are accused and those who accuse are part of the same community. This is important because it means that the duties that a person is accused of having violated are specifically correlated with rights to a fair process in determining whether those duties were in fact violated. Such correlations can be maintained by those who are not one's peers. But the thought is that peers will respect such rights because they can better identify with what it is like to have these rights not respected. The idea that one has peers, and that they are the ones who have convicted the accused, is important for establishing respect for the accused as a rights-holder.

However, there is a very important practical problem – namely that in international criminal law a true jury of one's peers would have to be drawn from the community the complaining party comes from, and that may well be half a world away from where the trial is to take place. And these jury members would have to be transported to The Hague, for instance, and housed potentially for several years. In addition, many parts of the world do not have a tradition of trial by jury, and if the complaining party comes from that part of the world, then there is a serious problem concerning how to get the members of his or her society to the point where they understand what it means to sit as a jury of his or her peers. And, finally, there is the problem that issues in international law tend to be rather more complex than domestic issues and so there is reason to think that a jury of one's peers will find it difficult even understanding the issue to be decided upon.

One way to respond to some of these objections is to restrict the scope of such trials or perhaps, as we will explore in the next chapter, initially to make them more like administrative hearings rather than full-blown trials. Hearings sometimes have small juries, and this would make things easier given the above difficulties. In addition, those hearings could be held initially in situ, as a fact-finding matter, and then the determination of applicable international law could be determined back in the place where the international tribunal or administrative panel regularly meets.

What is more important is that the spirit of trial by jury prevails rather than the letter. So, in this context what is crucial is that there are some people who are deciding major issues of the trial, especially factual matters, who are not merely drawn from the elite of the society and thus may not have much sympathy for a marginalized member of that society who appears before them. Indeed, the role of juries is to decide factual issues rather than issues of law in any event, so the complexity of the law is not necessarily an impediment to having trials with juries instead of merely trials with banks of jurists drawn from regions of the world that are quite different from the region where the defendant resides.

The issue of whether to have trial by juries is primarily one of affording to the individual defendant some kind of guarantee that his or her interests will not be significantly discredited because the people judging do not share those interests or even understand them. And there are various ways to help here, perhaps if we construct a progressive list of things that would lead to robust jury trials but would also include less robust institutional checks. On this list would be:

1) multiple-judge panels that have some jurists from the defendant's region;
2) multiple-judge panels that have some jurists from the defendant's State;
3) preliminary hearing panels that contain the defendant's peers;
4) juries that contain some of the defendant's peers;
5) juries that contain mainly the defendant's peers.

In each of these alternatives, we move progressively closer to true trial by jury in international trials.

If we think even more creatively, we can imagine other types of hearings, especially administrative hearings, which can partially serve the spirit of the principle of trial by a jury of one's peers.[15] In domestic contexts it is common to have these proceedings conducted by members of the professional class. But this need not be the case, as is sometimes true in small claims courts in the US or in alternative dispute resolution proceedings. In such proceedings it is possible to give the defendant a veto power over the mediator or even a more direct say in who should be the mediator, chosen from a list of approved mediators. The principle undergirding trial by jury can be seen here in these various alternatives to proper trials as well. It is commonly objected that international law cannot accommodate the procedure of trial by a jury of one's peers. But, as I have argued, this is too simplistic a response. In spirit, if not in letter, this procedure can be accommodated to various degrees in international law today. And in doing so, it will be possible to embrace the principles that undergird trial by a jury of one's peers.

It is also the case that the spirit of trial by a jury of one's peers is related to the idea that no one should be deprived of the right of being subject to international law. The very idea of a person being judged by those who are his or her co-nationals, or fellow members of a smaller group such as State membership in a federal system of States, is an idea that implicates the right to be a subject of the law. For without being a subject of a legal regime, there really are no peers that one has that could constitute a jury of one's peers. This does not rule out, as I argue at the end of this chapter, that one can be subject to more than one legal regime. What has motivated my study is the idea that some people have been denied the protection of legal subject status. And part of what this means is that such other rights as the right to trial by jury are also called into question when a person is deprived of being a legal subject. On the other hand, having the right to be judged by a jury of one's peers makes it harder for a person to be systematically deprived of his or her legal status.

10.5 CITIZENS OF WHAT?

The objection I wish to take up at the end of this chapter has to do with the idea of world citizenship with which I began. For there to be citizens of the world, there must be a world community that would in some sense correspond to a nation-State, or else there would not be any entity for the

---

[15] For a discussion of related issues about who is the subject of the administrative regulatory action, see Benedict Kingsbury, Nico Krisch, and Richard B. Stewart, "The Emergence of Global Administrative Law," *Law and Contemporary Problems*, vol. 68, Summer/Autumn 2005, 24.

people to be citizens of. Indeed, there seems to be something of a category mistake to say that there are citizens and yet for it to be unclear what political community these citizens are connected to. I shall address this objection by suggesting that there is enough of a world community for the idea of world citizens to begin to make sense, but that this does not commit me to full-scale cosmopolitanism.

Cosmopolitanism is the thesis that morality only or primarily concerns individuals. According to this view, the rights of individuals in the world, human rights, are not to be subjugated to the interests or rights of States. The State has no moral standing and indeed should not count in moral deliberations. Most cosmopolitans then make the leap to politics and argue that the individual is also the main unit of global politics, with the State greatly reduced in importance. And cosmopolitans are highly critical of attempts to talk of even a society of States. Yet their perspective, much more so than mine, falls prey to the charge that it is simply utopian to think that there is anything like a global community that would be morally or politically prior to communities in States.

I subscribe to the view that is often called "the society of States" perspective.[16] The international community is a community composed primarily of States and only secondarily of individuals. Nonetheless, there are human rights that are the rights of people qua human, not merely civil rights that are rights of State citizenship. The question is what to make of claims about world citizenship. My view is that such claims are partly metaphor and partly reality, but that it is indeed utopian to talk of full-scale world citizenship. People have citizenship rights that relate to the States they are members of. But people also have subsidiary citizenship rights to the global community that their States are the primary members of. Human rights are normally mediated through States, although there are important exceptions when it comes to those who are Stateless or whose rights are not being protected by their States. In my view, there is enough of a global community to speak non-metaphorically of a global community insofar as we focus on the community or society of States.

People are "citizens of the world" in two senses of that term. First, most people are citizens of some State that is part of a society of States. Second, for those who are not citizens of States or for whom States do not protect their rights, these people have a non-mediated right of citizenship in the world community. This latter category of citizenship is of a limited sort. The rights in question are rights to basic human rights and basic

---

[16] See Simon Caney, *Justice Beyond Borders*, Oxford University Press, 2005, especially pp. 10–13.

procedural rights, including the Magna Carta legacy rights I have been discussing. And when these rights are abridged, either States should redress their infringement or, failing that, these people still can pursue their rights claims directly in the international arena. The international "community" is then a stand-in for the society of States plus the protection mechanisms set up to deal with gaps that exist when people are Stateless or when States have clearly demonstrated that they will not protect the human rights of their citizens.

People are citizens of the world metaphorically, in that they have human rights that their States should protect creating a situation in which it is as if there were true citizenship rights of the world. And in those cases of Statelessness or failure of a State to protect the human rights of its citizens, there is a non-metaphorical sense in which people are global citizens insofar as they can press their human rights claims for direct redress by various international institutions. In this way it is possible to answer the question of what people are citizens of when it is said that they are citizens of the world.

It could still be objected that there is not enough of a world community for there to be anything other than the metaphorical sense of being a global citizen. In the remainder of this section I will attempt to respond to this variation of the objection I discussed above. There is a rudimentary international community in the sense that there are interlocking institutions that facilitate trade and health information and aid around the world. And such a community is as much as we need in order for there to be sufficient community of interest around the globe. In fact, the emerging consensus about the most important substantive rights in international law gives one hope that a similar consensus could emerge about procedural rights in international law as well. Such a consensus would provide fuel to the idea that there is generally an emerging idea of global citizenship.

A related objection is that in thinking about the problems of this book in global terms I have neglected the fact that many global problems result from what States have done and it is States that can and should be the ones to remedy those problems. This is the position that David Miller defends in his book *National Responsibility and Global Justice*.[17] Miller argues that we must treat individuals as agents and not merely as patients in terms of global problems having to do with those who are poor or refugees. The poor or those who are refugees are inhabitants of States, and often those States have contributed to these problems. Such considerations are not irrelevant.

---

[17] Miller, *National Responsibility and Global Justice*.

Indeed, it may mean that refugees do not have an absolute right to leave their home States and become members of another State.

My response to this objection is to point out that pursuing global solutions does not rule out also considering State-based solutions. Indeed, since I am not a cosmopolitan I do not have to worry about attacks like those of Miller as much as cosmopolitans do. My model remains that of the ICC, with its principle of complementarity. In many ways this international court is really only a back-up and deterrent device to prod States to redress substantive rights violations. The various models I will examine in the next chapter concerning how to redress procedural rights violations are also meant to be back-up alternatives to what States can often do best if properly motivated. There is, of course, the special case of people who have no State to appeal to, where international courts or other institutions will be the primary forum for their complaints. But these cases will be exceptional.

My view is that there is nothing wrong with the idea that most people are citizens or subjects of multiple legal realms. The two most important memberships are State and global. Being a citizen of the US and also a citizen of the world is not significantly different from being a citizen of Missouri and a citizen of the US, or perhaps a better analogy is to those people who hold dual citizenships. In any event, as I have indicated, being a citizen of the world in the sense that one has significant rights by virtue of being human does not necessarily indicate where those human rights are best protected, and certainly does not mean that one can press such rights claims only in an international or national forum.

David Weissbrodt has stated: "The architecture of human rights law is built on the premise that all persons, by virtue of their essential humanity, should enjoy all human rights."[18] This right to equality before the law has been promulgated by various international bodies including the United Nation's Human Rights Committee. But in the case of non-citizens, whether "migrants, refugees, stateless persons, and others, they share common experiences of discrimination and abuse."[19] Few deny that human rights protections should be extended to all; what is at issue is how this should be implemented, and especially to what extent a State's security interests can trump the protection of the right to equal protection of international law to all. In the final two chapters I will take up these issues.

[18] Weissbrodt, *The Human Rights of Non-Citizens*, p. 45.
[19] Ibid., p. 241.

In this chapter I have discussed the right not to be outlawed or rendered outside the protection of law, the rights of those who are Stateless, procedural rights against discrimination and abuse of non-citizens of various kinds, and the related right to have a trial by jury of one's peers. And I have ended by addressing the vexing question of what entity individuals are primarily subjects of when questions of international law are in play. Throughout I have argued that one of the most important rights is the right to be a legal subject, and that one of the most important international rights that one has is the right to be subject to international law. The right to be subject to international law is a procedural right that has its roots in certain aspects of Magna Carta and also is a lynchpin in the international rule of law. I will next explain the pros and cons of various international institutional options and how best to adjudicate conflicts that arise between global rights and national security.

PART IV

Security and global institutions

CHAPTER II

Alternative institutional structures

In previous chapters I have indicated that I prefer to solve some of the procedural infirmities by means of a new court, a world court of equity, or some other international institution. But I have only gestured at the reasons for this. In this penultimate chapter I will explore the idea of a world procedural court and several institutional alternatives to it. I should state at the outset that I have a preference for some kind of court on the model of the ICC. But I do not have a strong view about which of the alternatives should be pursued first. Indeed, my sense is that several alternatives could be explored at once. In what follows I will consider each of the options and then offer some tentative remarks at the end.

Institutional design is only now beginning to get uptake in more theoretical quarters. In political philosophy in particular, there has been very little work on how to approach the assessment of institutional alternatives. I will venture into this area by referring largely to literature in public and international law. But even the methodology of comparative institutional structures in international law is itself contested. And the tentativeness of my conclusions will also be due to the fact that I see many positive features of the three institutional structures I will examine: a world court, an administrative regime, and an enhancement of the existing human rights council. But, as I have already indicated, I think that something more needs to be done than is currently on offer in the system of regional commissions and courts of human rights. The regional system of rights protection, along with protection offered domestically, has given us the situations in Guantanamo Bay, Bagram Air Base, and Christmas Island, as well as refugee centers that resemble Hobbesian states of nature, which is a very regrettable position to be in. International law will remain infirm unless something more robust is developed.

Looking back at our model of how English law developed after Magna Carta, it is fair to remark that there were a number of alternatives that were employed. There was indeed a slow development of a court of equity, the Chancellor's Court. But, in addition, there were various attempts to codify a set of administrative practices, some of which resulted in tremendous abuse and some of which were successful. Indeed, an increasingly assertive court of equity seems to have emerged in part to curb the abuses that a looser form of administrative review of matters of equity had countenanced. There was nothing like the present UN-affiliated Human Rights Council, but there was an attempt to deal with some of the procedural rights issues in the common law courts of England as they slowly emerged to take an autonomous role as well. Indeed, the common law courts gradually emerged as playing a significant role in redressing rights violations of individuals against the Crown, in ways that would have been hard to predict at the time of the signing of Magna Carta itself.

In the first section of this chapter I will begin to explore the alternative of an international court of equity, setting out reasons in favor of its development, but also discussing its drawbacks. In the second section I will look at the pros and cons of developing a set of global administrative remedies. In the third section I will provide the same sort of analysis of an expanded role for the UN's Human Rights Committee and the new Human Rights Council. In the fourth section I will talk a bit about which of these alternatives should be tried first and whether it makes sense to try a combination of all three alternative institutional structures. Here I will also discuss how States are likely to react to this progressive development of international oversight and accountability. Finally, I will offer some brief thoughts about which questions still need to be addressed in future work. While only offering some preliminary suggestions about very practical institutional matters, this chapter will try to put such matters into the theoretical context that has been explored in the previous chapters.

11.1 A WORLD COURT OF EQUITY

The previous sections have pointed toward the need for an enforcement mechanism at the global, not merely the regional, level so as to protect basic procedural rights. I here briefly sketch what kind of institution I favor and then spend the rest of this section defending it against a set of objections that could be, and have been, raised against similar ideas. On one level, what I envision could be simply understood as a court of appeals from the regional courts and commissions of human rights. On another level, such a court could also, in a limited set of contexts, be a court of first impression where one did not first have to exhaust remedies before these regional courts. On yet another level, the court I envisage could also be an appellate court from decisions rendered by domestic courts, although again this would have to be quite limited in scope if it is ever to be acceptable in a system of strong State sovereignty. And, finally, this could be a court that fills in the gaps in areas such as Guantanamo Bay, Bagram Air Base,[1] or Christmas Island that some States have claimed to be legal black holes internationally.

Specifically, I envision a court that has the power to hear appeals from individual detainees who have not had their claims challenging the legitimacy of their detention heard or properly adjudicated in their home States or in regional courts. Denial of habeas corpus or non-refoulement would be a kind of international tort.[2] Setting things up as torts rather than as crimes or declaratory judgments has the advantage of making the system less straightforwardly intrusive into the sovereign affairs of States. Of course, for the system to be effective, the tort fines would have to be serious enough to get the attention of States and their leaders. And some kind of system of collecting such tort fines would also have to be put in place, perhaps through the UN. But, as I have been indicating, the hope is that the shame and embarrassment that comes from an international trial that holds a State responsible for mistreatment of an individual is the main way that deterrence will work.

The world court of equity could also be thought of as ancillary to other already-existing international courts, especially the ICC. Again the model could be taken from American law where habeas corpus proceedings are civil law matters that are nonetheless intimately connected to the criminal justice system. Habeas corpus in the US is a collateral attack on incarceration or detention where the civil law court is asked to assess what had happened at the criminal law proceedings that led to the detention or incarceration. As I have indicated above, denial of habeas corpus in the US is seen as a matter of equity, but also of other aspects of the legal system that is implicated when the legitimacy of a person's detention or incarceration is called into question.

Recognizing what some authors have called "world habeas corpus"[3] is a way to bring review and oversight to proceedings of State governments, perhaps in a

---

[1] For more on Bagram, see Kal Raustiala, "Is Bagram the New Guantanamo? Habeas Corpus and *Maqaleh v. Gates,*" *ASIL Insight,* vol. 13, Issue 8, June 17, 2009, 1–4.

[2] I am very grateful to Mark Drumbl for pushing me to be more specific about the form that court proceeding and remedy would take.

[3] See Luis Kutner, *World Habeas Corpus,* Dobbs Ferry, NY: Oceana Publications, 1962.

way that will not be seen as a significant challenge to their sovereignty if handled in a manner like the way Magna Carta was handled with regard to King John and the feudal barons. The American legal theorist Roscoe Pound said of such efforts of extending habeas corpus internationally:

If a complete regime of universal peace may be an ultimate objective, any step toward it in achieving a regime of securing paramount individual natural rights through a legal remedial process would be of the highest significance.[4]

It is true that there will be resistance from States, especially likely from the US, but the end of the Cold War in the 1980s, like the death of King John in 1216, has opened up new possibilities that in prior times seemed impossible.

Some legal theorists have contended that habeas corpus and other Magna Carta legacy rights are not as important as I have suggested, or that they are somehow rendered redundant by other rights. One such theorist, Christoff J. M. Safferling, says:

Common law recognizes the writ of *habeas corpus ad subjiciendum*. Its use according to its original purpose, that is, to secure the release of a suspect held without charge by the police, has largely been made redundant by the provisions of PACE governing police detention.[5]

But Safferling is wrong to think that this is the original purpose, or even the main purpose of the right of habeas corpus. And even if he is right to think that PACE (the Police and Criminal Evidence Act), a parliamentary Act of 1984, has made habeas corpus redundant in the UK,[6] it is not true in other countries or generally in international law.

Earlier ideas of a world habeas corpus court saw the court addressing all substantive and procedural appeals from State court jurisdictions.[7] My idea of a world court of equity is more restrictive than the earlier proposals for a world habeas corpus court. At least in part, this is because I have a much less expansive view of habeas corpus than did Luis Kutner and Roscoe Pound. I do not see habeas corpus as a stand-in for all human rights challenges, but only for basic human rights, even as I see habeas corpus as itself necessary for the full protection of all the other human rights. But rather than dwell on the differences between Kutner's and my

---

[4] Roscoe Pound, Preface to Luis Kutner's *World Habeas Corpus*, ibid., p. viii.
[5] Christoff J. M. Safferling, *Toward an International Criminal Procedure*, NY: Oxford University Press, 2001, p. 40.
[6] See also Colin Rogers and Robert Lewis, *Introduction to Police Work*, Cullompton: Wilan Publishing, 2007, p. 239.
[7] See Kutner, *World Habeas Corpus*, Chapter 1.

views, I wish instead to discuss at the beginning of this chapter the ways in which our views converge, especially in seeing how habeas corpus and other Magna Carta legacy rights, understood as *jus cogens* in international law, would indeed advance the goals of equity.

If there are to be human rights understood as international rights, various defects in the UN structure must be corrected. Hans Kelsen said: "Individuals can have international legal rights only if there is an international court before which they can appear as plaintiffs."[8] Recognizing habeas corpus and non-refoulement as *jus cogens* means that these rights will be seen as rights that States cannot derogate from. In protecting habeas corpus and non-refoulement internationally there will be an added layer of protection for all other human rights, and in that sense there is a kind of gap-filling role for a world court of equity.

Since at least the time of Thomas More, equity has been a means for bridging the divide between legality and morality, especially concerning issues of fairness. The Chancery Court was empowered to be the "conscience of the king" in that it could consider cases that had failed to achieve resolution in the common law courts, but where there was a strong case on the grounds of fairness that resolution should be achieved.[9] Insofar as international law is supposed to afford protection against that which "shocks the conscience of the world," it is natural to think of international equity in these terms. International equity concerns the idea that international law should not have gaps. As I have indicated, it may be possible to have global protection of habeas corpus and non-refoulement through domestic or regional courts, but the record on these matters has not been promising in the last few years.

In the next sections I will address two alternatives to the establishment of a new world court of equity, one having to do with a regime of international administrative rules and the other an expansion of already-existing international human rights institutions. I will consider each of these proposals and then end by defending the view that all three of these institutional alternatives could be put on the table at the same time, or at least in some kind of progressive development of these institutions to form a coherent response to the problems I have identified in earlier chapters of this book. My preference, though, is for something like a court of equity, which historically has had more teeth than the other alternatives.

---

[8] Hans Kelsen, *General Theory of Law and State*, Cambridge University Press, 1945, p. 343.
[9] See Joseph Story, *Commentaries on Equity Jurisprudence*, London: Stevens and Haynes, 1884.

II.2 GLOBAL ADMINISTRATIVE LAW

Throughout this book I have argued that the way to begin to solve the infirmity of international law is by developing a world court of equity that would protect the Magna Carta procedural rights that I have here discussed. I here wish to discuss an alternative proposal, concerning a system of global administrative law that moves away from a specifically judicial solution to the problem of gap-filling in international law, especially concerning the fact that many people seem to have simply no protection for internationally recognized rights.[10]

In a seminal article Benedict Kingsbury and colleagues described an emerging model of global administrative law, with a large variety of institutions that contribute to this new global administrative order including:

> globalized interdependence in such fields as security, the conditions on development and financial assistance to developing countries, environmental protection, banking and financial regulation, law enforcement, telecommunications, trade in products and services, intellectual property, labor standards, and cross border movements of populations, including refugees.[11]

The great variety of institutions mentioned by Kingsbury give us a sense of the breadth of the global administrative order that he and his colleagues believe is emerging on the world stage and that could be as significant as other more highly-publicized developments, such as the increasing number of international courts today.

Kingsbury and his colleagues then provide a definition of global administrative law:

> the mechanisms, principles, practices, and supporting social understandings that promote or otherwise affect the accountability of global administrative bodies, in particular by ensuring that they meet adequate standards of transparency, participation, reasoned decision, and legality, and by providing effective review of the rules and decisions they make.[12]

The little-understood area of administrative action is the centerpiece of their concept of this emerging area of international law. The forms of administrative action, they tell us, include: "rulemaking, administrative

---

[10] I am grateful to Kim Rubenstein for pushing me to consider this alternative institution.
[11] Benedict Kingsbury, Nico Krisch, and Richard B. Stewart, "The Emergence of Global Administrative Law," *Law and Contemporary Problems*, Summer/Autumn 2005, vol. 68, p. 16.
[12] Ibid., p. 17.

adjudication between competing interests, and other forms of administrative decision and management." Kingsbury admits that many of the components of global administrative law "operate below the level of highly publicized diplomatic conferences and treaty-making," yet in actuality "they regulate and manage vast sectors of economic and social life through specific decisions and rulemaking."[13]

Let me begin by saying that even on the most optimistic analysis, global administrative law is only emerging, and considered just on its own appears to have significant gaps. So, global administrative law is, like the rest of international law, in need of gap-filling. But put another way, expanding global administrative law might be able to fill some of the gaps that I have identified to exist at the more publicized level of treaties and international courts, just as is often true at the domestic level. So, while I still see the need for a new international court, it is certainly possible that an expanded global administrative law could fill some of the same gaps that a new international court could fill. And, at the very least, in the short run focusing on strengthening global administrative law could aid the project of strengthening the international rule of law until a world court of equity could come on board.

I would also point out that habeas corpus and non-refoulement are sometimes treated in domestic law as an administrative matter.[14] And I have great sympathy for seeing administrative or quasi-administrative matters as very important in the development of the international rule of law. I will rehearse some of the benefits and detriments of such an approach. Administrative law is indeed the great unrecognized avenue for the protection of rights, especially in common law societies, but also in some Continental systems of law. Generally, I do not see this project as necessarily at odds with my proposal for a world court of equity, even though administrative law often sees itself as somewhat antithetical to proper judicial proceedings.

Here we might initially think about the fact that habeas corpus in the US and elsewhere involves both judicial and administrative proceedings. There is certainly no incompatibility between the various ways habeas corpus is protected in the US, although as I argued earlier there is a practical problem in that even with both judicial and administrative

---

[13] Ibid.
[14] See Stephen H. Legomsky, "Refugees, Asylum, and the Rule of Law in the USA," in Susan Kneebone (ed.), *Refugees, Asylum Seekers, and the Rule of Law*, Cambridge University Press, 2009, pp. 122–170.

avenues open habeas corpus still has not closed all of the gaps that have allowed such travesties as Guantanamo Bay to develop. Similarly, the combination of these judicial and administrative remedies did not prevent the abuses in Afghanistan at the Bagram Air Base or in Australia that led to the Christmas Island debacle either. Indeed, this is a reason to think that even more is needed than the current combination of administrative and regional judicial remedies. I will say something about the additional need to have Executive authority as well – although this is not now possible at the international level, at least not to the same extent that it is currently available at the national level. Perhaps one day there will be a world State or at least a world Executive that could play this additional role in the protection of global rights.

I began this work by discussing the infirmity of international law, an infirmity largely perceived to have arisen due to the lack of Executive power at the global level. The creation of a world State is often thought to be the only way that a fully functioning international legal system can be developed. Throughout this book I have cast considerable doubt on that proposition. In looking back to Magna Carta, I argued that the development of a legal system does not need for there first to be a strong Executive branch of an existing State. Indeed, historically what was often the first thing was a set of procedural rules that were gradually protected locally and then increasingly in a broad and uniform manner. For this to happen, perhaps counter-intuitively, a strong Executive was not initially needed. But it is true that eventually such an Executive power seemed to be needed to cure those infirmities that seemed especially resistant to the gradual process of development.

So, let me say just a bit about what sort of Executive power is indeed needed for the proper development of a system of international law. The main thing is the coercive enforcement structure that seems to be needed when there are recalcitrant States that do not wish to go along with the rest of the States and that do not see that their own interests are indeed advanced by a system of international rules. Coercive sanctions are generally not needed since the majority of States, as is also analogously true of the majority of citizens within a State, see that their cooperation and conformity with the rules is so clearly in their own interests. But just as there are outlier citizens, so there are outlier States in the global order who will need the incentive to obey that comes from worry about coercive sanctions. So, while those incentive sanctions are not necessary to achieve quite a lot of conformity, they are sometimes needed to get over the last hurdles.

One of the most intriguing dimensions of global administrative law is that, like its domestic law equivalent, it operates with very subtle forms of coercion. Since international law is indeed infirm at the level of explicit sanctions, this fact is especially important, at least in the short run, as we attempt to fill the gaps in an international system of law which still lacks the strong sanctions that characterize domestic legal systems. I will return to the question of how best to integrate global administrative law with courts and other alternative institutions later in this chapter.

11.3 ENHANCEMENT OF INTERNATIONAL HUMAN RIGHTS INSTITUTIONS

The UN's institutional system has a human rights committee as well as a Human Rights Council (formerly called the Human Rights Commission) that are often overlooked in these debates, largely because their enforcement mechanisms appear, at least on first sight, to be so weak. The former, the Human Rights Committee, is a body created by multi-lateral treaty when the International Covenant on Civil and Political Rights (ICCPR) was formed by its State parties. This Committee monitors compliance with the ICCPR, and issues regular reports on how these rights are being implemented. The latter, the Human Rights Council, is an inter-governmental body within the UN system. The current human rights council was created by the UN General Assembly on March 15, 2006. This group sees its main role to be one of "institution-building" to create ways to respond to human rights crises. These two organizations are often ignored in discussing the kinds of issues I have been highlighting, but it is fair to say that there is much good that has been done here, and much more good that could be done with some emendations to these organizations.

I propose to ask whether it appears that enhanced human rights institutions already in place could be made more effective, especially concerning the protection of procedural rights. Initially, it is perhaps too easy to see the sanctioning power, or its lack, as a major impediment to the effective functioning of the Human Rights Committee and the Human Rights Council that has been recently formed as well. But, as we dig deeper, there is reason to think that these human rights institutions have been somewhat effective and certainly hold out the promise of being more effective in the future.[15]

---

[15] I am grateful to Hilary Charlesworth for urging me to consider this alternative institutional structure.

In a previous chapter I criticized the working of the regional human rights commissions and courts for ineffectiveness. At this point I wish to revisit this issue in terms of the international Human Rights Committee and Council. As with the regional commissions, reports are issued and recommendations are made. But it seems to me that there is more publicity that can be shed on human rights problems by employing these truly international institutions than merely employing regional institutions. In any event, the problems identified in the regional human rights regime can be useful in attempting to discern how enhancements of the current international human rights institutions might render them more effective. And I will also indicate why it is more likely that this enhancement will bear fruit in the international than in the regional context.

One of the things that the Human Rights Council has been most effective at is constructing and nurturing a partnership between civil society and non-governmental organizations (NGOs) to have highly public monitoring of human rights abuses across the globe, especially concerning human rights troublespots. And this is an important consideration in light of the criticisms that Charlesworth and others have made about the focus of formal organizations on public sector problems. NGOs have also been highly effective at monitoring matters in the "private" sector, through funding domestic human rights groups as well as development programs.[16]

Of course, one of the reasons why the Human Rights Committee has not taken up those issues that most concern women is that it is constitutionally designed to focus on the ICCPR, not the International Covenant on Economic, Social, and Cultural Rights (ICESCR). There is a parallel institution that is supposed to monitor compliance with the ICESCR, but it has not had the resources or international attention that the Human Rights Committee has had. Of course, it is relatively easy to say that this should change, and I would be one of the first to lend my support to such an idea. As I have indicated, a focus on global procedural rights does not mean that one focuses only on civil and political rights, although most of my examples have indeed come from that domain. When we shift to thinking of refugee camps instead of formal prisons, then social and economic rights violations come more into view

---

[16] See Anne Marie Devereux, "Selective Universality? Human-rights Accountability of the UN in Post-conflict Operations," in *The Role of International Law in Rebuilding Societies After Conflict*, Brett Bowden, Hilary Charlesworth, and Jeremy Farrall (eds.), Cambridge University Press, 2009, pp. 198–217.

and we can begin to see how procedural rights such as those concerning expanded rights of non-refoulement and habeas corpus would have a strongly positive effect on social and economic rights as well as civil and political rights.

I would follow Henry Shue's important contribution to these debates. Shue argued that we should focus on basic rights, a category of rights that spans the divide between civil and political rights on the one hand and social and economic rights on the other hand.[17] And in this respect, even more than in terms of the substantive basic rights that Shue focuses on, basic procedural rights span the divide between types of rights by focusing on the procedures necessary to protect personal security in all of its forms. Indeed, those who are deprived of procedural rights protection in refugee camps constitute such a large number of detained people in the world that this group should have pride of place in any discussion of global procedural rights, such as the discussion in this book.

Enhancing the existing international human rights institutions will have the effect, as is also true of increased global administrative institutions, of filling gaps in the international system of law. Indeed, there has been very good work carried out already by the Human Rights Committee. One good example concerns *Ng v. Canada*.[18] There the Committee held that Canada had violated the rights of Ng by extraditing him to the US where he faced the reasonably foreseeable possibility of being sentenced to death, in contravention of the ICCPR's prohibition against cruel, inhuman, or degrading treatment or punishment. Such rulings, very much like more straightforward judicial rulings, clearly fill some of the gaps in international law, especially in the area of enforcement of human rights treaty obligations of States. This linkage of human rights and extradition is the kind of linkage that closes gaps and brings us closer to a full-blown international rule of law.

11.4 A PROGRESSIVE DEVELOPMENT OF ALTERNATIVES

In principle, and even in practice, there is nothing wrong with trying all three of these alternatives or of trying some combination of them. Since the idea of yet another international court is probably the most

[17] Henry Shue, *Basic Rights: Subsistence, Affluence, and U.S. Foreign Policy*, Princeton University Press, 1980.
[18] UN Doc. CCPR/C/49/D/469/1991 (1993), 98 ILR 479. See also John Dugard and Christine Van den Wyngaert, "Reconciling Extradition with Human Rights," *The American Journal of International Law*, vol. 92, no. 2, April, 1998, 187–212, especially 191–193.

controversial, it certainly makes sense to start with the other two alternative institutional structures. And the combination of expanding the domain of an already-existing Human Rights Committee and Council is certainly compatible with also aiding in the advancement of the increasing movement toward a global administrative law regime. Indeed, the human rights organizations, which mainly operate by publicizing abuses of rights, could be a good complement to the administrative regimes that often need a bit of added publicity and sanctioning power. Of course, in this respect, eventually adding a court with compulsory jurisdiction would advance the goal of strengthening sanctions even more, and this is why I have earlier supported the idea of a world court of equity. But in the meantime, the combination of the other two alternatives could significantly advance the goal of protecting procedural rights globally that has been the focus of this book.

The fact that a world court of equity with compulsory jurisdiction is at the moment highly controversial is no reason not to work toward its eventual implementation even as one also works to adopt the other two alternative institutional structures. Indeed, working toward the institution of a world court of equity may help advance the other institutional structures by calling attention to the need to do something about the current lack of protection for global procedural rights. In the rhetoric of human rights protection and promotion, any attention given to international procedural rights will be to the good and will not likely work at cross-purposes to the other more easily realizable institutional alternatives.

With these non-court alternatives, it will be harder although not impossible to get the kind of accountability oversight, especially in terms of visibility, that I have suggested is ultimately the key to the international rule of law. Administrative oversight is still oversight, as is true of oversight by the existing Human Rights Committee and Council. And surely it is a better position to be in than without such oversight. Just as the pressure of court oversight offers a paradigmatic incentive to States to remedy rights abuses on their own, so this is also true, although not as strongly so, for the oversight of administrative review or of the Human Rights Council. Oversight can be more or less effective, and the effectiveness does not necessarily depend on the strength of the sanctions that are threatened. Courts will be the best at achieving this goal, but the other institutions discussed above can accomplish this goal as well.

In the progressive development of the international rule of law, the great impediment is getting States to agree to relinquish some of their sovereign prerogative. If we start with relatively unobtrusive oversight and accountability institutional structures, States may be less resistant to go along than if we start with some of the most obtrusive, namely international court oversight and even judicial review with the possibility of veto of Executive decision. Indeed, it may be that the administrative and human rights regime oversight works so well that a world court of equity is never needed. Even if this happy result occurred, I believe it is still important to keep the idea of a world court of equity on the table in order to add one more very strong layer of incentives to those others so as to encourage States to monitor and redress both substantive and procedural rights abuses in their countries.

There are also cost factors to consider. Criminal justice systems are generally quite costly matters, and various States or even a world State may not have the resources to provide oversight for all detentions and incarcerations in the world. This is especially true of jury trials, as I have indicated above in Chapter 10. States, and the community of States, may find it easier to support institutional structures that are less costly than a world court of equity. Since it is not possible to eliminate all unfairness and arbitrariness from these matters, we must think of degrees of protection for those who are detained or incarcerated.[19] And here surely any increase in protection is better than none.

I do not want to end this discussion without stressing yet again that optimally all three approaches should be linked to each other, with a new world court of equity eventually being the cornerstone of protection of procedural rights such as those that I have discussed in this book. The court may be the most controversial but it is my belief that it is also the most likely to bring with it a fully functioning international rule of law. This is only to stress that strong institutions will be needed, even as I also recognize that the practical difficulty of bringing those institutions into play now means that pursuing alternative institutions is also certainly part of the progressive development toward the goal of a fully realized international rule of law.

11.5 DUE PROCESS INSTITUTIONS

Throughout this book I have tried to redirect some of our attention in the discussions of global justice toward procedural issues that normally fly very much below the radar screen in human rights and global justice

[19] See James W. Nickel, *Making Sense of Human Rights*, second edn, Oxford: Blackwell, 2007, pp. 111–112.

discourse. In particular, I have addressed a range of "due process" issues rather than more colorful issues like genocide and crimes against humanity. In treatments of human rights, whether in international human rights documents or in theoretical discussions, it is common to have some discussion of due process rights, but these are typically not given pride of place. And when it is said that certain rights cannot be abridged, even in times of emergency, it is common for due process rights to be suspendable.[20] Indeed, as I said above, the habeas corpus clause of the US Constitution is referred to as "the suspension clause," indicating that it can best be seen as something that can be suspended rather than something that should not be abridged.

The terrorist events in the early part of the twenty-first century have caused the kind of reaction that many would not have thought possible prior to September 11, 2001. In the US, but also in many other parts of the world, people were detained or stripped of their citizenship rights or rendered outlaws merely on the grounds of suspicion of terrorist connections. In Australia, the US, and the UK, for instance, the governments created detention centers that held those who were deemed a threat to security.[21] In some cases those individuals could not be returned to their countries of origin either because those States would not take them back or because their lives would be threatened by such deportations. In many cases the government simply decided to incarcerate these people because of the threat they posed, and since there were no hearings held there was no visibility or accountability for these decisions and no appeals process open to the detainees. As in the US and the UK, these people were kept in detention facilities for indefinite periods of time.

One can certainly imagine a time in the not too distant future where even States like the US, Australia, and the UK will be willing to allow their own courts more oversight over Executive or Legislative decisions in order to avoid succumbing to international oversight. Indeed, there is evidence that this is just what happened in the Bush administration's reluctance to challenge the *Boumedienne* case, and in British Prime Minister Gordon Brown's decision not to challenge the 2008 House of Lord's rejection of his attempt to increase the amount of time that citizens of the UK could be incarcerated without charge. In Australia the calls

---

[20] See James Nickel's very useful discussion of this issue in *Making Sense of Human Rights*, pp. 112–116.

[21] See Susan Kneebone, "Conclusions on the Rule of Law," in *Refugees, Asylum Seekers, and the Rule of Law*, Susan Kneebone (ed.), Cambridge University Press, 2009, pp. 281–309.

for the closing of immigration detention facilities may also have been influenced by such international pressure.[22]

My book has been in large part a response to such recent events. But these recent events have merely been a graphic way to have our attention focused on a problem that has existed for a very long time and that is especially problematic in light of the fast pace of globalization in other domains. I have tried to broaden the issue by discussing it initially in terms of Magna Carta, which is obviously not of recent vintage and not ripped from the front pages of the world's newspapers. And I have also tried to broaden the issue by a conceptual discussion in terms of the category of procedural rights, especially procedural rights in the context of global justice. As I explained at the beginning, the debates about global justice, both in political philosophy and in international law, are often conducted exclusively in terms of substantive rights. But such a focus has led to a piecemeal approach to global justice, rather than an approach that works toward understanding international law in terms of a system of rules, as well as an international rule of law.

As I have indicated, procedural issues do not stir the collective conscience in the way that substantive issues do. It is not easy to mount international campaigns against procedural rights abuses, even those abuses that are on the scale and notoriety of Guantanamo Bay. Institutionally, even more is needed to curb abuses of procedural rights than to curb abuses of substantive rights. This is one reason why I have been pushing the idea of a world court of equity, along with a global administrative set of rules and an enhanced role for the international Human Rights Council. Multiple avenues need to be explored as potential ways to fill in the gaps that have allowed individuals to slip through the cracks and be rendered effectively rightless.

Kingsbury ends his provocative study of international administrative law with these words, which are especially apt to my attention on global procedural justice:

Work on normative issues is likely both to deepen transnational and global democratic theory and to raise challenging questions about its application to specific administrative structures. Normative inquiries will also enrich operational understandings of the place of diversity, equality, and equity in global administrative law.[23]

---

[22] James Massola, "Release Asylum-Seekers 'Within a Year,'" *The Canberra Times*, Tuesday, December 2, 2008, pp. 1, 4.
[23] Kingsbury *et al.*, "The Emergence of Global Administrative Law," 61.

The same things could be said of the other alternative institutions I have explored. Indeed, my stress has been on equity, but equality, especially equality before the international law, and diversity of cultural contexts are also extremely important topics in a general account of how to assess alternative global institutions in terms of global procedural justice.

I see the development of these various international institutional alternatives as advancing what Aristotle called the natural part of justice and what Fuller called the procedural natural law.[24] Many have focused on the need for greater protection of substantive rights in international law, but not enough attention has been given to the equally important area of procedural rights and to the idea that such rights could attain *jus cogens* status along with their better known substantive rights, such as the rights against aggression and genocide.[25]

International law is moving toward becoming a true system of law that is able to protect human rights across the globe, but it is definitely not there yet. Just as the the development of Magna Carta's procedural rights took a long time in England, so the development of international procedural rights will also take a long time globally. It is important to map out the various avenues to traverse to bring international law to the point of becoming a fully mature legal system. Heeding the lessons of Magna Carta provides important sources of guidance. In this book I have pursued that route. Surely there are also other routes that could be pursued. Hopefully others will also offer advice concerning the creation or emendation of international institutions. I next turn to the conflict between security and rights protection as well as to some other concluding thoughts.

---

[24] See the discussion of these views at the beginning of Chapter 4.
[25] See Mark Janis, "The Nature of *Jus Cogens*," *Connecticut Journal of International Law*, vol. 3, 1988, 361.

CHAPTER 12

Global procedural rights and security

In this final chapter I will explore the relationship between procedural rights and security. There is a wide-ranging debate about how best to understand security. Some see it as narrowly focused on keeping States safe from external and internal assaults. There is another group, though, that sees security in a much broader light, in terms of the security of persons, both groups and individuals. Indeed, the UN Charter speaks of a broader conception of security when it links both State sovereignty and human rights to the idea of global security. In what follows I will focus on what has come to be called human security, not merely the security of States, even as I also think that State security is an important topic – one about which I have previously written a volume.[1]

As I indicated at the beginning of Chapter 1, most of the recent literature on global justice and human security in political philosophy has focused on substantive issues, such as claims of economic distributive justice of those in poor countries, or the rights against persecution and genocide. Such rights are extremely important. But, as I have been arguing throughout this book, there is a class of issues that have been given little attention, namely procedural rights such as the right of habeas corpus or non-refoulement at the global level. These rights are arguably just as important for the security of peoples across the globe and yet there is little discussion of them and few effective global institutions that currently consider them. In this chapter I will address this issue in the context of both human and State security in an increasingly interconnected world.

In the first section of this chapter I will rehearse some of the main international documents that have linked human rights with security, paying special attention to the Charter of the UN. In this section I will explain the various meanings of security and will also discuss both its

---

[1] See Larry May, *Aggression and Crimes Against Peace*, NY: Cambridge University Press, 2008.

value and subjects. In the second section I will attempt to respond to various objections to seeing procedural rights as crucial to global security, especially concerning what should happen when security and rights conflict. I will offer a tentative solution to the security/rights conflict by conceptualizing both sides of the conflict in similar terms. In the third section I will explain how habeas corpus and non-refoulement bear on global security. And, finally, I will summarize some of the earlier sections of the book by linking habeas corpus to the other rights of Magna Carta. I will argue that these four Magna Carta legacy rights form a coherent set of rights that could partially constitute a rule of law in the international realm, acting as a bulwark against abridgement of personal security.

12.1 HUMAN RIGHTS, PEACE, AND SECURITY

The Preamble of the Charter of the UN states that the Peoples of the United Nations are determined "to reaffirm faith in fundamental human rights" as well as "to unite our strength to maintain international peace and security." There is no explicit linkage between fundamental human rights on the one hand and peace and security on the other hand. And most of the rest of the Charter continues to talk of peace and security but not much about human rights. Yet it is well recognized today that such a linkage was indeed contemplated by the drafters of the Charter, even if the linkage between these ideas was not well articulated.

One of the best bits of evidence to support the link between human rights and peace or security comes in a hortatory document. The UDHR, adopted by the UN shortly after it was itself established, explicitly links peace with the protection of human rights when it declares: "Whereas recognition of the inherent dignity and of the equal and inalienable rights of all members of the human family is the foundation of freedom, justice, and peace in the world." And since peace and security are linked together throughout the Charter, it appears that human rights protection must also be linked to security. Conceptually, there is both a crucial link and a significant difference between the idea of human rights and the idea of peace and security. I will explore the differences in the final section of this chapter.

Security can be of the person or the State. No one denies that security has very high value, indeed many would say that the value of security is paramount, especially if one does not indicate what kind of security is at issue. Security is indeed a value, but its extent is different for nearly each person or entity subject to it. At one end of the spectrum, security means not being attacked, or at least reducing the risk of attack until it is very low. At the other end of the spectrum, security means being able to flourish without interference, or at least with only a very small risk of interference. What lies in between the ends of this spectrum includes all of the liberties and rights that individuals may be said to have by virtue of our common humanity. Not all forms of security are of equal value or of paramount importance.

Security can be understood in three distinct ways: personal, collective, and national. The *jus ad bellum* and *jus in bello* considerations of the Just War tradition are aimed at each of these ways of understanding security. The *jus in bello* norms are primarily aimed at protecting the personal security of combatants and civilians in armed conflicts. The provisions of The Hague and Geneva Conventions, modeled on these Just War considerations, have become the gold standard of personal security protection during those most insecure of times, namely when war is afoot. The *jus ad bellum* norms are aimed at protecting States from aggression by other States. And the Security Council has been authorized, in Chapters VI and VII of the Charter of the UN, to enforce the norm against aggression. There is also a sense that both sets of norms are aimed at protecting collectivities, especially social groups, from harm. Soldiers are treated as a group for some of the *jus in bello* considerations, as are civilian populations.[2]

There are three subjects in need of security protection in armed conflict: States, especially those that have been unjustly attacked, civilians caught in the crossfire of wars, and combatants, especially those who have been captured. It is clear that atrocities like aggression and genocide harm the international community in that they destabilize security for many of those who are affected: individuals, social groups, and States alike. When NATO decided to send troops into Kosovo, it was because of a concern that the ethnic cleansing campaign in the Balkans had already risked spreading into a wider European problem. The genocide in the Sudan is not merely a horrific humanitarian crisis for the people who are being starved to death; it is also a major factor destabilizing collective security of ethnic peoples and States, as well as individuals, in the region. Atrocities like genocide and aggression can thus be understood in terms of their effects on security: personal, collective, and national. Norms of armed conflict aim to protect each form of security.

---

[2] See my paper "Contingent Pacifism and the Moral Risks of Participation in War," forthcoming.

The UDHR, in Article 3, says: "Everyone shall have the right to life, liberty, and the security of persons." The ICCPR sought to provide specificity to the provisions of the UDHR. Of special note are Article 9's provision against "arbitrary arrest or detention" and Article 13's provision against removal of an alien without review by "competent authority." So, in one sense the rights that I have discussed throughout this book have already been recognized as important human rights. And one could ask why I spent so much time, especially in the previous chapter, discussing new international institutional structures when the extant system of international institutions already recognizes what I have been advocating.

As we have seen, the problem is that the current international institutional regime has been largely ineffective at the level of procedural rights. In particular, the specific provisions having to do with the treatment of those who are incarcerated, or who are in detention centers and camps, have not been afforded the highest standing, of being *jus cogens* or non-derogable. As a result, the procedural rights I have been discussing are thought to be abridgeable, especially when security interests of a given State are at issue. And there are no international institutions, on the order of the ICC, where someone can appeal when denied these procedural rights. As a result, these rights have not been properly recognized or protected internationally. Yet these rights are crucial for personal security.

This book is an attempt to call attention to a new direction in security having to do with norms of armed conflict. The first set of issues comes under the label of what I have called "global procedural justice." Here I would again mention two global procedural rights that need to be protected to secure individuals and populations: habeas corpus and non-refoulement. Habeas corpus rights, including the right not to be arbitrarily incarcerated, and non-refoulement rights, including the right not to be deported to a State where one's life will be put in jeopardy, are the cornerstones of procedural rights that protect security of individuals as well as those of groups. The latter claim is most plausible concerning members of groups that are currently being persecuted in a given State. Such procedural rights take on added importance during situations of non-traditional armed conflict, such as the US's war on terrorism, where special detention facilities were established in Guantanamo Bay, Cuba and Bagram Air Base in Afghanistan. Contrary to current international instruments, the US has failed to provide hearings and has also employed extraordinary rendition by returning prisoners back to States that will torture them.

Habeas corpus and non-refoulement are basic security rights but they are also primarily procedural rather than substantive in that they set limits on a process, imprisonment in the case of habeas corpus and deportation or immigration in the case of non-refoulement. For habeas corpus, the limit is that there must be a publicly declared charge against the prisoner, and the imprisonment must be for a definite and relatively short period of time until a preliminary trial is held. For non-refoulement, the limit is that no one should be deported to a State where it is likely that the prisoner will be put in serious jeopardy of harm. These rights are procedural and negative, and are at least as important as substantive and positive rights. A new global focus on such procedural matters is needed but is currently lacking.

As I have argued throughout this book, new global institutions should be established to guarantee basic procedural rights. Not only is there a significant risk that denial of these rights will adversely affect individuals and be used to persecute disfavored groups, but since human rights abuses can easily spread across borders, this is also a matter of security for States. So, there are good self-interested reasons for States to accept the greater protections of human rights I have indicated here. It is time for a serious discussion of a new institutional regime to protect security in light of the problems I have been addressing.

12.2 CONFLICTS BETWEEN SECURITY AND RIGHTS

Perhaps the best example of where there is a disparity between the protection of rights, especially between procedural rights such as habeas corpus and non-refoulement on the one hand and threats to security on the other hand, is in the fight against terrorism in the US. The US has consistently claimed that it is not possible to protect the rights of detainees and at the same time protect national security. I do not agree with the position of the US government on this issue, but I agree that there is a serious problem about how to afford maximal personal security rights protection to those who are accused of being a security threat to a State.

Let us begin by considering the standard rights that defendants have during trials and how the exercise of such rights might conflict with security interests of the State where the trial is occurring. Trial by jury is often thought to be problematic when considering the testimony of those who have been incarcerated, especially when it is thought that they have information that if conveyed could pose security threats. Once such testimony has occurred, it is difficult to control its dissemination if jurors are merely selected randomly from the population and not required to be screened for security clearance. Indeed, even letting defense attorneys hear this evidence without requiring that they also get security clearance could pose a serious national security problem. And even if the jury and defense counsel are screened, it will be nearly impossible to put the defendant through security clearance, leaving open the possibility that sensitive information could be passed from the defendant to acquaintances during or after the trial takes place.

Yet, if the defendant is denied representation by counsel of his or her choosing, serious rights violations have occurred. And if the defendant himself or herself is not allowed to hear certain testimony or to examine certain evidence, the very ability for there to be a fair trial is seriously undermined. The right to confront one's accuser, and, by implication, the evidence presented by one's accuser, is a fundamental procedural trial right that butts up against such national security concerns. Of course, one can try to challenge the idea that the mere dissemination of information that could be learned at trial presents a serious risk to national security. And I would not object to taking such a critical position. But even the most skeptical must acknowledge the possibility that the expression of procedural trial rights could contribute to a serious security problem.

One question to ask though is whether adjudicating the conflict between security and rights should lead to a full-throated approval of a "balancing" approach. As I indicated in Chapter 9, a recent case before the European Court of Human Rights, *Saadi v. Italy*, said that States were not permitted "to balance the security threat the person poses" against the basic rights of the person.[3] The UK had argued in an earlier case, and Italy argued in the current case, that it was appropriate to balance its security interests against these rights issues. And what that amounted to was the overriding of basic procedural rights whenever national security seemed threatened by the protection of these rights. Both claims were strongly rejected by the European Court of Human Rights. But the various courts to consider this issue have allowed that the security issues of States are relevant considerations, but not necessarily ones that can be straightforwardly balanced as if they were equal to considerations of fundamental procedural rights.

The *Saadi* case concerned a young man convicted of conspiracy to terrorism. He was sentenced to four years in prison, at the end of which he

[3] See Ashley Deeks, "*Saadi v. Italy*: ILM Introductory Note," 47 ILM 542 (2008), reprinted in *Newsletter of the American Society of International Law*, July/September 2008, p. 8.

was to be deported to Tunisia. Saadi claimed that if he were deported, there was a strong likelihood that he would be tortured, and various NGOs supported this contention. Italy cited national security concerns and appealed for an emergency exception to the application of Article 3 of the European Convention for the Protection of Human Rights and Fundamental Freedoms. The Court held that:

Article 3, which prohibits in absolute terms torture and inhuman or degrading treatment of punishment, enshrines one of the fundamental values of a democratic society. Unlike most of the substantive clauses of the Convention and its Protocols Nos. 1 and 4, Article 3 makes no provision for exceptions or derogations from it is permissible under Article 15, even in the event of a public emergency threatening the life of the nation ... the nature of the offence allegedly committed by the applicant is therefore irrelevant for the purposes of Article 3.[4]

In recognizing the *jus cogens* nature of non-refoulement, the Court ruled out any compromise on grounds of security. Even if there was a clear conflict between fundamental rights and security, in this case the Court held that security must give way.

In my view, though, the cases of straightforward conflict between rights protection and security will be few and far between. When the conflicts do arise, the benefit of the doubt should go to the right holder, since when the individual is made less secure there is a diminishment of the aggregate security of the larger society. If rights are claimed to be offset by a mere *risk* of loss of security to the larger society, we must dig deeper and discover what the extent and likelihood of that risk to society is. If it is determined that the risk to society should outweigh the risk to the individual person, then it must be clear that this is an exceptional case and not one that changes the general balance between State and personal security. And most of all, it must not be allowed that a State like the US could use the threat to national security as a mere pretext to detain individuals for lengthy periods of time, long after the strong threat to State security has passed, and to deprive them of habeas corpus appeal to challenge such incarceration.

The other example I have spent time considering involves the right of non-refoulement. It may be very difficult indeed to find a State to take a detainee who the home State believes constitutes a continuing threat, merely by one's presence in that State. And here there seem to be only

---

[4] *Saadi v. Italy*, Application no. 37201/06, European Court of Human Rights, judgment of 28 February 2008, para. 127.

two choices: deport the person to a State that is highly likely to mistreat him or her, or submit the person to open-ended detention even though there has been no judicial decision that the person indeed deserves punishment through incarceration. It seems that no matter what is done to protect security, some rights of the detainee will be abrogated, and these rights will be of the most fundamental sort, including jeopardizing the security interests of the persons to be deported. Collective detention in such cases, especially if the detention facility is horrible, as is true of nearly all refugee camps, makes the solving of this problem of considerable urgency.

Again, I favor a system that puts the benefit of the doubt on the side of the person to be deported. Deporting a person is to send the person outside a State's jurisdiction and control. The State that does the deporting has a responsibility to make sure that the person deported is not likely to be harmed by the host State since, in handing over the person, the home State is ceasing to protect the human rights of that person and remains responsible for him or her until another State secures those rights. David Miller has defended such ascriptions of national responsibilities most recently in his book *National Responsibility and Global Justice.*[5] He starts Chapter 5 of that work by saying "In everyday political discourse, we often make judgments that seem to involve holding nations responsible for their actions, or for the consequences that follow from those actions."[6] As Miller rightly says, "Often when states are held responsible for the outcomes they produce, they are being judged as agents of the people they are supposed to serve."[7]

One way to respond to these problems concerning habeas corpus or non-refoulement is to articulate an emergency exception to even fundamental procedural rights.[8] But if we are to pursue this strategy, I would propose that we also consider, at the same time, exceptions to the assumed priority of security as well, so that we have a kind of compromise achieved where neither rights nor security should be unduly sacrificed for the other. Such an arrangement – let us call it the security/rights compromise – is premised on the idea that rights can really only be protected when there is a modicum of security, and that security only has value when it is in the service of rights protection.

[5] David Miller, *National Responsibilities and Global Justice*, NY: Oxford University Press, 2007, Chapter 5.
[6] Ibid., p. 111.   [7] Ibid.
[8] See Michael Walzer, "Emergency Ethics," in his book *Arguing About War*, New Haven, CT: Yale University Press, 2004, pp. 33–50.

The security/rights compromise can also be characterized not in compromise terms if we take seriously the interdependent relationship between security and rights. Indeed, there is a sense that the most important considerations of security and of rights have to do with method and procedure. So, as we search for an appropriate adjusted relationship between rights and security in emergency situations, we should focus on the correct methods and procedures for dealing with people and problems. And here the common denominator is that the emergency regime should itself be one that is fair in that the methods and procedures of the emergency regime are ones that people from all perspectives will find acceptable.

Emergency situations, like most other hard cases, make for bad rules. But this is not to say that we should avoid discussing them – just that we should not radically alter our original conceptualizations in order to accommodate them. This is an aspect of fairness that seems to elude government officials in times of crisis. Government officials often use emergency situations to reframe the relationship between security and rights in their desired direction long after the crisis is over. Such maneuvers are unfair in that they exploit the crisis in ways that readjust the security/rights divide initially portrayed as a one-time response to an emergency crisis in ways that the overall population would not find acceptable once the crisis was over. Indeed, such rights violations are violations of equity.

In the recently decided case of *Boumediene v. Bush*, Justice Kennedy, writing for the US Supreme Court, discusses the role of the historical doctrine of habeas corpus I have outlined: "Remote in time it may be, irrelevant to the present it is not."[9] Kennedy cites the case of *Schlup v. Delo* as holding that habeas corpus "is at its core an equitable remedy."[10] As I have indicated in previous chapters, equitable considerations have played an important, if controversial, role in habeas corpus proceedings in the US. Consider the circumstance addressed in the *Boumediene* case where new potentially exculpatory evidence arises after a trial has occurred. In *Boumediene*, the Court declared:

There is evidence from 19th century American sources indicating that, even in States that accorded strong res judicata effect to prior adjudications, habeas corpus courts in this country routinely allowed prisoners to introduce exculpatory evidence that was either unknown or unavailable to the prisoner.[11]

---

[9] *Boumediene v. Bush*, 128 S. Ct. 2229, 2277 (2008).
[10] Ibid. at 2267, citing *Schlup v. Delo*, 513 U.S. 298, 319 (1995). [11] Ibid. at 2267.

While controversial in some respects, *Boumediene* affirms this doctrine today:

> If a detainee can present reasonably available evidence demonstrating there is no basis for his continued detention, he must have the opportunity to present this evidence to a habeas corpus court ... The role of an Article III court in the exercise of its habeas corpus function cannot be circumscribed in this manner.[12]

As the Court recognized, these considerations make habeas corpus an equitable remedy.

The habeas corpus court, seen as an equity court, acts as the conscience of the republic by making sure, in these circumstances for instance, that no innocent prisoner remains incarcerated. Another way to think about it is that, as fundamental law, habeas corpus and related rights bring basic moral considerations into the legal system. And just as the foundation is not always part of the structure itself, so habeas is equitable in that it is fundamental to but not necessarily a proper part of the legal system itself. As I have argued, this gives us the conceptual space to see equity as a bridge between morality and law.

Seeing habeas corpus as an equitable remedy also allows us to understand how such a simple proceeding could constitute a challenge to the legitimacy of an action by a properly authorized Executive decision-making body. Justice Kennedy said, "Within the Constitution's separation-of-powers structure, few exercises of judicial power are as legitimate or as necessary as the responsibility to hear challenges to the authority of the Executive to imprison a person."[13] Just as the old courts of equity (as the Chancellor's Court) acted to overturn abuse in either the common law or king's courts, so habeas corpus is understood today to have the same equitable function. And this is to say that habeas corpus brings in a certain set of basic moral considerations into a legal system. It also allows for equity to be a gap-filler for situations where the law is silent or where the law as applied would be unfair, and hence would cause law and justice to separate. Considerations of national security should not be allowed to trump considerations of the conscience of the people.

12.3 LINKING THE RIGHTS OF MAGNA CARTA

The procedural rights embedded in Chapter 29 (39) of Magna Carta all have roughly the same rationale, namely the principle of visibleness. The right to habeas corpus is meant to give to the detainee the right to

---

[12] Ibid. at 2273. See also Larry May and Nancy Viner, "Actual Innocence and Manifest Injustice," *St. Louis University Law Journal*, vol. 49, no. 2, 2004, 481–497.   [13] *Boumediene* at 2277.

challenge his or her incarceration by being brought into the light of day where the charges against him or her can be made public and challenged. The prohibition against arbitrary exile or outlawry is normatively grounded in the idea that a person's other rights cannot be secure if he or she can be rendered invisible by being sent overseas or sent outside of the visible protection of the courts. The right to trial by jury is not as easily seen as falling under the principle of visibleness, because in part it is not merely a procedural right in any event. But even this right has to do with being brought before one's peers and made visible to the jury, rather than in a possibly semi-secret proceeding of jurists. Jury trials have historically functioned, among other things, as a protection against what Blackstone saw as a great scourge, the arbitrary treatment by magistrates.

If one can be secreted away in prison or in rendition, Blackstone is surely right to say that none of one's rights are secure. I have tried to indicate why the minimal sense of habeas corpus is so important, especially for the security of persons. I have also argued that a somewhat expanded idea of habeas corpus, which included minimal judicial review and due process considerations, was even more significant for the security of people, especially in times of emergency such as when there have been terrorist attacks against a given State. And I have also argued that the other rights that I have extracted from Magna Carta can be similarly defended, despite the fact that the right to trial by jury remains highly controversial in the international sector.

The idea is that the Magna Carta legacy procedural rights all protect people from being arbitrarily deprived of any of their basic substantive rights. As I said, even the minimalist understanding of habeas corpus gives some significant protection to those who are in prison or otherwise detained. Non-refoulement protects individuals against being arbitrarily deported or otherwise exiled in cases where their life or liberty is likely to be jeopardized. The right to be subject to international law, or not to be rendered an international outlaw, obviously protects against arbitrary deprivation of one's rights, even one's human rights insofar as one's human rights are primarily protected by States. The right to trial by jury is a more subtle protection against arbitrariness. The idea is that a group of random citizens is much less likely to be corrupt than is a single judge, or even a small set of judges, drawn from the elite realm of the society.

There is a kind of descending order to the four rights I have extracted from Magna Carta. The most uncontroversial is the right of habeas corpus, at least in its minimalist form articulated by Bracton that I discussed in Chapter 5. If we then add a rudimentary idea of due process to habeas corpus, it is still highly likely to meet with assent from the vast majority of people in the world. The right of non-refoulement is a bit more controversial since it is so closely linked to the prerogative of States to control their borders. But again there is a less controversial version of this right that would allow for exceptional cases where national security is at risk. The expanded notion of non-refoulement is even more controversial and for the same reasons, but it is still something that seems at the moment at least to have widespread support, especially in the international condemnation of the extremes to which the US government was willing to put its doctrine of extraordinary rendition. The right not to be rendered an outlaw or Stateless person is more controversial than the other rights since it really does set the beginnings of a global legal order in ways that the other rights do not. And, finally, the right to trial by jury, as we briefly saw in Chapter 10, is far and away the most controversial on the international plane, yet it is nonetheless interesting how uncontroversial such a right in criminal proceedings is in many domestic settings in large parts of the world, and in any event there are more and less controversial ways to implement this right, as we have seen.

The four procedural rights in question form a set of procedural rights that partially constitutes a rule of law. In all four cases, officials who would abuse their power are forced to follow procedures that will expose possible abuse to the light of day and to public scrutiny. This is one of the most rudimentary, and also highly effective, forms of oversight and accountability. Indeed, the very idea of being held to account presumes that the person who is placed to do this is not himself or herself subject to abuse this power. This is where, in my view, trial by a jury of one's peers connects in such significant ways with the other three Magna Carta legacy rights. A public trial by a jury of one's peers is in many ways the epitome of accountability, especially when it is the leaders of the State who can find themselves in the dock.

For all four Magna Carta legacy rights, what matters is that a process is followed. In the seemingly innocuous following of this process, the substantive rights of the person in question stand a much greater likelihood of being protected. And in a system of law where such important rights-protecting procedures are adhered to, it is also much more likely to be a system of laws that has priority over the whim and abuse of individual leaders. This is just what it means to have a rule of law.[14] When the whim of leaders can be in effect overturned by a jury of one's peers, and when the unfairness and arbitrariness of unchecked governors is made public, progress is made of the sort that would allow for a truly robust system of law to emerge. When this occurs at the international level, then it will no longer be clear that international law is infirm in the way that H. L. A. Hart worried about fifty years ago.[15] And it reminds us of how important procedural matters are even for, and perhaps especially for, "natural law" considerations.[16]

Due process considerations should be at the forefront of discussions of global justice today. As in the various cases I have highlighted, such as Guantanamo, Bagram, and Christmas Island, if there are gaps in international law, there will be places where there is no justice for those who are arbitrarily detained. And in the end, if people can be arbitrarily detained, none of their rights are secure and it is as if these people had lost even their human rights. Contrary to what seems to be true of the name "human" rights, at least minimal procedural protection is needed for anyone to have these human rights effectively protected.

Here I should once again underline the way that procedural rights are primarily guarantors of a certain status, even as they are also very important for protecting specific liberties. The idea that there are human rights is grounded in the idea that being human, or at least being recognized as human, carries with it the idea that every human person is to be treated with at least a minimum of respect for who he or she is. Whether we characterize this status in terms of basic dignity or in terms of being "citizens" of the world, the core idea is roughly the same. The key status concerns a person's right to be subject to an international legal regime. Of course, the status of being human also carries with it significant obligations and responsibilities.[17] I have argued that international law concerns the status rights of humans and relatedly I have indicated that more attention needs to be paid to procedural rights than is currently on offer.

Twenty-five hundred years ago Plato made this point in *The Republic.* In Book Two, he discusses the Ring of Gyges, where the motivation to be

---

[14] For more on this important topic, see Brian Z. Tamanaha, *On the Rule of Law: History, Politics, Theory,* NY: Cambridge University Press, 2004.

[15] H. L. A. Hart, *The Concept of Law,* Oxford: Clarendon, 1961; see especially the final chapter.

[16] Lon Fuller, *The Morality of Law,* New Haven, CT: Yale University Press, 1964, especially Chapter 2.

[17] See Larry May, *Sharing Responsibility,* University of Chicago Press, 1992. See also Larry May, "Collective Inaction and Shared Responsibility," *Nous,* vol. 24, no. 2, April 1990, pp. 169–177.

just is said to turn on whether one is "put to the proof" in terms of "the fear of infamy." To be clothed in justice, it cannot be that one can escape by becoming invisible.[18] The seemingly innocuous set of Magna Carta legacy rights is crucial for global security rights, putting those who would abuse such basic rights "to the proof." I hope this book will provide the theoretical framework to advance the development of global fairness and the international rule of law.

---

[18] Plato, *The Republic*, Book II, Jowett translation.

Bibliography

Ake, Claude. "The African Context of Human Rights," *Africa Today*, vol. 34, no. 142, 1987, 5–13, reprinted in *Applied Ethics: A Multicultural Approach*, Larry May, Shari Collins-Chobanian, and Kai Wong (eds.), fourth edn, Englewood Cliffs, NJ: Prentice Hall, 2006, pp. 111–116.

Alexander, Larry. "Are Procedural Rights Derivative Substantive Rights?" *Law and Philosophy*, vol. 17, no. 1, January 1998, 19–42.

Amnesty International Report on United States Immigration Detentions (2009), reported in *International Law in Brief*, ASIL, April 17, 2009, pp. 2–3.

An-Na'im, Abdullahi Ahmed. "Islam, Islamic Law, and the Dilemma of Cultural Legitimacy for Universal Human Rights," in *Asian Perspectives on Human Rights*, Claude E. Welch and Virginia Leary (eds.), Boulder, CO: Westview Press, 1990, reprinted in *Applied Ethics: A Multicultural Approach*, Larry May, Shari Collins-Chobanian, and Kai Wong (eds.), fourth edn, Englewood Cliffs, NJ: Prentice Hall, 2006, pp. 101–110.

Arendt, Hannah. *The Human Condition*, University of Chicago Press.

Aristotle, *Nicomachean Ethics*, Terence Irwin (trans.), second edition, Indianapolis, IN: Hackett Publishing, 1999.

Bayles, Michael D. *Procedural Justice*, Dordrecht: Kluwer Academic Publishers, 1990.

Bell, Daniel A. *East Meets West*, Cambridge University Press, 1999, reprinted in *Applied Ethics: A Multicultural Approach*, Larry May, Shari Collins-Chobanian, and Kai Wong (eds.), fourth edn, Englewood Cliffs, NJ: Prentice Hall, 2006, pp. 117–132.

Blackstone, William. *Commentaries on the Laws of England* (1765), University of Chicago Press, 1979, vol. I.

Borelli, Silvia. "Casting Light on the Legal Black Hole: International Law and Detentions Abroad in the 'War on Terror,'" *International Review of the Red Cross*, vol. 87, no. 857, March 2005, 39–86.

Boseley, Sarah. "Britain is Criticized for Deporting HIV Patients," *The Guardian*, Monday, December 1, 2008, p. 1.

Bracton, *De Legibus et Consuetudinibus Angliae* (London: Longmans, 1883), Sir Travis Twiss (ed.), quoted in William F. Duker, *A Constitutional History of Habeas Corpus*, Westport, CT: Greenwood Press, 1980.

Caney, Simon. *Justice Beyond Borders*, Oxford University Press, 2005.

Chan, Joseph. "A Confucian Perspective on Human Rights for Contemporary China," in *The East Asian Challenge for Human Rights*, Joanne R. Bauer (ed.), reprinted in *Applied Ethics: A Multicultural Approach*, Larry May, Shari Collins-Chobanian, and Kai Wong (ed.), fourth edn, Englewood Cliffs, NJ: Prentice Hall, 2006, pp. 117–132.

Charlesworth, Hilary and Christine Chinkin, "The Gender of *Jus Cogens*," *Human Rights Quarterly*, vol. 15, 1993, 63–76, reprinted in *Philosophy of Law: Classic and Contemporary Readings*, Larry May and Jeff Brown (eds.), Oxford: Wiley/Blackwell, 2010, pp. 610–619.

Christiano, Thomas. "Debate: Estlund on Democratic Authority," *The Journal of Political Philosophy*, vol. 17, no. 2, 2009, 228–240.

Clark, David and Gerard McCoy. *Habeas Corpus: Australia, New Zealand, The South Pacific*, Sydney: The Federation Press, 2000.

Commentary on Geneva Convention IV, Jean S. Pictet (ed.), Geneva: International Committee for the Red Cross, 1958.

Cook, Walter Wheeler. "'Substance' and 'Procedure' in the Conflict of Laws," *Yale Law Journal*, vol. 42, 1933, 333–357.

Cooper, Jeremy. "Poverty and Constitutional Justice: The Indian Experience," *Mercer Law Review*, vol. 44, 1993, 611–635, reprinted in *Philosophy of Law: Classic and Contemporary Readings*, Larry May and Jeff Brown (eds.), Oxford: Wiley/Blackwell, 2010, pp. 569–584.

Convention Relating to the Status of Refugees (1951), Article I.A(2).

Criddle, Evan J. and Evan Fox-Decent, "A Fiduciary Theory of Jus Cogens," *Yale Journal of International Law*, vol. 34, Summer 2009, 331–387.

Dan-Cohen, Meier. "Decision Rules and Conduct Rules: On Acoustic Separation in Criminal Law," *Harvard Law Review*, vol. 97, 1984, 625–677.

Darcy, Shane. *Collective Responsibility and Accountability under International Law*, Leiden: Transnational Publishers, 2007.

Deeks, Ashley. "*Saadi v. Italy*: ILM Introductory Note," 47 ILM 542 (2008), reprinted in *Newsletter of the American Society of International Law*, July/September 2008, p. 8.

Devereux, Anne Marie. "Selective Universality? Human-rights Accountability of the UN in Post-conflict Operations," in Brett Bowden, Hilary Charlesworth, and Jeremy Farrall (eds.), *The Role of International Law in Rebuilding Societies After Conflict*, Cambridge University Press, 2009, pp. 198–217.

Dobson, R. B. and John Taylor, *The Rymes of Robin Hood: An Introduction to the English Outlaw*, London: Sutton Publishing, 1977.

Drumbl, Mark. *Atrocity, Punishment, and International Law*, NY: Cambridge University Press, 2007.

Dugard, John and Christine Van den Wyngaert. "Reconciling Extradition with Human Rights," *The American Journal of International Law*, vol. 92, no. 2, April 1998, 187–212.

Dworkin, Ronald. *Law's Empire*, Cambridge, MA: Harvard University Press, 1986.

"The Model of Rules I," *Taking Rights Seriously*, London: Duckworth, 1977.

Estlund, David. "Debate: On Christiano's *The Constitution of Equality*," *The Journal of Political Philosophy*, vol. 17, no. 2, 2009, 241–252.

Democratic Authority: A Philosophical Framework, Princeton University Press, 2007.

Fawcett, J. E. S. *The Application of the European Convention on Human Rights*, NY: Oxford University Press, 1987.

Feinberg, Joel. "The Nature and Value of Rights," *The Journal of Value Inquiry*, 1970, 243–260.

Feller, Erika, Volker Turk and Frances Nicholson. *Refugee Protection in International Law*, NY: Cambridge University Press, 2003.

Franck, Thomas M. *Fairness in International Law and Institutions*, NY: Oxford University Press, 1995.

Freeman, Mark. *Truth Commissions and Procedural Fairness*, NY: Cambridge University Press, 2006.

Fuller, Lon L. *The Morality of Law*, New Haven, CT: Yale University Press, 1962.

"Positivism and Fidelity to Law: A Reply to Professor Hart," *Harvard Law Review*, vol. 71, 1958, 630–672.

Gardner, James. "Community Fines and Collective Responsibility," *American Journal of International Law*, vol. 11, no. 3, 1917, 511–537.

Geldart, W. M. *Elements of English Law*, London: Thornton Butterworth, 1933 [1911].

Gibney, Matthew J. "'A Thousand Little Guantanamos': Western States and Measures to Prevent the Arrival of Refugees," in *Displacement, Asylum, and Migration*, Kate E. Tunstall (ed.), Oxford University Press, 2006, pp. 139–169.

Gough, J. W. *Fundamental Law in English History*, Oxford University Press, 1955.

Grenfel, Laura. "Legal Pluralism and the Challenge of Building the Rule of Law in Post-Conflict States: A Case Study of Timor Leste," in *The Role of International Societies After Conflict*, Brett Bowden, Hilary Charlesworth, and Jeremy Farrall (eds.), Cambridge University Press, 2009, pp. 157–176.

Gross, Michael. *Moral Dilemmas of Modern War: Torture, Assassination, and Blackmail in an Age of Asymmetric Conflict*, NY: Cambridge University Press, 2010.

Gross, Oren and Fionnuala Ni Aolain, *Law in Times of Crisis: Emergency Powers in Theory and Practice*, NY: Cambridge University Press, 2006.

Grotius, Hugo. *De Jure Belli Ac Pacis (On the Law of War and Peace) (1625)*, Francis W. Kelsey (trans.), Oxford: Clarendon Press, 1925.

Haggenmacher, Peter. "Grotius and Gentili," in *Hugo Grotius and International Relations*, Hedley Bull, Benedict Kingsbury, and Adam Roberts (eds.), Oxford University Press, 1990.

Hannikainen, Lauri. *Peremptory Norms (Jus Cogens) in International Law*, Helsinki: Finnish Lawyers Publishing Company, 1988.

Hart, H. L. A. *The Concept of Law*, Oxford University Press, 1984 [1960].

"Positivism and the Separation of Law and Morals," *Harvard Law Review*, vol. 71, 1958, 593–629.

"Problems of the Philosophy of Law," in *The Encyclopedia of Philosophy*, Paul Edwards (ed.), NY: Macmillan Publishing, 1967, vol. 6, pp. 264–276.

Hathaway, James. "Forced Migration Studies: Could We Agree to Just Date?" *Journal of Refugee Studies*, vol. 20, 2007, 349–369.

The Rights of Refugees under International Law, Cambridge University Press, 2005.

Hertz, Randy and James S. Liebman. *Federal Habeas Corpus Practice and Procedure*, Charlottesville: Lexis Law Publishing, 1998, fourth edn 2001.

Hill, Michael and David Winkler. "Juries: How Do They Work? Do We Want Them?" *Criminal Law Forum*, vol. 11, no. 4, 2000, 397–443.

Hobbes, Thomas. *Leviathan* (1651), Richard Tuck (ed.), NY: Cambridge University Press, 1996.

Hobsbawm, E. J. *Bandits*, London: Pelican Books, 1972 [1969].

Howard, A. E. Dick. *Magna Carta: Text and Commentary*, Charlottesville: University of Virginia Press, 1998 [1964].

Inada, Kenneth K. "A Buddhist Response to the Nature of Human Rights," in *Asian Perspectives on Human Rights*, Claude E. Welch and Virginia Leary (eds.), Boulder, CO: Westview Press, 1990, reprinted in *Applied Ethics: A Multicultural Approach*, Larry May, Shari Collins-Chobanian, and Kai Wong (eds.), fourth edn, Englewood Cliffs, NJ: Prentice Hall, 2006, pp. 133–142.

International Law Association, declaration of 1921.

International Military Tribunal (Nuremberg) Judgment and Sentences October 1, 1946.

Jacobs, Francis and Robin White. *The European Convention on Human Rights*, third edition edited by Clare Ovey and Robin White, NY: Oxford University Press, 2002.

Janis, Mark. "The Nature of *Jus Cogens*," *Connecticut Journal of International Law*, vol. 3, 1988, 359–363, reprinted in *Philosophy of Law: Classic and Contemporary Readings*, Larry May and Jeff Brown (eds.), Oxford: Wiley/Blackwell, 2010, pp. 184–186.

Kelsen, Hans. *General Theory of Law and State*, Cambridge University Press, 1945.

Kemp, Kenneth W. "Punishment as Just Cause for War," *Public Affairs Quarterly*, vol. 10, no. 4, October 1996, 335–353.

Kingsbury, Benedict, Nico Krisch, and Richard B. Stewart. "The Emergence of Global Administrative Law," *Law and Contemporary Problems*, vol. 68, Summer/Autumn 2005, 15–61.

Kneebone, Susan. "Conclusions on the Rule of Law," in *Refugees, Asylum Seekers, and the Rule of Law*, Susan Kneebone (ed.), Cambridge University Press, 2009, pp. 281–309.

Kneebone, Susan (ed.). *Refugees, Asylum Seekers, and the Rule of Law*, Cambridge University Press, 2009.

Koskenniemi, Martti. *The Gentle Civilizer of Nations: The Rise and Fall of International Law 1870–1960*, Cambridge University Press, 2001.

Kramer, Larry. *The People Themselves*, NY: Oxford University Press, 2004.

Kutner, Luis. *World Habeas Corpus*, Dobbs Ferry, NY: Oceana Publications, 1962.

Kutz, Christopher. "On Visibility in International Criminal Law," in *The Hart-Fuller Debate in the Twenty-First Century*, Peter Cane (ed.), Oxford: Hart Publishing, 2010, pp. 97–105.

Lane, Melissa. "Response to Matthew J. Gibney, 'A Thousand Little Guantanamos,'" in *Displacement, Asylum, and Displacement*, Kate E. Tunstall (ed.), Oxford University Press, 2006, pp. 170–175.

Langford, Ian. "*Fair Trial*: The History of an Idea," *Journal of Human Rights*, vol. 8, no. 1, January–March 2009, 37–52.

Lauterpacht, Elihu and Daniel Bethlehem, "The Scope and Content of the Principle of Non-refoulement: Opinion," in *Refugee Protection in International Law*, Erika Feller, Volker Turk, and Frances Nicholson (eds.), NY: Cambridge University Press, 2003, pp. 87–181.

Lauterpacht, Hersch. *The Development of International Law by the International Court*, Oxford University Press, 1958.

Law Reform Commission, Report 1 (1966) – Application for Writs of Habeas Corpus and Procedure to be Adopted, September 26, 1966.

Legomsky, Stephen H. "Refugees, Asylum, and the Rule of Law in the USA," in *Refugees, Asylum Seekers, and the Rule of Law*, Susan Kneebone (ed.), Cambridge University Press, 2009, pp. 122–170.

Lieber Code, Instructions for the Government of the Armies of the United States in the Field, General Orders No. 100 (1863).

McKechnie, William Sharp. *Magna Carta: A Commentary on the Great Charter of King John*, Glasgow: John Maclehose and Sons, 1914.

Maine, Henry. *Dissertations on Early Law and Custom*, NY: Henry Holt and Company, 1886.

Maitland, Frederick W. *The Forms of Action at Common Law*, Cambridge University Press, 1971 [1909].

Massola, James. "Release Asylum-Seekers 'Within a Year,'" *The Canberra Times*, Tuesday, December 2, 2008, pp. 1, 4.

May, Larry. *Aggression and Crimes Against Peace*, NY: Cambridge University Press, 2008.

  "Collective Inaction and Shared Responsibility," *Nous*, vol. 24, no. 2, April 1990, 169–177.

  "Contingent Pacifism and the Moral Risks of Participation in War," forthcoming.

  Crimes Against Humanity: A Normative Account, NY: Cambridge University Press, 2005.

  Genocide: A Normative Account, NY: Cambridge University Press, 2010.

  "International Criminal Law and the Inner Morality of Law," in *The Hart-Fuller Debate in the Twenty-First Century*, Peter Cane (ed.), Oxford: Hart Publishing, 2010, pp. 79–96.

Sharing Responsibility, University of Chicago Press, 1992.

The Morality of Groups, University of Notre Dame Press, 1987.

War Crimes and Just War, NY: Cambridge University Press, 2007.

May, Larry and Stacey Hoffman (eds.), *Collective Responsibility: Five Decades of Debate in Theoretical and Applied Ethics*, Savage, MD: Rowman & Littlefield, 1991.

May, Larry and John C. Hughes. "Is Sexual Harassment Coercive?" in *Moral Rights in the Workplace*, Gertrude Ezorsky and James Nickel (eds.), Albany, NY: State University of New York Press, 1987, pp. 115–122.

May, Larry and Nancy Viner. "Actual Innocence and Manifest Injustice," *St. Louis University Law Journal*, vol. 49, no. 2, 2004, 481–497.

Miller, David. *National Responsibility and Global Justice*, NY: Oxford University Press, 2007.

Mohawk, John. "Epilogue: Looking for Columbus," in *The State of Native America*, M. Annette Jaimes (ed.), Boston, MA: South End Press, 1992, pp. 439–444.

Murphy, Colleen. "Lon Fuller and the Moral Value of the Rule of Law," *Law and Philosophy*, vol. 24, no. 3, 2005, 239–262.

Nickel, James, W. *Making Sense of Human Rights*, second edn, Oxford: Blackwell, 2007.

Nielsen, Kai. "There is No Dilemma of Dirty Hands," in *Cruelty and Deception: The Controversy Over Dirty Hands in Politics*, Paul Rynard and David P. Shugarman (eds.), Peterborough, ONT: Broadview Press, 2000, pp. 139–155.

Nozick, Robert. *Anarchy, State, and Utopia*, NY: Basic Books, 1974.

Nussbaum, Martha. "Judging Other Cultures: The Case of Genital Mutilation," in *Sex and Social Justice*, Oxford University Press, 1999, reprinted in *Applied Ethics: A Multicultural Approach*, Larry May, Shari Collins-Chobanian, and Kai Wong (eds.), fourth edn, Englewood Cliffs, NJ: Prentice Hall, 2006, pp. 15–26.

Orakhelashvili, Alexander. *Peremptory Norms in International Law*, Oxford University Press, 2006.

Osiel, Mark. *Making Sense of Mass Atrocity*, NY: Cambridge University Press, 2009.

Oxford Manual on the Laws of War, Oxford: Institute of International Law, August 9, 1913.

Plato, *The Republic*, Desmond Lee (trans.), second edn, NY: Penguin Books, 1974.

Pocock, J. G. A. *The Ancient Constitution and the Feudal Law*, Cambridge University Press, 1957.

Pogge, Thomas. *World Poverty and Human Rights*, Cambridge: Polity Press, 2002.

Roscoe Pound, Preface to *World Habeas Corpus*, Luis Kutner (ed.), Dobbs Ferry, NY: Oceana Publications, 1962, pp. v–viii.

Raustiala, Kal. "Is Bagram the New Guantanamo? Habeas Corpus and *Maqaleh v. Gates*," *ASIL Insights*, vol. 13, no. 8, June 17, 2009, 1–4.

Rawls, John. *A Theory of Justice*, Cambridge, MA: Harvard University Press, 1971.

Raz, Joseph. *The Authority of Law*, Oxford University Press, 1979.

Riedel, Eibe. "Standards and Sources: Farewell to the Exclusivity of the Sources Triad in International Law?" *European Journal of International Law*, vol. 2, no. 1, 1991, 58–84.

Reidy, David and Rex Martin (eds.). *Rawls's Law of Peoples: A Realistic Utopia?* Malden, MA: Blackwell Publishers, 2006.

Robison, Wade L. "The Great Right: Habeas Corpus," in *Coercion and the State*, David A. Reidy and Walter J. Riker (eds.), Dordrecht, The Netherlands: Springer, 2008, pp. 161–173.

Rogers, Colin and Robert Lewis. *Introduction to Police Work*, Cullompton: Wilan Publishing, 2007.

Safferling, Christoff J. M. *Toward an International Criminal Procedure*, NY: Oxford University Press, 2001.

Savage, Charlie. "Senator Proposes Deal on Handling of Detainees," *The New York Times*, March 4, 2010, p. A20.

Shue, Henry. *Basic Rights Subsistence, Affluence, and U.S. Foreign Policy*, Princeton University Press, 1980.

"Torture," *Philosophy & Public Affairs*, vol. 7, no. 2, 1978, pp. 124–143.

Slote, Michael. "Dirty Hands in Ordinary Life," in *Cruelty and Deception: The Controversy Over Dirty Hands in Politics*, Paul Reynard and David P. Shugarman (eds.), Peterborough, ONT: Broadview Press, 2000, pp. 27–41.

Solum, Lawrence B. "Procedural Justice," Public Law and Legal Theory Research Paper No. 04–02, in possession of author, 1–126.

Stateless Persons Convention, Article 1.2 (iii)(b).

Story, Joseph. *Commentaries on Equity Jurisprudence* (1834), London: Stevens and Hayes, 1884.

Sulum, Jacob. *Reason Magazine*, January 21, 2009, pp. 1–2.

Tamanaha, Brian Z. *On the Rule of Law: History, Politics, Theory*, NY: Cambridge University Press, 2004.

Thompson, Faith. *Magna Carta – Its Role in the Making of the English Constitution 1300–1629*, Minneapolis, MN: University of Minnesota Press, 1948.

Timmerman, Jacobo. *Prisoner Without a Name, Cell Without a Number*, Toby Talbot (trans.), Madison, Wisconsin: University of Wisconsin Press, 2002.

Tittemore, Brian D. "Guantanamo Bay and the Precautionary Measures of the Inter-American Commission on Human Rights: A Case for International Oversight in the Struggle against Terrorism," *Human Rights Law Review*, vol. 6, no. 2, July 2006, pp. 378–402.

Toensing, Victoria. "KSM Deserves Military Justice," *The Wall Street Journal*, Tuesday, March 2, 2010, p. A23.

Tomuschat, Christian. "Concluding Remarks," in *The Fundamental Rules of the International Legal Order: Jus Cogens and Obligations Erga Omnes*, Christian

Tomuschat and Jean-Marc Thouvenin (eds.), Leiden: Martinus Nijhof, 2006.

Tully, Stephen. "Australian Detainee Pleads Guilty before the First Military Commission," *ASIL Insights*, vol. 11, issue 11, April 23, 2007.

United Nations Charter, Article 39.1.c.

Universal Declaration of Human Rights, U.N.G.A. Res. 217A, 3 U.N. GAOR, U.N. Doc. A/810, at 71 (1948).

Vienna Convention on Law of Treaties, May 23, 1969, 1155 U.N.T.S 331, 8 International Legal Materials 679 (1969), Art. 53.

Vitoria, Francisco. *De Indis et de Ivre Belli Relectiones (Reflections on the Indians and on the Laws of War)* (1557), John Pawley Bate (trans.) and Ernest Nys (ed.), Washington, DC: Carnegie Institution, 1917.

Waldron, Jeremy. "The Core of the Case Against Judicial Review," *Yale Law Journal*, vol. 115, 2006, pp. 1346–1406.

"Positivism and Legality: Hart's Equivocal Response to Fuller," *New York University Law Review*, vol. 83, no. 4, 2008, 1135–1169.

Walzer, Michael. "Emergency Ethics," in *Arguing About War*, New Haven, CT: Yale University Press, 2004, pp. 33–50.

Walzer, Michael. "Political Action: The Problem of Dirty Hands," *Philosophy & Public Affairs*, vol. 2, no. 2, 1973, 160–180.

Wellman, Carl. *Real Rights*, Oxford University Press, 1995.

Weissbrodt, David. *The Human Rights of Non-Citizens*, Oxford University Press, 2008.

Yoo, John. *The Powers of War and Peace: The Constitution and Foreign Affairs*, University of Chicago Press, 2005.

LIST OF CASES

Boumediene v. Bush, 128 S. Ct. 2229 (2008).

Case Concerning the Barcelona Traction, Light, and Power Co., Limited, Second Phase, *Belgium v. Spain*, 1970 International Court of Justice 3, 1970 WL 1.

Chahal v. United Kingdom, 108 ILR 385 (1997).

In re Kappler, Italy, Military Tribunal of Rome, 20 July 1948, Case no. 151.

In re McDonald, 16 F. Cas. 17, 21 (E.D. Mo. 1861) (No. 8, 751).

In re Ross, 149 U.S. 453 (1891).

Jean-Bosco Barayagwiza v. Prosecutor, ICTR Appeals Chamber, 3 November 1999.

Marbury v. Madison, 5 U.S. 137 (1803).

Moore v. Dempsey, 261 U.S. 86, 87–88 (1923).

Ng v. Canada, UN Doc. CCPR/C/49/D/469/1991 (1993), 98 ILR 479.

Prosecutor v. Anto Furundzjia, International Tribunal for Yugoslavia, Trial Chamber Judgment, Case No. IT-95–17/1-T, December 10, 1998.

Prosecutor v. Fernando Nahimana, Jean-Bosco Barayagwiza, and Hassan Ngeze, International Criminal Tribunal for Rwanda, case no. ICTR-99–52-A, Appeals Chamber Judgment, November 28, 2007.

Prosecutor v. Joseph Kanyabashi, International Criminal Tribunal for Rwanda, Trial Chamber II, Case No. ICTR-96–15-I, May 23, 2000, Decision of the Defence Extremely Urgent Motion on Habeas Corpus and for Stoppage of the Proceedings.

Reid v. Covert, 353 U.S. 1, 75 (1955).

Saadi v. Italy, Application no. 37201/06, European Court of Human Rights, judgment of February 28, 2008.

Schlup v. Delo, 513 U.S. 298, 319 (1995).

Soering v. United Kingdom, 11 European Court of Human Rights, (ser. A) (1989).

X. v. United Kingdom, Judgment No. 46, European Court of Human Rights (5.11.1981).

Index

accountability
  and deterrence, 97
  and due process, 108
  and judicial review, 118
acoustical separation
  and distinguishing procedural from
    substantive rights, 62
Alexander, Larry
  on value of procedural rights, 55–56
American Convention on Human Rights, 135
anti-majoritarian
  as distinct from anti-democratic, 112
  judicial review as, 110
Aquinas
  on just war, 150
arbitrariness
  and democratic legitimacy, 63–64
  and habeas corpus, 54, 56, 99
  and procedural rights, 52–54, 102, 231
  and rule of law, 56
Arendt, Hannah
  on Statelessness, 60
Aristotle
  on equity, 127
  on rule of law, 66
Augustine
  on just war, 151
Australia
  recent habeas corpus rulings in, 137–140

Barcelona Traction
  and jus cogens norms, 124
Bayles, Michael
  on distinguishing procedure from substance, 47
Bethlehem, Daniel
  on non-refoulement, 169, 173, 174
Bill of Rights
  and Magna Carta, 25
Blackstone, William
  on due process, 108
  on habeas corpus, 57, 88, 93

Boumediene v. Bush
  and habeas corpus, 134, 229–230
Bracton
  on habeas corpus, 89, 105
Charlesworth, Hilary
  criticisms of jus cogens norms, 140
Chinkin, Christine
  criticisms of jus cogens norms, 140
Christiano, Thomas
  on procedural fairness, 63
claims
  and the disappeared, 94
  and Guantanamo prisoners, 45
  and procedural rights, 46
  rights understood as, 45
  and substantive rights, 46
Coke, Edward, 24, 25, 27
collective detention
  and fairness, 159
  and human rights, 159
  and refugee camps, 157, 162
  and security, 228
collective punishment
  and collective responsibility, 150, 162
  detention as a form of, 154–155
  and deterrence, 149
  fines as form of, 153
  and the Just War tradition, 150–152
  and protective retribution, 153
  range of sanctions, 148
  various forms of, 147–148
collective responsibility
  and collective punishment, 146–150, 162
  as justification for war, 150
complementarity
  and cultural pluralism, 40
  and the International Criminal Court, 31, 33, 200
  and judicial review, 118
Constitution
  and fundamental law, 76

US. *see* US Constitution
Convention Against Torture and other Cruel,
    Inhuman or Degrading Treatment or
    Punishment
    and non-refoulement, 169
Convention on the Elimination of all Forms of
    Racial Discrimination
    and Statelessness, 190
Convention on Trafficking
    misuse of, 177
Convention Relating to the Status
    of Refugees
    and non-refoulement, 156, 168
    and Statelessness, 190
Convention Relating to the Status of Stateless
    Persons, 190, 191
Cook, Walter Wheeler
    on distinguishing procedure from
        substance, 50
cosmopolitanism
    and society of States, 198
Courts of the Hundred, 22
Covenant on Civil and Political Rights
    and non-refoulement, 169
    and security, 224
    and UN Human Rights Committee, 213
Covenant on Economic, Social, and Cultural
    Rights, 214
Criddle, Evan
    on *jus cogens* norms, 122
cultural imperialism, 37–41
    and human rights, 38
custom
    and cultural imperialism, 37
    and fundamental law, 76
    and *jus cogens* norms, 122, 181
    and Magna Carta, 27

Declaration of the Rights and Duties
    of Man, 135
desseised
    and Magna Carta, 25
detention
    and outlawry, 190
    protective, 158
    and refugee camps, 155
    and security, 155
deterrence
    and accountability, 97
    and collective punishment, 149
    and habeas corpus, 90–92, 102
    and the Just War tradition, 151
    and publicity, 91–93
dirty hands
    problem of, 164
    vicarious, 166–168

disappearance (disappeared)
    and habeas corpus, 99
    habeas corpus as protection against, 93–95
    and loss of rights, 94
    and outlawry, 188
Drumbl, Mark
    on collective penalization, 163
due process, 108–109
    and accountability, 108
    and fairness, 74
    and gap-filling, 32
    and global justice, 17, 119, 233
    and habeas corpus, 107
    and human rights, 117, 218
    and international courts, 35
    and judicial review, 109
    and Magna Carta, 26
Dworkin, Ronald
    on anti-majoritarianism of judiciary, 112

equity
    and arbitrariness, 64
    and fairness, 48, 127, 159
    and gap-filling, 77, 158, 209, 230
    and habeas corpus, 230
    and human rights, 158
    and international law, 35
    and *jus cogens* norms, 126–129
    and personal security, 127
    and procedural justice, 13
    and rule of law, 129
    under emergency conditions, 229
Estlund, David
    on non-arbitrariness, 63
    on procedural fairness, 54
European Convention for the Protection of
    Human Rights and Fundamental Freedoms
    and *Saadi v. Italy*, 227
European Convention on Human Rights
    and habeas corpus, 130–132
    and non-refoulement, 173
European Court of Human Rights
    and non-refoulement, 173
    and *Saadi v. Italy*, 226
Executive power
    and the development of international law, 212

fairness
    and collective detention, 159
    and equity, 127, 159
    and gap-filling, 128
    and judicial review, 112
    and *jus cogens* norms, 126
    and minimally moral procedures, 59
    and non-refoulement, 170
    procedural or substantive end, 48, 56

fairness (cont.)
  and procedural rights, 76, 102
  and rule of law, 130
  and status, 49
  and trial by jury, 195
  under emergency conditions, 229
  and visibleness, 64
  whether intrinsically valuable, 54
Feinberg, Joel
  Nowheresville, 44
  on procedural rights, 46
  on rights as claims, 44–47
fiduciary duties
  as distinct from stewardship duties, 123
  as source of *jus cogens* norms, 123
Fox-Decent, Evan
  on *jus cogens* norms, 122
Franck, Thomas
  on equity, 127, 129
  on fairness, 52
  on process fairness and moral fairness, 58
Freeman, Mark
  on due process in truth commissions, 118
Fuller, Lon
  on due process, 74–75
  on habeas corpus, 75
  on procedural versus substantive law, 73
  and procedural rights, 27
  on rule of law, 72–73
fundamental law, 26
  criticisms of, 77
  not identical with Constitution, 76
  and procedural rights, 76–78

Geneva Conventions
  intended to be gapless, 158
  and Statelessness, 190
Gibney, Matthew
  on refugees, 190
global administrative law, 210, 211
global citizenship. *see* world citizenship
global justice
  and due process, 119, 233
  and habeas corpus, 51
  and procedural rights, 58–60, 219
Grotius, Hugo
  on collective punishment, 151
  on outlawry, 10
  on society of States, 8
  and substantive rights, 107
Guantanamo
  and claims to rights, 45
  and habeas corpus, 46, 134
  and Inter-American Commission on Human
    Rights, 134

and non-refoulement, 136
and procedural rights, 47, 58

habeas corpus
  and arbitrariness, 54, 55, 99
  in Australian jurisprudence, 137–140
  beyond minimalist conception of, 117
  and cultural imperialism, 37, 39
  and deterrence, 90–92, 102
  and due process, 107
  emergency exception to, 228
  and equity, 230
  and gap-filling, 32, 69, 102, 131
  and global justice, 51
  and Guantanamo, 46, 134
  and international law, 34, 37
  and judicial review, 75, 109, 132
  and Magna Carta, 25
  minimalist conception of, 104–106
  and non-refoulement, 164, 171
  and principle of visibleness, 100
  procedural or substantive right, 50–51, 62
  and procedural rights, 101, 106
  and rule of law, 55, 80
  and security, 224, 231
  and substantive rights, 106
  and the disappeared, 93–95
  and torture, 95–97
  and US Constitution, 155
  in US jurisprudence, 211
  value of, 55–56, 88–90, 99–100
  and visibleness, 100–102
Hague Regulations
  on collective punishment, 152
harm principle
  as source of *jus cogens* norms, 125
Hart, H. L. A., 6
  on international law, 67–70
  on natural law, 70
  on primary and secondary rules, 48
  theory of jurisprudence, 82
Hathaway, James
  on refugees, 168, 182, 188
Hicks, David
  habeas corpus petition, 138
Hill, Michael
  on trial by jury, 194
Hobbes
  on outlawry, 9
Howard, A. E. Dick, 30
human rights
  and cultural imperialism, 38
  and due process, 117, 218
  and equity, 35, 158
  loss of, 160

and non-refoulement, 179
normative vs. empirical, 41
and outlawry, 187
and procedural rights, 51, 58, 233
and refugee camps, 157
and security, 222
and substantive rights, 51
and world citizenship, 198
and world community, 159
human security, 14

inner morality of law
and internal perspective, 73
Inter-American Commission on
Human Rights, 136
and Guantanamo, 134
Inter-American Court of Human Rights, 133
internal perspective, 68–69
and gap filling, 69
and inner morality of law, 73
and natural law, 71
International Court of Justice (ICJ)
and *Barcelona Traction*, 124
International Criminal Court (ICC)
and complementarity, 31, 33, 118, 200
and international law, 6, 8
and security, 224
International Criminal Tribunal for Rwanda
(ICTR)
and habeas corpus, 35, 78–79
International Criminal Tribunal for Yugoslavia
(ICTY)
on non-refoulement, 175
international tort
as penalty for denial of procedural rights, 207

Janis, Mark
on *jus cogens* norms, 176
judicial review
and accountability, 118
and anti-majoritarianism of Judiciary, 110
and complementarity, 118
and due process, 109
and fairness, 112
and habeas corpus, 75, 109, 132
at international level, 117
and judicial overreach, 113
and New Deal settlement, 114
and procedural rights, 115, 116
jus cogens norms
and custom, 122, 181
and equity, 126–129
and fairness, 126
fiduciary theory of, 122
and gap-filling, 128

and harm principle, 125
and moral minimalism, 128
and natural law, 122
and non-refoulement, 177, 227
and procedural rights, 126, 130, 176
proposed sources of, 120–125
and torture, 174
and vulnerability, 123
and women's interests, 140
Just War tradition
and collective punishment, 150–152
and deterrence, 151
and security, 223
justice
global. *see* global justice
procedural. *see* procedural justice

Kelsen, Hans
on need for international court of rights, 209
Kingsbury, Benedict
on global administrative law, 210
Kramer, Larry
on judicial accountability, 110–112
on New Deal settlement, 114
Kutz, Chris, 81

Langford, Ian, 41
Lauterpacht, Elihu
on non-refoulement, 169, 173, 174
Lieber Code
on collective punishment, 152

Magna Carta
and custom, 27
and due process, 32, 107
and English law, 22–26
and Guantanamo, 4
and international law, 30–34, 36
and non-refoulement, 173, 178
and outlawry, 9, 184, 185
and procedural rights, 25, 27, 230
and rule of law, 37
and trial by jury, 193
Maine, Henry, 29, 101
Maitland, Frederick, 23, 29
Marbury v. Madison, 115
McKechnie, William
on Magna Carta, 24
Mill, J. S.
harm principle, 125
Miller, David
on the right to be subject to international law, 192
on State responsibilities, 199, 228
moral minimalism
and *jus cogens* norms, 128

municipal courts
  and international law, 33
MV Tampa
  and habeas corpus rights of refugees, 139

natural law
  and procedural rights, 107
  as source of *jus cogens* norms, 122
New Deal settlement, 114
Nielsen, Kai
  on problem of dirty hands, 165
non-refoulement
  emergency exception to, 228
  and fairness, 171
  and Guantanamo, 136
  and habeas corpus, 164, 171
  and human rights, 179
  and international law, 36, 37
  as *jus cogens* norm, 177, 227
  and Magna Carta, 26, 173
  potential misuse of, 177
  and problem of dirty hands, 166
  as procedural right, 170
  and refugees, 156
  and rendition, 171, 178, 179
  and rule of law, 170
  and security, 224, 227
Nowheresville, 44
  and Guantanamo, 45
Nozick, Robert
  on procedural rights, 60–61
nullification
  by jury, 110

Orakhelashvili, Alexander
  on *jus cogens* norms, 121
Organization of American States
  and Guantanamo, 135
outlawry, 185–187
  and detention, 190
  and the disappeared, 188
  and Hobbes, 9
  and human rights, 187
  in international law, 189–191
  and Magna Carta, 9, 184, 185
  and Statelessness, 189

Plato
  Ring of Gyges, 98, 233
Police and Criminal Evidence Act (PACE), 208
Pound, Roscoe
  on international habeas corpus, 208
procedural justice, 11–14
procedural norms, 7, 32
  and Magna Carta, 38

procedural rights, 29
  applications to public and private life, 141
  and arbitrariness, 52–54, 102, 231
  and claims, 46
  and cultural imperialism, 39
  and fairness, 48, 76, 102, 170
  and fundamental law, 27, 76–78
  and gap-filling, 14, 77
  and global justice, 58–60, 219
  and Guantanamo, 35, 47, 58
  and habeas corpus, 50–51, 101, 106
  and human rights, 51, 58, 233
  and judicial review, 115
  and *jus cogens* norms, 126, 130
  as *jus cogens* norms, 176
  and Magna Carta, 27, 230
  and natural law, 107
  and non-refoulement, 170
  and refugee camps, 214
  as related to substantive rights, 39, 43, 46,
    47–50, 102
  and rule of law, 57, 232
  and security, 221
  and status, 46
  and visibleness, 34, 57, 80
protective retribution
  and collective punishment, 153
publicity
  deterrent effect of, 91–93
  and due process, 108

Rawls, John
  on distributive justice and moral minima, 59
  and procedural justice, 11
Raz, Joseph
  on arbitrariness, 53
refugee camps. *see also* refugees
  and collective detention, 155, 157, 162
  and human rights protection, 157
  and procedural rights, 214
Refugee Convention. *see also* Convention
  Relating to the States of Refugees
Refugees. *see also* refugee camps
  and non-refoulement, 36
  as Stateless, 190
rendition
  difficulty of detecting, 180
  and non-refoulement, 171, 178, 179
  and principle of visibleness, 172
  and problem of dirty hands, 166
right to be subject to international law, 193, 233
  and trial by jury, 197
rights
  human. *see* human rights
  procedural. *see* procedural rights

substantive. *see* substantive rights
Ring of Gyges, 98–99, 233
Robin Hood
  as outlaw, 9, 186
Rome Statute
  and Magna Carta, 34
rule of law
  and arbitrariness, 56
  and equity, 129
  and fairness, 130
  and habeas corpus, 56, 80
  international, 8, 216
  and Magna Carta, 29
  and non-refoulement, 170
  and procedural justice, 13
  and procedural rights, 57, 102, 232
rules
  primary, 48
  secondary, 48
Russian roulette
  as unreliable procedure, 61

Saadi v. Italy
  and the security/rights compromise, 227
Safferling, Christoff J. M.
  on habeas corpus, 208
security
  and collective detention, 155
  and equity, 128
  and habeas corpus, 224, 231
  and human rights, 222
  and the ICC, 224
  and the Just War tradition, 223
  and non-refoulement, 224, 227
  personal and State, 222
  and procedural rights, 221
  and trial by jury, 225
security/rights compromise, 161, 228
Shue, Henry
  on basic rights, 125, 215
Slote, Michael
  on problem of dirty hands, 165
society of States, 12
  and cosmopolitanism, 198
  and Hugo Grotius, 8
Solum, Lawrence
  Participation Principle, 53
  on procedural vs. substantive
    rights, 62
Statelessness
  de facto vs. de jure, 188
  in international law, 189–191
  and outlawry, 189
  and refugees, 190
  and world citizenship, 187, 199

status
  and fairness, 49
  and procedural rights, 47
stewardship duties
  as distinct from fiduciary duties, 123
Story, Joseph
  on equity, 127
substantive norms, 7, 32
substantive rights, 29
  and claims, 46
  and cultural imperialism, 39
  and gap-filling, 31
  and global justice, 16
  and habeas corpus, 50–51, 106
  and human rights, 51
  as related to procedural rights, 43, 46, 47–50, 102

Timmerman, Jacobo, 56, 93
Tomuschat, Christian
  on *jus cogens* norms, 129
Torture Convention. *see* Convention Against
    Torture and Other Cruel, Inhuman or
    Degrading Treatment or Punishment
trial by jury
  costs associated with, 194, 217
  and cultural imperialism, 37
  and fairness, 195
  and international law, 36
  and Magna Carta, 25, 193
  and principle of visibleness, 231
  and right to be subject to international law,
    193, 197
  and security, 225

UN Human Rights Committee
  and gap-filling, 215
UN Human Rights Council, 213
  and accountability, 216
Universal Declaration of Human Rights (UDHR), 5
  and habeas corpus, 37
  and human security, 14
  and security, 222
  on security, 224
US Constitution
  and habeas corpus, 155
  and judicial review, 115
  and Magna Carta, 25, 30

Vienna Convention on the Law of Treaties
  and *jus cogens* norms, 121, 175
visibleness (visibility)
  and administrative law, 216
  and arbitrariness, 56
  and cultural imperialism, 39
  and fairness, 64

visibleness (visibility) (cont.)
  and habeas corpus, 28, 100–102
  principle of, 100
  and procedural rights, 34, 80
  and refugees, 10
  and rendition, 172
  and trial by jury, 231
Vitoria, Francisco
  on war as collective punishment, 150
Von Neurath
  on collective punishment, 153
vulnerability
  as source of *jus cogens* norms, 123

Waldron, Jeremy
  on H. L. A. Hart, 71
  on judicial review, 110
Weissbrodt, David
  on human rights, 200
will of the people
  and procedural rights, 77

Willheim, Ernst
  on *MV Tampa* decision, 139
Winkler, David
  on trial by jury, 194
world citizenship
  and human rights, 198
  and idea of world community, 197
  and Statelessness, 187, 199
  two senses of, 198–199
world community
  and human rights, 159
  and world citizenship, 197
world court of equity
  and human rights, 216
  and the ICC, 205, 207
  and *jus cogens* norms, 209
  proposal for a, 209

Yoo, John
  on presidential power, 113